Jesse H. Shera:
THE FOUNDATIONS OF EDUCATION FOR LIBRARIANSHIP

Charles T. Meadow:
THE ANALYSIS OF INFORMATION SYSTEMS, Second Edition

Stanley J. Swihart and Beryl F. Hefley:
COMPUTER SYSTEMS IN THE LIBRARY

F. W. Lancaster and E. G. Fayen:
INFORMATION RETRIEVAL ON-LINE

Richard A. Kaimann:
STRUCTURED INFORMATION FILES

Thelma Freides:
LITERATURE AND BIBLIOGRAPHY OF THE SOCIAL SCIENCES

Manfred Kochen:
PRINCIPLES OF INFORMATION RETRIEVAL

Dagobert Soergel:
INDEXING LANGUAGES AND THESAURI: CONSTRUCTION AND
MAINTENANCE

Robert M. Hayes and Joseph Becker:
HANDBOOK OF DATA PROCESSING FOR LIBRARIES, Second Edition

Andrew E. Wessel:
COMPUTER-AIDED INFORMATION RETRIEVAL

Lauren Doyle:
INFORMATION RETRIEVAL AND PROCESSING

Charles T. Meadow:
APPLIED DATA MANAGEMENT

Andrew E. Wessel:
THE SOCIAL USE OF INFORMATION—OWNERSHIP AND ACCESS

Hans H. Wellisch:
THE CONVERSION OF SCRIPTS: ITS NATURE, HISTORY, AND UTILIZATION

Eugene Garfield:
CITATION INDEXING—ITS THEORY AND APPLICATION IN SCIENCE,
TECHNOLOGY, AND HUMANITIES

Frederick W. Lancaster:
INFORMATION RETRIEVAL SYSTEMS: CHARACTERISTICS, TESTING AND
EVALUATION, Second Edition

Andrew E. Wessel:
THE IMPLEMENTATION OF COMPLEX INFORMATION SYSTEMS

The Implementation of
Complex Information Systems

The Implementation of Complex Information Systems

Andrew E. Wessel

With contributed cases
by

DONALD L. DRUKEY
HERMANN J. GRAML
PATRICIA M. McDONNELL
DIETRICH SEYDEL
IVO STEINACKER

A WILEY-INTERSCIENCE PUBLICATION

JOHN WILEY & SONS
New York • Chichester • Brisbane • Toronto

Thanks for their permission to reprint two lines
from T. S. Eliot's "Choruses from 'The Rock'"
in *Collected Poems 1909-1962* go to
Faber & Faber Ltd, London, and to
Harcourt Brace Jovanovich, Inc., New York.

Copyright © 1979 by John Wiley & Sons, Inc.

This publication is designed to provide accurate and
authoritative information in regard to the subject
matter covered. It is sold with the understanding that
the publisher is not engaged in rendering legal, accounting, or other professional service. If legal advice or
other expert assistance is required, the services of a
competent professional person should be sought.
*From a Declaration of Principles jointly adopted by a
Committee of the American Bar Association and a
Committee of Publishers.*

Library of Congress Cataloging in Publication Data

Wessel, Andrew E
    The Implementation of complex information systems.

    (Information science series)
    "A Wiley-Interscience publication."
    1. Information storage and retrieval systems—
Case studies. 2. Electronic data processing—Case
studies. I. Title.

Z699.W44   029.7   79-9892
ISBN 0-471-02661-1

Printed in the United States of America

10 9 8 7 6 5 4 3 2 1

Information Sciences Series

Information is the essential ingredient in decision making. The need for improved information systems in recent years has been made critical by the steady growth in size and complexity of organizations and data.

This series is designed to include books that are concerned with various aspects of communicating, utilizing, and storing digital and graphic information. It will embrace a broad spectrum of topics, such as information system theory and design, man—machine relationships, language data processing, artificial intelligence, mechanization of library processes, non-numerical applications of digital computers, storage and retrieval, automatic publishing, command and control, information display, and so on.

Information science may someday be a profession in its own right. The aim of this series is to bring together the interdisciplinary core of knowledge that is apt to form its foundation. Through this consolidation, it is expected that the series will grow to become the focal point for professional education in this field.

Preface

This book, which includes five contributed case histories, is concerned with showing users, managers, and technologists how to go about developing and using better methods, attitudes, and technologies for the implementation of complex information systems. It is hard-hitting. However, sharp critiques of certain methods, attitudes, and technologies should not be construed, by any reader exercising a modicum of care, as an attack upon those now afflicted with what is criticized.

Of course, one can offer the observation, "If the shoes pinch, there is no reason to keep on wearing them." But this is of little solace when better "shoes" are not available. In this light, some new methods, attitudes, and technologies are suggested, described, and illustrated. These are intended to encourage and permit users, managers, and technologists to undertake participatory development and implementation programs for complex information systems. Should the suggested approaches prove better fitting the needs, the credit will belong to those who try them out.

I would like to take this opportunity to thank all concerned with the making of this book, the contributors and the Wiley editors and production staff. They have done their best to make its reading, with that modicum of care, as painless as possible.

A. E. Wessel

Adelzhausen in Bavaria
March 1979

Contents

CHAPTER EIGHT

Reflections on the Implementation Problems of Complex Documentation Systems in Industry

by Hermann J. Graml

CHAPTER NINE

Toward Better Implementation Methods

CHAPTER TEN

An Example of an Experimental First Phase Implementation Project

CHAPTER ELEVEN

The Implementation of
Complex Information Systems

Chapter One

The Way Things Are

1.1 IMPLEMENTATION AS INTERACTIVE ADAPTATION

"Where is the wisdom we have lost in knowledge?
Where is the knowledge we have lost in information?"
From: "Choruses from 'The Rock,' " T.S. Eliot

Human mediation is a necessary activity for the transformation of data into information. Processing and exchange of data between machines, however efficient, leads to information, knowledge, and wisdom only within social or organizational frameworks—and, of course, not always then.

Human mediation within organizational and social frameworks is just as necessary with regard to the implementation of complex information systems. Getting such systems to work, to perform to some degree in accordance with the purposes for which they were developed, means a variety of implementation tasks must be accomplished successfully. But the accomplishment of implementation tasks does not take place within an ideal framework, a vacuum where friction and other extraneous factors can be, for all practical purposes, neglected. The implementation of complex information systems takes place within a human context of user environments, organizations, goals, and conflicts.

There are single-purpose, "simple" information systems, or, at least, many information systems start out that way. However, almost as soon as such simple information systems begin to operate, most of them grow more complex because of the extension of their usage and application. Everyone within an organization tries to get into a good act, to become a participant in progress. For our purposes, information systems functioning within a multipurpose, multiuser environment will be regarded as complex whether they are relatively simple data banks, more involved accounting or banking/credit systems, documentation systems, or middle and higher level management decision systems.

Search the literature as one may, neither the technocrats nor the administrators have developed coherent practical methods for the implementation of complex information systems. The specific problems are poorly identified. The costs are unclear but usually surprisingly high. The relevant management policies are in dispute, and the appropriate technologies associated with the implementation of complex information systems are either lacking or left to individual whim.

We do know that users are confronted with often overwhelming and unexpected tasks in attempting to get such information systems to work. Costs in time, manpower, and money for the implementation phases, while often hidden, are sometimes higher than the costs of development itself. We also know that even when partially successful, information systems seldom function in direct conformance with the original purposes. A significant degree of complex adaptation occurs during implementation—adaptations of user organization, system, system functions, and overall as well as specific system goals.

We have observed elsewhere that these adaptation and learning processes are truly interactive (1). Adaptation is not a one-way street. It applies to both the systemsware and user organization (machines *and* people).

We have to consider that a significant degree of unlearning is involved as well. To take a very simple case, the very same computer manufacturers who once provided us with systems so inflexible that changing an individual's address took months now seem to accept that "individuals should have access to information about themselves in record-keeping systems . . . There should be a way for individuals to correct or amend inaccurate records"(2).

Can we now expect the computer manufacturers to recall and correct, exchange and replace without cost to the users the inadequate or presumably dangerous systems they have put on the market?

The need for interactive adaptation and learning has been given lip service by many. That is not enough. Connected to this adaptive process is the need to take a rather detailed look at file interrogation processes and user/data base interfaces. It is precisely here that technology must adapt itself and provide society with systems more suited to interaction.

However, the requirement for flexible and easy interaction with data bases and information collections, the key to successful adaptation, and the interactive characteristics of the implementation processes themselves have been poorly understood by both system developers and administrators. We have had generalities, but the hard specifics of the adaptive/interactive processes are often ignored until they emerge, often quite late in the implementation phase. We simply do not have a consistent, generally accepted understanding of the feedback from over a decade of system development and implementation—the processes, the problems, the methods, and the tasks. What has been isolated from specific cases has never been taken seriously enough to affect the relevant technology or the user organizational procedures in timely fashion, during ongoing system development and design.

The world of complex information systems seems always new—the next case unrelated to the last! As such the errors are repeated and even intensify over a period of time. The results are high costs, unsatisfied expectations, low morale, poor performance, organizational chaos, administrative burdens. We have arrived at a stage today where complex information systems must be developed and implemented in an environment where managers fear and have contempt for technology in just about equal balance with the technocrats' fears and contempt for management.

From a conversation with a bank manager in Munich: "Just a few years ago I understood my bank, my people, the clerical processes, for which I am still responsible. However, today, I simply have to trust my EDP staff and their computer even though I do not know enough about what goes on inside them and it and they have even less knowledge about what goes on inside me and my bank. This may be progress but it is not a very happy situation."

From the EDP staff of a bank in Chicago: "We certainly can't afford to waste our time explaining EDP processes to the bank manager. Thank God, he is too dumb to either ask us or to understand what we might answer"(3). These attitudes are not unique. However understandable, they need to be changed.

Let us make the attempt.

1.2 SOME WORKING PREJUDICES

We intend to take a close look at existing developmental and implementation practices associated with complex information systems. In doing so, the variety of implementation tasks is described in both general and specific terms including the methods for accomplishment. However, the description of current implementation practices is not sufficient. We intend to suggest certain significant and rather specific changes of approach and methodology. These changes in implementation processes are essential should we wish to improve information systems performance and to achieve better system operations at less real cost. Those now satisfied with current costs and the means to hide them, or current system performance and the means to justify it could find certain results of our explorations offensive. There are vested beliefs, prejudices, and interests involved. As the specific case histories later discussed illustrate, there are more prejudices and beliefs than scientific principles in this field. However, the attainment of a degree of enlightenment about current implementation processes and their results and some critically needed options for a different and better methodology involves a degree of risk roughly equal to the clarity and specificity attempted.

In dealing with the implementation problems associated with complex information systems we are entering the preserves of specialists who prefer to call themselves information or management scientists. The self-announced birth of a new science may help with the funding for academic departments and governmental or industrial projects. It also may recruit interested professionals and produce useful accomplishments. However, it does tend to raise prejudices to the status of scientific principles. Rather than mask prejudices, under the existing circumstances, it is better to state them explicitly as such.

Unfortunately, some information scientists still seem to feel that information systems can be designed, developed, and implemented as if information, people, and electronic computers could be treated like little round balls on a billiard table, that the interactions among these could be determined by something like Newtonian mechanics (4). We reject this view. The complex interactions among information, people, and computers, the building blocks of contemporary information systems, are not determinable by applications of Newtonian physics. Perhaps the latest versions of solid state physics or the "eightfold way" of recent atomic physics may have much to offer concerning advanced computer design itself, but we are dealing with information as a social product within complex information systems. Just as important, the means to describe, transfer, process, store, and retrieve information are social products, and so are the people in their organizations and social contexts who want, need, use, or have information forced upon them or hidden from them. Different models or theories are required rather than last century's classical mechanics or today's physics.

Thus our basic prejudice is: "Information, information systems, people, and their organizations are social products."

Left as is, this prejudice may seem trivial or, perhaps, odd. It is neither. First of all it does mean that we cannot simply treat information as data and concern ourselves solely with data transmission, storage, processing, and retrieval, nor can we treat information systems solely as if they were data processing systems.

It is clear that some management scientists presume to treat information, people, electronic paraphernalia, and organizations as resources to be manipulated or used. Some information scientists presume to treat people and information as data. True enough, information, people, and organizations can be represented by forms of data and handled as such by computers. True enough, information, people, organizations, and information systems can be interpreted as resources. However, anyone who has had the responsibility for actually managing information, people, information systems, or organizations has discovered that these types of resources and data have the disturbing habit of jumping out of such confining interpretations.

Just as soon as a piece of data is used by people, it begins to behave as information. People, more often than not, function as people rather than as resources, particularly when they are dealing with poorly functioning computer systems. And, to date, information systems have refused to behave in any manner permitting confinement to the rigid boundaries of the computer room.

Our basic prejudice means that we must treat information as information, people within organizations and social contexts as people within organizations and social contexts, and treat computers, when functioning as proper parts of information systems, as the social products of which they are a part. This is hardly odd. Spelling out this viewpoint about information systems further would mean:

a. Whatever the form of data may be that we use as the means to process information, we are dealing with what begins as information, and we must end up with what is regarded by the people who use it as information.

b. Computers as proper parts of information systems had best be treated as idiot robots. We should not expect idiot robots to accomplish successfully anything requiring intelligence (what people have and sometimes use) for the satisfactory accomplishment of information systems.

c. Treating people as idiot robots is not merely immoral. As this attempts to reduce people to idiots, it is also rather wasteful. Computers make far better idiots than people.

d. Blaming people for the failures and costs of systems that so mistreat both people and computers does not achieve successful information systems.

e. Such general prejudices as these may be of interest and useful for clarification of viewpoint, but without specific detail about their influence upon development and implementation, they remain mere starting points. However, once the details are supplied, an interesting result may be obtained. Once we learn, ourselves, how to build and implement systems taking these prejudices seriously, we may not have to apply the fashionable term "science" to what we information and management specialists call information systems. Our works may speak for themselves. That would hardly be trivial.

We intend to explore and illustrate quite thoroughly implementation methods under various circumstances and in accordance with differing perspectives. In so doing, our starting points may be emphasized, clarified, and transformed. Before starting, however, a short survey of the recent views expressed by various information scientists about these same matters is appropriate. Some recent trends indicate that our working prejudices may have become more respectable.

1.3 THEORETICAL AND METHODOLOGICAL FOUNDATIONS

The requirement for theory development and both a more rigorous and realistic description of the methodological foundations for the information sciences has been stated by Vladimir Slamecka: "So far, the well-meaning intention and hard work of the research community of information science have been no match for the elusiveness of its goal to formulate theoretical foundations . . ."(5). ". . . theoretical research in information science . . . takes place in a real political world, the behavior of which strongly determines both the support and the constraint on such search"(6). "Studies in communication theory, logics, representation theory, linguistics, and the like (had been established during the fifties and sixties as prestigious areas for which funding could be obtained) to participate in the national 'mission' to strengthen science and technology"(7).

According to Slamecka, the recent shift in political and social fashion presents an opportunity for information science to focus on the problem domains relevant for the 1970s and 1980s. He concludes that this problem domain is "the management of man's knowledge as a social and national resource"(8).

The shift from the more abstract research favored in the 1950s and 1960s toward the development of theory for information sciences which regards information as essentially a human product in a social context began in roughly 1975. This was expressed by James G. Williams and Chai Kim, who concur with James Dickoff (9) in concluding that "factor-relating theories" (typology) must be developed for the information sciences as the basic grounds upon which "situation-relating theories which include predictive theories . . ." and "situation-producing theories (prescriptive theories)" can be developed (10).

Interestingly enough, and as a comment on the pre-1975 research fashions, Nancy van de Water, Neil Surprenant, B.K.L. Genova, and Pauline Atherton found that it cannot be said ". . . that research in our field is scientific . . . a systematic and rigorous gathering and analysis of data . . . with the long-term goal of developing a set of logically interrelated propositions which describe, predict, and explain . . ."(11) despite the then current fashions of borrowing from such abstract, related fields as formal communications theory, linguistic analysis, and mathematics (topology and formal representation theory, etc.).

The trend away from treating information as data (the Shannon definition) and toward regarding information as a human product in the social context grew stronger in 1976. Articles by Norman Roberts (12), Nicholas J. Belkin and Stephen E. Robertson (13), Peter P.M. Meincke and Pauline Atherton (14), and Börje Langefors (15) discuss this trend. Of this group, only Meincke and Atherton continue to use the older, borrowed terminology (in this case borrowed from vector analysis), but they make a distinction between " 'vectors' for a field of knowledge represented in a multi-dimensional space, and the 'state vectors' for a person based on his understanding . . . and the 'representational vectors' for information items which might be in a retrieval system . . ."(16).

More typically, the relationship between system and user and information and user with both relationships understood in their organizational and social contexts was emphasized as the key element characterizing information for the information sciences. This particular trend has already spread from the United

States to Great Britain and Sweden. Furthermore, it has continued. It is not surprising to find in the journal *Computers and People* an article by Bharat Maldé, where these themes are emphasized (17). However, it is significant to note the penetration of these ideas into the worlds of the computer scientist and the computer industry as indicated by Robert A. Kahn (18) and Alan Kay (19) in *Computer*.

This approach towards theory and methodological foundations for the information sciences is, of course, not novel. There were earlier proponents as indicated by my own RAND Corporation papers of the late 1960s cited in ''Computer-Aided Information Retrieval'' and ''The Social Use of Information'' (20). In fact, by 1973, the thesis that a transactional analysis of user requirements and needs was the basic foundation for building information and documentation systems could be found in an article by Frederic F. Scheffler in the *Journal of the American Society for Information Science*(21).

1.4 USER PARTICIPATION

The issue of user participation in the design, development, as well as implementation of information systems has always provoked a certain degree of controversy. Experts and professionals generally prefer to tell laymen (the ''patients'') what they should have and do, rather than to listen even to each other. We have argued that serious user participation is the best way to enhance the required learning processes about information systems. These learning processes involve both the system scientists and engineers, on one hand, and the system managers and users on the other (22). Furthermore, it seems that the best and only realistic way to determine user requirements, needs, and problems is by direct observation of the user as an interactive participating element of the information system itself.

Bharat Maldé points out that various studies, including one recently conducted by the University of Georgia, have concluded that the human intermediary ''is an integral component of the interface (for information and documentation systems)'' (23). In order to successfully design and implement meaningful forms of information and documentation systems, we must not only comprehend what the computer is good at, such as ''mass storage of information, fast and accurate retrieval, fast and accurate information processing, following predefined instructions,'' but also study and understand what the user must accomplish in interaction with computers. ''Pattern recognition, goal formulation, identifying new ideas, resolving ambiguity and uncertainty'' (24) are examples. Thus, it becomes clear that user research must be directed at providing better means to determine user needs and requirements and providing better methods of user participation in the design, development, and implementation of information and documentation systems. However, perhaps most important of all, research must be undertaken to explore and determine the most appropriate ways to permit the users to perform their functions and human work interactively as part of the overall information and documentation system functions. System design that proceeds without such understanding, as we shall see, is one of the major culprits, producing many of the difficulties encountered during implementation.

1.5 NETWORKING

The change of focus for the information sciences just indicated has had a corresponding change in network theory and problems. It is not so much that the essentially technical aspects involved in providing telecommunications networks have become less important, but rather that a new dimension of problems and theory have grown out of the attempt to construct networks for information and documentation bases and the organizations associated with the development, maintenance, and utilization of these informational resources. At first, the emphasis was on what was called "computer networks." For example, W. David Penniman quotes Farber's (25) definition of a computer network as ". . . an interconnected set of dependent or independent computer systems which communicate with each other in order to share certain resources such as programs or data—and/or for load sharing and reliability reasons" (26).

By 1976 it was recognized that even for computer networks, which differ from information or documentation base networks, telecommunication technology and models were not sufficient. According to H. Frank, "within the last few years, computer networking has emerged as a discipline. Modeling, analysis, and design techniques have made substantial progress, but the best results are still obtained by the artistic blend of theory, experience, and pragmatism" (27).

As early as 1973, Ruth M. Davis demonstrated that research into computer networks must consider not only computer applications and technology, but specifically address itself to "customer population, productivity, management and decision-making, performance of public services" (28). She also states that such aspects "are of national concern and of direct Federal interest" (29).

Thus, while the technical aspects of network theory are still relevant, J. H. McFadyen states that such networks are supposed to "enhance the exchange of information among a diverse group of operators, application programs, and devices," and not just machines (30).

H. Frank has said that not only are we concerned with such problems as "circuit versus packet switching" and "network survivability and reliability", but also that emphasis must be placed upon "centralized versus distributed data bases," "user models," "network management," and "network protocol theory" (31).

J. F. Sherlock also concurs with the view that when considering networks for information and documentation bases, the relationship of the user and system, man and machine, becomes central (32).

It also appears that some of the relatively new technical problems have more to do with establishing methods of intellectually linking differing information and documentation bases than with the linking of hardware elements. In fact, a project along these lines is being considered by the West German Ministry of Research and Technology as part of the development to be undertaken for the creation of a German national network of information centers.

1.6 EVALUATION AND ECONOMICS

Related to the problems of information system networks are general questions about their evaluation and economics. The fundamental issue would seem to be whether any of the accepted so-called economic models, evaluation and performance models, or analytic techniques are of any value whatsoever when applied to information and documentation systems.

I have shown elsewhere that cost and effectivity models, singly or in combination, are rather tricky affairs when applied to information and documentation systems, and that reliable measures of performance are hard to achieve (33). While such efforts as Cleverdon's at Cranfield and Lancaster's with MEDLARS, and Salton's comparison of MEDLARS and SMART were believed by many to be reliable, Don R. Swanson has shown that these efforts were dubious, if not seriously flawed (34). According to Swanson, in Cranfield II, "it has been shown that this method (of pre-identifying relevant documents to permit later evaluation of performance) very likely missed about 90 percent of the relevant documents," that Lancaster's MEDLARS study "involved a method for determining 'recall' (the percent of relevant documents retrieved) that could be misleading," and that Salton's MEDLARS/SMART comparison in addition to the previous objections provided "no evidence to support an inference (that automatic systems should replace those based on manual indexing) for very large document collections" (35).

Rowena Weiss Swanson points out that "the retrieval powers of indexing languages have been compared . . . and retrieval effectiveness has been assessed in terms of relevance judgments . . . (however) studies of other elements of information systems, for example the coverage of data bases, document delivery capabilities of systems, and use of information products by customers, are far less numerous" (36). Rowena Swanson quotes Debon and Montgomery in defining information systems as "environments composed of people, equipment, and procedures organized to achieve specific information objectives (37). These objectives, operationalized to performance requirements, constitute the criteria for evaluating systems." There is a "paucity of studies that assess operations in relationship to designs'' (38). Further ''although methodology (how to measure) is important, it is secondary to conceptualization of a study (what to measure and why)'' (39). Evaluation must be ''more than isolated investigations of indexing languages, file structures, single products or services, etc . . .'' (40).

What seems clear is that cost/effectivity comparisons and efficiency studies seem to be of dubious worth in any environment where the differing information and documentation systems are effective (or not) in quite different ways, and costly (or cheap) only in comparison to other systems with differing goals or purposes and performance criteria. It might be well to take a step back from the economic models, the cost/effectivity theorists, and efficiency experts, and start by making an attempt to define and determine the variety of values and services information and documentation systems offer in their differing organizational and social contexts. Whether general evaluation criteria would result from such an investigation may be disputed, but certainly a far better understanding of the realities involved in comparing costs to performance(s) for specified objectives would be obtained.

1.7 SUMMARY AND CONCLUSIONS

While attempts continue to define the fields of information science(s) and documentation, to debate their scientific status, to offer highly technical solutions to problems invented in the laboratories, a shift of effort toward addressing more realistic problems has occurred. This increasingly includes serious attempts to provide information systems on a more realistic basis for governmental, industrial, and public sector applications. More rational analyses are being attempted covering such areas as funding contraints, requirements for the extension of documentation and library facilities, network utilization, user interests and needs, and even the potential impact (good and bad) on the society as a whole. These trends do not ignore technological development itself; they assume technical comprehension but focus upon who sets the goals, how evaluations can be performed, who pays the costs, what are the benefits within differing organizational contexts, and how the benefits are distributed.

In summary, it can be shown that more carefully defined applications of scientific methods in the information sciences have become more evident as distinct from the more pseudo-scientific generalities and pretensions of the past. Further, a more careful and realistic assessment of the technology, current and near-term future, applicable to information systems, is being developed. Specifically, it would appear that:

a. The notion of information for the information scientist (as distinct perhaps from the communications network or computer sicentist) must include the human dimension within a social-economic framework.

b. Despite emphasis upon theory building, information science may be becoming a practice-oriented field, at least to the extent that there now exists a good fifteen years of information and documentation applications based upon computer systems technologies.

c. As such, there exists a relevant mass of data concerning systems operations and utilization in providing access to information for people within a wide range of differing organizational and social contexts. It is certainly time to gather and analyze this data both to improve practice and develop theory.

d. Realistic assessments of the contemporary technological state-of-the-art remain critical to the development of the information sciences and to the development of national and international information systems.

e. Given the rapid pace of technological development with its profound impact on capabilities, costs, and efficient networking, such technological assessments must be made at relatively frequent intervals to keep up to date.

f. User requirements cannot be solely determined from on high or left to the discretion of the manufacturers or systems engineers.

g. The economics and efficiencies of information and documentation systems are more complex than previously believed, and evaluation methods that neglect relevant measures of systems and information usage within a social or organizational framework give misleading, if not false, results.

h. Information networking is not solely an engineering task.

i. Information systems, as implemented, produce new social problems in the economic, organizational, and social domains requiring new standards and definitions about criminal and industrial law, and the rights of citizens.

j. National developments of information and documentation systems have important, if unexpected, national and international effects.

k. The neglect of any of these factors simply ensures that the resulting problems will surface with explosive impact.

Taken individually and as a whole, these conclusions remain controversial. This is precisely why we have willingly identified such theses earlier as prejudices.

What cannot be doubted, however, is that there is indeed a trend toward these conclusions and that this trend is found in the literature over the last decade. For readers interested in further explanation of these topics, many additional citations have been listed at the end of this chapter. In any event, it is now time to turn from the literature to the real world of information systems as they have been and are being implemented.

NOTES

1. A.E. Wessel, "The Social Use of Information," John Wiley & Sons, New York, 1976; and "Computer-Aided Information Retrieval," John Wiley & Sons, New York, 1975 (Melville Publishing Company, Los Angeles).

2. IBM advertisement between pp. 4 and 4B, *Newsweek, International Edition,* November 21, 1977. It is nice to see the problem advertised; one would have liked still more to see the IBM solutions. Should we junk all the inflexible systems that make just this sort of file change routinely difficult? Can we expect better and more useable file change routines from IBM?

3. Names withheld upon request.

4. See R. T. Kimbler, review of Wessel, Computer-Aided Information Retrieval, *Journal of Documentation,* September 1976, pp. 239-241

5. Vladimir Slamecka, "Pragmatic Observations on Theoretical Research in Information Science," *Journal of the American Society for Information Science (ASIS),* Vol. 26, No. 6, November—December 1975, pp. 318—320 (p. 318).

6. Ibid., p. 319.

7. Ibid.

8. Ibid.

9. James Dickoff, "Theory in Practice Discipline," *Journal of Nursing Research,* Vol. 17, No. 5, 1968, p. 418

10. James G. Williams, Chai Kim, "On Theory Development in Information Science," *Journal of the ASIS,* Vol. 26, No. 1, January—February 1975, pp. 3—8 (p.7).

11. Nancy van de Water, Neil Surprenant, B.K.L. Genova, and Pauline Atherton, "Research in Information Science: An Assessment," *Information Processing & Management,* Vol. 12, pp. 117—123 (p. 120), Pergamon Press, 1976. Printed in Great Britain.

12. Norman Roberts, "Social Considerations Towards a Definition of Information Science," *Journal of Documentation,* Vol. 31, No. 4, December 1976, pp. 249—257.

13. Nicholas J. Belkin, Stephen E. Robertson, "Information Science and the Phenomenon of Information," *Journal of the ASIS,* Vol. 27, No. 4, July—August 1976, pp. 197—204.

14. Peter P.M. Meincke, Pauline Atherton, "Knowledge Space: A Conceptual Basis for the Organization of Knowledge," *Journal of the ASIS,* Vol. 27, No. 1, January—February 1976, pp. 18—24.

15. Börje Langefors, "Information Systems Theory," *Information Systems,* Vol. 2, pp. 207—219, Pergamon Press, 1977.

16. Meincke, Atherton, "Knowledge Space," p. 18.

17. Bharat Maldé, "The Human Intermediary in the Use of Computers," *Computers and People,* Vol. 26, No. 2, January 1977, pp. 22—23.

18. Robert A. Kahn, "Public Access to Personal Computing: A New Role for Science Museums," *Computer,* April 1977, pp. 56—66.

19. Alan Kay, Adele Goldberg, "Personal Dynamic Media," *Computer,* March 1977, pp. 31—41.

20. Wessel, Computer-Aided Information Retrieval (CAIR) and Social Use of Information (SU).

21. Frederic L. Scheffler, "A Novel Philosophy for the Design of Information Storage and Retrieval Systems Appropriate for the '70's," *Journal of the ASIS,* Vol. 24, No. 3, May—June 1973, pp. 205—209.

22. Wessel, CAIR and SU.

23. Maldé, "The Human Intermediary," p. 22.

24. Ibid., p. 23.

25. D. Farber, "Networks: An Introduction," *Datamation*, April 1972, pp. 36−39.
26. W. David Penniman, Richard E. Krohn, Gabor J. Kovacs, "A Framework for the Study of Emerging Network Technology," *Journal of the ASIS*, Vol. 25, No. 6, November−December 1974, pp. 378−380 (p. 378).
27. H. Frank, "Computer Networks: Art to Science to Art," *Networks*, Vol. 5, No. 1, January 1975, pp. 7−32 (p. 29).
28. Ruth M. Davis, "Computing Networks: A Powerful National Force," *Computer*, April 1973, pp. 14−18 (p. 18).
29. Ibid., p. 18.
30. J.H. McFadyen, "Systems Network Architecture: An Overview," *IBM System Journal*, Vol. 15, No. 1, 1976, pp. 4−23 (p. 22).
31. H. Frank, "Computer Networks."
32. J.F. Sherlock, "Design and Simulation of Man-Machine Systems Using Network Models," *Computer-Aided Design*, Vol. 9, July 3, 1977, pp. 151−156.
33. Wessel, SU, Chapters 2 and 9.
34. Don R. Swanson, "Information Retrieval as a Trial-and-Error Process," *Library Quarterly*, Vol. 47, No. 2, 1977, pp. 128−148.
35. Ibid., p. 129.
36. Rowena Weiss Swanson, "Performing Evaluation Studies in Information Science," *Journal of the ASIS*, Vol. 26, No. 3, 1975, pp. 140−141 (p. 140).
37. Ibid., p. 140.
38. Ibid., p. 140.
39. Ibid., p. 141.
40. Ibid., p. 141.

BIBLIOGRAPHY

Philip H. Abelson, Allen L. Hammond, "The Electronics Revolution," *Science*, Vol. 195, March 18, 1977, pp. 1087−1091.

The American University, Center for Technology and Administration, "Information Technology Serving Society," program for a series of seminars occurring February through March, 1977. College of Public Affairs. The American University Intergovernmental Bureau for Informatics, Pergamon Press, 1977.

Howard Anderson, "IBM Versus Bell in Telecommunications," *Datamation*, May 1977, pp. 91−95.

C. Warren Axelrod, "The Economic Evaluation of Information Storage and Retrieval Systems," *Information Processing & Management*, Vol. 13, pp. 117−124, Pergamon Press, 1977.

Nicholas J. Belkin, "Information Concepts for Information Science," *Journal of Documentation*, Vol. 34, No. 1, March 1978, pp. 55−85.

Ivan Berenyi, "Computing's Youngest Grandchild—An Accident," *Data Processing*, April 1977, pp. 40−43.

Abraham Bookstein, William Cooper, "A General Mathematical Model for Information Retrieval Systems," *Library Quarterly*, Vol. 46, No. 2, 1976, pp. 153−167.

John M. Carroll, "The Computer 'Discredit Bureau'—An Extension of a Community Information Utility," *Proceedings of the 37th ASIS Annual Meeting,* Vol. 11, American Society for Information Science, Washington, D.C., 1974, pp. 18–23.

John M. Carroll, "Prospects for Parallelism and the Computer Crunch," *Journal of the ASIS,* Vol. 27, No. 1, January–February 1976, pp. 63–69.

Thomas Childers, "The Neighborhood Information Center Project," *Library Quarterly,* Vol. 46, No. 3, 1976, pp. 271–289.

Dixon R. Doll, "Telecommunications Turbulence and the Computer Network Evolution," *Computer,* February 1974, pp. 13–22.

Linda Flato, "One Step at a Time—The Many Approaches to Automating the Patent Office," *Datamation,* June 1977, pp. 173–177.

Mauro Guazzo, "Retrieval Performance and Information Theory," *Information Processing & Management,* Vol. 13, pp. 155–165, Pergamon Press, 1977.

Louis-Gavet Guy, "A Mathematical Formulation of Keyword Compression for Thesauri," *Information Processing & Management,* Vol. 13, pp. 189–200, Pergamon Press, 1977.

J. Havatny, W.M. Newman, M.A. Sabin, "World Survey of Computer–Aided Design," *Computer–Aided Design,* Vol. 9, No. 2, April 1977, pp. 79–98.

(Please note the international character of this report with one author from the Hungarian Academy of Science, the second from the United Kingdom, and the third from the Palo Alto Research Center, Xerox Corporation, Palo Alto, California).

Nicholas Henry, "Public Policies for Information Management: An Overview," *Information Processing & Management,* Vol. 11, pp. 67–74, Pergamon Press, 1975.

Gerald R. Johnson, Robert A. Mueller, "Automated Generation of Cross–System Software for Microcomputers," *Computer,* January 1977, pp. 23–31.

E. Michael Keen, "On the Generation and Searching of Entries in Printed Subject Indexes," *Journal of Documentation,* Vol. 33, No. 1, March 1977, pp. 15–45.

Donald H. Kraft, "A Decision Theory View of the Information Retrieval Situation: An Operations Research Approach," *Journal of the ASIS,* Vol. 24, No. 5, September–October 1973, pp. 368–376.

Ferdinand F. Leimkuhler, "Operational Analysis of Library Systems," *Information Processing & Management,* Vol. 13, pp. 79–93, Pergamon Press, 1977.

Ian A. Macleod, "Towards an Information Retrieval Language Based on a Relational View of Data," *Information Processing & Management,* Vol. 13, pp. 167–175, Pergamon Press, 1977.

W.A. van der Meulen, P.J.F.C. Janssen, "Automatic Versus Manual Indexing," *Information Processing & Management,* Vol. 13, pp. 13–21, Pergamon Press, 1977.

Calvin N. Mooers, "Preventing Software Piracy," *Computer,* March 1977, pp. 29–30.

The National Commission on Libraries and Information Science, "A National Proposal for Library and Information Services: A Synopsis of the Second Draft Program," *Information Storage and Retrieval,* Vol. 10, Nos. 9/10, September–October 1974, Pergamon Press, New York, pp. 343–348.

R.N. Oddy, "Information Retrieval Through Man-Machine Dialogue," *Journal of Documentation,* Vol. 33, No. 1, March 1977, pp. 1–14.

P.C. Patten, "Data Organization and Access Methods," Section 8, "Summary and Conclusions," *Advances in Information Systems Science,* Vol. 5, 1974, pp. 85−91. Plenum Press, New York, London, ed. Julius Troll.

Gerald J. Popek, "Protection Structures," *Computer,* June 1974, pp. 22−23.

Marc U. Porat, "Structures of the Specialized Common Carrier: Implications for the Information Utility Industry," *Proceedings of the 37th ASIS Annual Meeting,* Vol. 11, ASIS, Washington, D.C., 1974, pp. 13−17.

C.J. van Rijsbergen, "A Theoretical Basis for the Use of Co−Occurrence Data in Information Retrieval," *Journal of Documentation,* Vol. 33, No. 2, June 1977, pp. 106−119.

S.E. Robertson, "Progress in Documentation—Theories and Models in Information Retrieval," *Journal of Documentation,* Vol. 33, No. 2, June 1977, pp. 126−148.

S.E. Robertson, K. Sparck Jones, "Relevance Weighing of Search Terms," *Journal of the ASIS,* Vol. 27, No. 3, May−June 1976, pp. 129−140.

William B. Rouse, "A Library Network Model," *Journal of the ASIS,* Vol. 27, No. 2, March−April 1976, pp. 88−99.

Tefko Saracevic, "Questions About the Notion of Information Utilities," *Proceedings of the 37th ASIS Annual Meeting,* Vol. 11, ASIS, Washington, D.C., 1974, pp. 1−7.

"Security: The Only Means to Privacy," (Rubric: News in perspective), *Datamation,* May 1977, pp. 240−241.

Petr Sgall, Jarmila Panevova, Svatava Machova, "A Linguistic Approach to Information Retrieval—II," *Information Processing & Management,* Vol. 11, pp. 147−153, Pergamon Press, 1975.

K.S. Shankar, "The Total Computer Security Problem: An Overview," *Computer,* June 1977, pp. 50−62.

Dagobert Soergel, "Is User Satisfaction a Hobgoblin?", *Journal of the ASIS,* Vol. 27, No. 4, July−August 1976, pp. 256−259.

F.H. Spaulding, R.O. Stanton, "Computer-Aided Selection in a Library Network," *Journal of the ASIS,* Vol. 27, No. 5, September−October 1976, pp. 269−280.

Peter A. Thomas, "Micropublishing and Libraries in the Future," *Aslib Proceedings,* 30 (5), May 1978, pp. 165−171.

Erwin Tomash, Dataproducts Corporation, "SOS: The Next 11111 Years," *Computer,* December 1976, pp. 11−21.

I.L. Travis, "Design Equations for Citation Retrieval Systems: Their Role in Research and Analysis," *Information Processing & Management,* Vol. 13, pp. 49−56, Pergamon Press, 1977.

A.E. Wessel, "Einsatz von Minicomputern in der Dokumentation−Perspectiven und Probleme," *Nachrichten für Dokumentation,* Vol. 28, No. 3, 1977, pp. 99−104 (in German only).

A.E. Wessel, "Wesentliche Aufgaben der Informationswissenschaft," *Informationswissenschaft,* ed. W. Kunz; R. Oldenbourg Verlag, Munich and Vienna, 1978, pp. 205−210 (in German only).

Howard D. White, "A Directory of Public Services: Utopian Notes," *Information Processing & Management,* Vol. 13, pp. 177−187, Pergamon Press, 1977.

Martha E. Williams, "The Impact of Machine—Readable Data Bases on Library and Information Services," *Information Processing & Management,* Vol. 13, pp. 95—107, Pergamon Press, 1977.

T.D. Wilson, "Factors Affecting the Coordination of Information Agencies to Form Public Information Utilities," *Proceedings of the 37th ASIS Annual Meeting,* Vol. 11, ASIS, Washington, D.C., 1974, pp. 3—12.

Stanley Winkler, Lee Danner, "Data Security in the Computer Communication Environment," *Computer,* February 1974, pp. 23—31.

Harold Wooster, "An Experiment in Networking: The LHNCBC Experimental CAI Network, 1971—1975," *Journal of the ASIS,* Vol. 27, No. 5, September—October 1976, pp. 329—337.

Chapter Two

The Implementation Paradigm

This chapter covers the basic steps of the implementation of complex information systems. It is a general discussion offering an introduction to the topics and will be followed by detailed case histories leading to more specific recommendations as to the approaches to implementation.

There is probably no one general scheme or representation of the varied phenomena involved in and surrounding the implementation of complex information systems. Accuracy requires the specific analysis of each actual or potential case. What follows then is best understood as a listing and description of topics for discussion. Clarification must precede a logical and temporally sequential itemization of the implementation phase. However, most actual cases must deal with or accomplish the items listed below however different the methods of decision or accomplishment may be. As such, a paradigm of information system implementation would include these basic steps:

a. The decision to automate (or further automate).
b. The determination of requirements.
c. The system design and/or determination of system configuration.
d. The determination of system design or system configuration costs.
e. System requirements, design, and configuration compromises as a result of d. and various types of cost/effectivity analyses.
f. System development or putting the pieces (software, hardware, and user organization) together.
g. The development of an implementation plan and program.
h. System delivery and start-up.
i. Training and initial system use.

j. One to three years of on-site problem discovery and partial solutions (shakedown).
k. Transformation of system operations, functions, and requirements combined with equivalent transformation of user operations, functions, and requirements.
l. System operational stages with various imperfections and many unresolved or newly discovered problems in a functioning system often costing more and doing other than expected. (The decision to live with the system as is and/or to revert back to manual processes, at least in part, must now be faced.)
m. After some period of time, return to a.

2.1 A GENERAL DISCUSSION OF THE IMPLEMENTATION PARADIGM

The old platitude about the repetition of history being the doom of those ignorant of history is well justified in application to implementation. Those beguiled by various "how to" manuals concerning automation to the extent that they ignore what actually has happened seem prone to make or find themselves and their organizations embroiled in the same repeated mistakes. Unfortunately, there is no simple and reliable "what happened" manual available. The uniqueness of each case or situation often has meant that the same mistakes are repeated, if in differing ways, just as the successes have been achieved in differing ways. Compounding such differences is the fact that the technology involved has changed much faster than it has been able to be used well or often to be understood particularly on its impact on the implementation processes.

Nonetheless, some understanding of what has happened is essential. We can hope to understand the range of variations and define, at least, the boundaries within which the attempts to accomplish the basic steps of our implementation paradigm have fluctuated. Honesty as well as prudence about future attempts require that mistakes be identified. But we attempt this more in the light of learning what could and should be accomplished better in future than in an attempt to offer the many "should have beens" of hindsight.

The general discussion of these implementation steps in this chapter will be expanded and illustrated by various detailed case histories presented later. However, even in this general discussion, we intend to isolate certain critical aspects of the implementation processes.

2.1.1 The Decision To Automate (or Further Automate)

Over the last twenty years at least the decision process has been studied, formalized, modeled, and debated within various disciplines ranging from operations research and management science to games theory, applied mathematics, and philosophy. Some of these efforts, applied to information systems automation and design, are discussed in the literature cited in Chapter One.

Most decision models are flawed in at least one or two ways. Either they are too simple, neglecting relevant factors in the real world, or they are too complex, requiring more and better information about the real world than is available normally. Both flaws often exist simultaneously. The more simple models usually require a significant amount of hard data not always obtainable for their calculations; the most complex models too often fail to show that important factors pertaining to the decision nonetheless are being ignored.

To the extent that any of the variety of available decision methods and models force a more rational gathering and use of information, and most do precisely that, they may be of value when deciding whether or not to automate. However, the very question of automation applied to existing information processes and services is legitimately raised only when the existing information apparatus has been deemed inadequate. The costs then of obtaining the required information with which to complete the decision model, given the inadequacies of the existing information system, may be extremely high. In fact merely to satisfy the informational requirements for a halfway reliable decision model may require automation. Thus the wish to possess the ability to use the modern methods of decision making becomes one fundamental ground for automating the existing inadequate information system.

On the other hand, the use of most decision methods and models too often appears to result in exactly the decisions already in the management's minds and about to be made anyway. To the extent that the use of modern decision making processes accommodates existing prejudices, and it usually does precisely that, it is as dangerous as the prejudices themselves. For one thing, opposed prejudices may not get equivalent weighting without going through the strenuous effort of developing a competing decision model. Constructive opposition is difficult enough within most organizational frameworks. It might be wise under the circumstances to use the best scientific traditions of confirmation by attempting to disprove the thesis at hand. This would mean using decision models and methods essentially in opposition to the trend of the ongoing decisions and to force consideration of the opposing positions. In the case considered here, of course, this would mean decision models should be used to oppose rather than to support whatever managerial decisions seem to be on top.

In actuality, however, the impact of decision theory, models, and methods used is likely to be all too slight at the point of decision. (The justification of the decision taken is another story, as we shall see.) There may be a myriad of expressed reasons to automate, but we think the basic grounds are few indeed. In fact most decisions to automate feel forced, that is, one automates because:

a. One must, in order to remain competitive.
b. One has to do or attempt new tasks the manual system appears unable to handle efficiently.

c. The work load is, or appears to be, increasing faster than it can be handled efficiently by any conceivable upgrading or expansion of the manual workers.

d. People problems and people organizations, such as unions and their management, appear to have become too time consuming, worrisome, unprofitable, or beyond control just when automation promises to replace people by unemotional machines for the care and feeding of which supposedly only electricity is required.

Behind seemingly free decisions to automate may stand someone, or some groups, who want to achieve more control and power within their organizations. Correspondingly, there may be those who do not want to lose their existing power and control, or who wish to be up-to-date. Then, too, some people have nothing else more interesting to do and have access to the funding at the time. Less frequently than one would like to think do the basic grounds for automation involve the wish to offer better and more efficient services to clients or customers or the publics served. Yet forced or free, this decision context applies even more clearly in the case of automation of complex information systems where organization politics come more powerfully into play rather than with the automation of production or process control.

Information, its flow and control lie at the heart of things. It is a necessary ingredient for making peace and war as well as pies, for doing and undoing business, for making hate as well as love. We have emphasized in Chapter One that information is a human product. The decision to automate when applied to complex information systems is a very human decision. This needs to be said every bit as strongly as the assertion that the decision to automate is or ought to be based on rational grounds, particularly since the grounds we consider when rationalizing a decision are influenced rather significantly by the actual grounds of the decision itself.

What has all this to do with the subsequent implementation processes? It is simply that the decision to automate, if carried out, involves so great an expenditure of money, time, and resources that most organizations require an extensive justification or rationalization of the decision. A question then arises in the next step, the determination of requirements: What sets the requirements, the original reasons behind the decision to automate or the grounds for automation developed for the justification of the original decision?

2.1.2 The Determination of Requirements

It turns out that the answer to this question is as confusing as the decision process is murky. Both the original grounds for the decision and the justificatory claims are relevant to the determination of requirements. So are all sorts of additional considerations which often combine with the former to produce an inconsistent and partially irrelevant mess. In any event, the next step for most complex cases and organizations is to initiate a requirements study. Often outside experts are hired to make the objective case that the decision makers want precisely what they should want. All the necessary numbers and charts are provided, which are nice to have. Also usually provided is a new, often quite detailed list of requirements several steps removed from the original decision to automate. Nonetheless, here is where the information kinds and rates of transfer, inputs, requests, storage and file update, accretions and changes, transmissions, reports and other forms of outputs are defined. And here is where those decision makers in charge of operations of the organization begin to lose control, begin to lose the feeling they may have had concerning "how things work and ought to work around here." They now may begin to wonder just what it was that they had decided, when the decision to automate was made.

Determining requirements also takes a good deal of time. The existing operations must be studied and to some degree understood. The stated and unstated grounds for automation must be comprehended and the probable direction of the technological art must be assessed. Rough notions of costs must be clarified. All this must be accomplished during the definition and specification necessary to produce the detailed statement of requirements. Thus, even assuming the automated system could be then designed, put together, and made operational in zero time, the time elapsed merely in determing detailed requirements is generally long enough to produce an outdated set of requirements. As such, even if accurate and well done, the requirements are usually misleading at best. That is to say that if the requirements are eventually actually satisfied, the result *when obtained* will prove disappointing because the needs satisfied will no longer be as central and important as they once may have been felt to be. Along with such a result come the many unforeseen side effects, those transformations of organization, jobs, functions, and costs which occur just because one has introduced significant changes within the information flow, patterns, distribution, and handling inside the organization.

Of course, neither the assumption about zero time for system construction and operation nor the assumption that any set of requirements is that accurate for a given organization at a given time or is that completely satisfied by any known information system, however automated, is valid. Much time passes and many errors mount as we begin system design and establish system configuration.

The determination of requirements for an information system within any given organization requires a clearer understanding of the business of the organization than is usually available. In order to describe the appropriate information flow—its generation, handling, processing, storage, retrieval, transformations, and cycling—the purposes for which information is produced and used must be clearly established. Without a clear understanding of organizational purposes and functions the detailed requirements for flow, feedback, amount, quality, speed, and kinds of information become a matter of intuition. At the same time the realistic performance capabilities and costs of the varieties of automated information systems must be clearly understood. Otherwise a meaningful statement of requirements cannot be accomplished. The critical question then arises: Who is going to learn whose business? This question deserves some thought.

The normal practice is to establish a group of data processing experts within the organization or to hire them through a consultant service. This group of experts is first given the task of learning organizational processes, functions, and purposes (the company's way of doing business and the whys of the ways). This is a first step toward establishing information system requirements in accordance with the managerial interests, usually expressed as a function of the decision to automate. This same group of experts is supposed to be knowledgable about the performance capabilities and costs of information systemsware.

Without proceeding directly to the implementation of a resultant system configuration and seeing what happens, is there any way for management to determine whether the experts know what they are doing and are supposed to know? Is there any way management can determine both that the organizational ways and whys of doing business have been sufficiently comprehended by the experts and that the experts know the realistic performance capabilities and costs of the plausible systemsware thought appropriate?

A typical approach to this sort of problem is to attempt to rely on the past performances of the experts, the successes and failures of this particular group of experts along similar lines. Reputation based merely on in-group status alone is of little use. Presumably that was the ground for choosing the staff of experts either in house or from consultant services. But how is management to know which experts did what with regard to any previous successes and failures along similar lines? How is management to know just how similar previous tasks were to the current tasks, to the present organization and information system? It would seem that the only reliable way for management, or that part of management concerned, to know how to evaluate the experts is for management to learn quite a bit about the business of the experts.

To hire or create in house a group of experts to learn enough about the ways and whys of the business of the organization in order to automate the required information system is to spend a great deal of time and money. This also means the time of top level managers in sufficient quantities to permit them to offer the necessary access to themselves, to express and explain the problems, current purposes and processes. If, on top of this, management must also understand the business of the experts sufficiently well to understand what they are doing and proposing, quite a lot of time and money is involved. It would seem logical for management to have done just this in the first place, before calling in the experts. The question about who should learn whose business can be answered by asserting that it is management's business to understand the art and expertise of data processing and information systems experts.

The roar of managerial, not to mention expert, indignation that such a suggestion produces is rather understandable. After all, why hire experts if one has to learn the expertise oneself? This very same question disturbs the experts as well for the simple reason that it could lead to the conclusion not to hire experts. However, this conclusion is no more outrageous than when management, without sufficient managerial knowledge of the field of expertise, hires experts. Experts are useful in conjunction with highly skilled and knowledgeable management. But, as some of the case histories to be discussed later seem to imply, experts may be worse than useless when hired by management ignorant (and proud of their ignorance) of the field of expertise. Certainly this point has merit when dealing with expertise purporting to know the utility of automated information systems. Whether it is taught at Harvard Business School or not, the principle that "if management doesn't first understand what it is trying to do, management oughtn't to do it" makes sense in the world of information systems. What a management that is relatively ignorant of this art ought to do will be discussed in detail later.

2.1.3 System Design and/or Configuration and Costs

System designers consider paradise a state where something quite new or never before attempted is desired and costs are of little consideration. However, even the most restrictive of circumstances ("Just give me what the competition has at half the price it cost him") can produce highly inventive system design. For one thing the Avis car rental system does not work quite like Hertz. Pan American Airways reservation systems do not function quite like Lufthansa's, and The Bank of America data processing systems do not perform quite like Dresdner Bank's. General Motors management systems cannot be exactly duplicated within Ford, and the technical libraries at Siemens AG do not perform in the same ways as do the technical libraries of General Electric or RCA or MIT. The Library of Congress has different goals and problems than the library services for the British Parliament, and information in Bavaria is treated in differing ways and accents than information in Ostfriesland, California, Bangladesh, or Uganda. In short, generally one cannot have exactly the system the other fellow has and get the same results at even twice the cost and chaos.

What may be less obvious is that usually one cannot opt merely to replace the existing manual system as is by an automated system that functions the way the manual system did. Perhaps this can be accomplished in the most simple case but, in general, the mere introduction of automation changes organizational functions both directly and indirectly in nontrivial ways. The more complex the system, the less trivial the changes stemming from automation.

Yet designers are all too often presented with the task of replication—that is, copying another's automation in a differing context or copying the manual system when automating, inevitably changing the context.

A significant degree of creativity is required in the design process. Such creativity has less to do with inventing new things than with understanding some rather old things in order to put them together in better and newer ways in a context where change is more evident than stasis. Furthermore, the design process itself has been radically transformed in less than two decades. Where not too long ago computer hardware was both expensive and inadequate for information system applications of any complexity, computer hardware systems today, with the exception of certain peripheral equipment, provide ever increasing capacity and high reliability at less cost.

The design task is to choose and to choose wisely among a great and often bewildering variety of hardware system components. Such design choices must moreover be made knowing that the continued rapid advance of technological development of hardware will make any choice look bad later. And not much later, at that, since hardware has been improving faster than systems have been implemented.

We have noted previously that system requirements and goals are transformed during implementation. With the available system hardware changing as well, the designer is forced to make the best selections and choices he can while everything around him is in flux. If the designer fails to fix on a system, no system gets implemented. If the fixed system gets implemented, by the time it becomes operational, better means of satisfying the then current goals and requirements have become available. This quite normal situation was once summed up in what could be called Genensky's Law: "Information system requirements and hardware are both not invariant with respect to time" (1). The creativity of the design process involves understanding and getting around this paradox.

System software is quite another story. Hardware constraints can no longer be blamed for the inadequacies of current software. For a variety of reasons, some of which are discussed elsewhere (2), software development has concentrated on the easy machine processing tasks, the basis of any automated system, or on the essentially impossible tasks of getting machines fully to perform human functions requiring human judgment and, at the least, human interaction.

The result is that we have very fine software for getting machines to accomplish processing tasks that humans may have previously accomplished but for which no significant human capabilities were required—the essentially rote and mechanical processes. Further, we have scores of unsuccessful attempts to provide software replacing or performing the essentially human tasks which require judgment and thought. And we have precious little in-between software, functional software that permits, encourages, and helps humans to interact with machines to do better work.

If the system designer then restricts selection to the off-the-shelf software packages (or attempts merely to adapt them to given hardware and operations), the resultant system may work, but it will hardly satisfy the basic goals of the decision maker who opted for automation. Automation of essentially mechanical tasks is not the kind of automation that will enable the construction of complex information systems.

On the other hand, if the system designer opts for the development of new, if needed, software, questions arise about what kind, at what cost, and with what results. Furthermore, these questions arise in an environment where organizational decision makers and top management have been sold on the notion that going the automation route no longer requires extensive or radical development. They want a plug-in system, not chancy development. The designer may well know that any such configuration of plug-in elements available will tend to increase rather than decrease the human work load surrounding any complex information system. He may well know that software development is necessary. But in today's climate, designers are not likely to offer this knowledge and lose the design job. After all, IBM and all the other computer firms are quite ready to step in at a moment's notice.

Here certainly we have focused on an area where much more can be accomplished than at present, an area at the heart of the implementation of complex information systems. The development and use of interactive software might well be aimed precisely at the implementation process itself. Here is where tools may be found that can transform our implementation paradigm, tools that aid the decision process about automation, the determination of requirements, and the design processes directly. But some very basic attitudes and notions will have to be changed as well.

The first of these has to do with what has been called interim versus complete solutions. Much of the preceding discussion, when properly understood, tends toward the conclusion that there are, at best, only interim solutions. But interim solutions are not greatly desired by anyone. Strangely even during the period of terribly inadequate hardware, managers and funders wanted the ultimate and final fix. For example, in the late 1950s, when vacuum tube computers represented the state of the art, the RAND Corporation's suggestion of an interim systems approach was rejected by the Strategic Air Command for their command and control system. Needless to say, SAC's option for an ultimate system merely resulted in the creation of one interim system after another over more than a decade, each interim system becoming outmoded by the changing requirements and technology, even before it had become operational.

In today's context of adequate but still rapidly improving hardware and continued inadequate software, only long and often bitter experience has tempered the demand for the complete, once and for all attainment of the wishbook. Those, for example, who sought, built, and paid for the ultimate in high fidelity systems shortly before the introduction of stereo, did the same again with stereo, but have to some degree tempered their rush to the ultimate quadro-sound system. The same experience has occurred with complex information systems, even though high fidelity in any form has never been obtained.

Another basic attitude that needs changing has to do with costs. Managers have been all too concerned with the cost itself of an automated system but surprisingly slow to focus on the sources of the most cost-producing factors. Designers have not been of much help in this regard. Or perhaps designers have been clever enough to define the boundaries of their systems in such a way that many of these cost-producing factors have remained beyond their responsibilities. Organizations need information as well as data processing systems (in the sense of the distinctions made in Chapter One). Designers have generally restricted themselves to consideration of costs within the boundaries of data processing. The sources of high costs, however, reside along the boundaries between the two, the conversion of data into information and vice versa.

A detailed cost study can be made showing the costs in time, labor, and/or money of current operations and resultant products of an existing information system. That is to say, the costs can be determined for the number of items of information handled, the number of books or documents indexed and filed, the number of search requests, the number of information items retrieved, the number of reports, special and typical or cyclic, produced, the duplication and distribution of these, and so forth. In more sophisticated fashion, such costs can be charted against an increasing or decreasing load, against time expended, or against any definable form of resource consumed. In most cases, automation is considered when the anticipated work load is expected to grow to the extent that the costs of the existing system performance go off the charts.

Further, the values or utility or, often, the absolute necessity and the priorities applicable to the existing products and services are given some quantifiable forms. Once this has been accomplished, various means of introducing automation can be costed and compared against each other and the existing system. Included here are analyses which attempt to show how close or how far, how well or how poorly, the various proposed automated improvements or systems come to meeting the statement of requirements, and more subtly, the goals of the decision makers and top management.

There are two elements in this sort of cost comparison and analysis process that we wish to emphasize at this point. One is simply that in determining and defining costs, certain costs get counted and others get ignored. Those costs that are easier to put into numerical form can be explicitly identified and can, by explicit agreement, be determined whether they do belong to the system. But many costs less easily put into numbers (impact on the organizational atmosphere, consumption of intangibles, feelings about job satisfaction, physical or phychological stresses...), are not put into the cost models because no one knows how to fit them in appropriately or at all. The same sort of omissions and inclusions pertain to utilities or values. In both cases, what counts as costs or utilities are, generally, what can be counted.

The second and more important point is that for the most part we simply do not have strictly comparable alternatives. Information containing products and services are what they are partly as a function of the way they were produced. Each variety of automated information system will satisfy and dissatisfy a differing set of purposes and goals. The spectrum of requirements to be satisfied will differ from system to system. Further, this same comparison problem applies between the existing system and any one of the automated alternatives. It is almost like betting on a horse race in which not only are all the horses different and each bet itself influences the odds and payoff but also where the race has already started and an identical fisnish line is undefinable for all horses in the race. Or to put this more exactly in the terms of our discussion, it is a race in which the odds and payoffs and the finish lines are constantly changing with time.

The costs of the hardware and software, the system configuration, itself, are relatively easy to determine. Development merely adds an order of magnitude or two of doubt. The costs of getting the hardware and software to work can also be estimated with a fair degree of reliability. We know how much the horse will cost and how much it will cost to get the horse to run. It is just that the odds of crossing the finish line (getting the system to do what you want it to do at the time it does anything useful) or even placing (coming close) and the finish line itself (when you can stop bothering about the system) keep changing.

These remarks about costs and some problems in their determination and comparison lead again to the proposition that we continue to deal with interim systems, interim comparisons, interim results, and interim costs. This in turn may lead us to consider whether it is the path toward automation for which alternatives can be defined, costed, and compared, rather than any of the given automated points and their alternatives along the sundry paths. We shall explore this viewpoint in some detail later. However, to put this viewpoint in the clearest terms we can, what we wish to propose for consideration is:

a. All complex information systems are interim.
b. The alternative points (given systems at a given time) can seldom be usefully compared, costed, or well designed and evaluated as if they were varying equivalent end stations.
c. There are alternative paths toward automation containing sometimes identical points representing the interim solutions or systems at given times.
d. We might do better to design, compare, evaluate, and cost the alternative paths.
e. Finally, perhaps only in terms of its position on the various paths toward automation can any given interim system be evaluated.

2.1.4 Compromises and System Configurations

As before in this chapter, we offer reflections rather than the details of an approach to be found in later chapters. We highlight certain difficulties for which we think there are solutions. Here we attempt to show that changes in technology have also produced differences in the kinds of compromises that were necessary in the selection of workable and economic system configurations.

Not so many years ago, not even the major manufacturers had a complete competitive line of hardware. For example, in the earlier major military systems efforts, a prime contractor such as IT&T would join forces with, say, IBM. IBM would supply the computer system, and IT&T the communications and certain peripheral items, such as on-line displays. Software was generally supplied by yet another contractor, say, SDC.

From the perspective of large-scale information systems, the basic compromises involved the sacrifice of flexibility and interactive functions in order to achieve efficiencies in file structures and the use of expensive and quite limited computer storage. The need for such compromises is less today but has by no means been eliminated. What persists, however, is a function of this older compromise. Although we have learned how to write efficient programs, we have still to learn how to make file structures and interactive functions flexible enough to easily incorporate changes in either files or functions. We may have learned by this time that the ambiguities of systems requirements definition and their refusal to stay fixed for any significant time period require software offering easy transformation of functions and files. But we have not quite achieved the art of producing the software that will successfully and flexibly accomplish such transformations.

Today we have a plethora of hardwares and hardware systems, peripheral devices, and intelligent terminals. Yet this embarrassment of riches will remain fool's gold as long as we fail to provide the effective software with which to make use of the current and coming hardware. Furthermore, system concepts gradually developed over the years are too often based on large central computers connected to unintelligent consoles and terminals via complex communications gear. Such system concepts were born also of the requirement for efficiency of central storage usage and computing capabilities, not to mention the high costs of distributing large-scale computers to all users of interest. The centralized system concept remains very much alive despite the distributed data processing possibilities offered by the newer hardware. Two related factors are involved. The first, already mentioned, is the lack of proper software. The second is the very strong desire for keeping the control of the system and its information and capabilities centralized, that is, in the hands of central or top management. This second factor may well see to it that the appropriate software for distributiong both the available information and the means to transform information into more useful and powerful forms will remain lacking or unimplemented.

The basic compromise today lies then in the determination of how far the system design and configuration shall go toward effective distribution of the system functions, how far out and/or down the system capabilities shall reach. This includes the most important system function of all—the ability to transform the system functions, rearrange the information files to better suit the variety of purposes and users for which they may be made available. A related compromise has to do with the choice of systemsware at a time when the systemsware is in rapid flux and transformation in quite radical ways, such as microprocessor systems with micro-micro memories.

But essentially the choices involved in the selection of a system configuration have not changed all that much. The tendency has been and still is to select systemsware that works, even though that kind of selection tendency has never been able to do what has been long promised. As a result we continue to compromise toward data processing system configurations instead of opting for truly functional information systems interactively connected to information makers and users. And interestingly enough, this result is often what is actually desired by those who make the initial decision to automate. An appropriately functioning information system among other things would provide the means to more objectively evaluate the top decision makers and management. Does anybody really want that?

Nationalistic and other political factors are also involved in equipment selection. But far more important, as various market share studies have demonstrated, is the availability of standardized systems and maintenance support provided by IBM. Few competitors come close here. Thus advanced technology is often given second place to standardization and maintenance services, even though what has been standardized may be far from a serious base upon which to build complex information systems. Given the rather poor, ambiguous statement of requirements, perhaps this drawback has seldom been emphasized.

2.1.5 Putting the Pieces Together, System Start-Up, and Training

Assuming that the defined data bases, information flow, machine processing tasks, human information handling and work loads, the specified inputs and outputs, and overall scheduling determined by the statement of requirements can be reasonably well accommodated by a variety of existing systems, what are the pieces that still have to be put together? Certainly we are no longer in the position of having to construct the data processing systemsware from an assortment of hardware and software. Whole systems are available with a variety of modular variations to suit a similar variety of requirements and presumed growth rate. It turns out that the pieces which must be put together are the assortment of organizational functions and services lying like Humpty Dumpty at the bottom of the wall after automation has struck in force. The organization begins to accommodate itself, often by attempting the quite organic reaction of trying to rid itself of the foreign bodies automation has introduced. That this is both a long and necessary process is indicated by the often made choice to maintain parallel processes (the old and the new systems operate at the same time). This is used as a safety factor to ensure that whatever the organization was doing before it will now continue to do. This sets up an additional battle between the old and the new and raises the question concerning which will get rid of which.

Neither the new nor the old system can be said to win this battle. During the implementation of the new system, new tasks, as well as differing ways of handling the old tasks, have to be accomplished. It becomes quite evident that the new system, with all its advanced machinery, cannot accomplish these tasks alone. The organization finds itself with a wide range of training problems to teach the work force the new required skills, to transform older practices and ways of doing work. Those opting for automation because it would lessen or do away with people problems discover that there is more and more difficult—not less human—work to be done during the short run at the least. As we have previously intimated, the long run may simply turn out to be a series of short runs. There may be no reliably finite way out of this situation.

Furthermore, most implementation programs focus upon the care and feeding of the machines. Seldom is it made clear how and what to teach human beings so they may function interactively within the new environment. In addition, there now exists a new group of machine care-and-feeding experts generally ignorant of and caring little to understand beyond the barest necessities the organizational functions for which the new system is supposed to provide support. Everyone else in the organization is encouraged to stay out of the machine room, to stay clear of the process, and to adapt without being told how. Better control of events and processes expected when opting for automation may exist somewhere, but most people have been placed several steps away from the process. An intervening and too often randomly variable system stands between management and the information it works with. And there are no training manuals to tell management what to do about this other than the continuing requirement to adjust to the system now or to consider doing it all over once again.

Sooner or later a flood of data, reports, answers begin to enter the information channels with little or no assurance about how such outputs were constructed nor what questions the answers were truly answering. Given enough time and patience, however, the new system works better than the older in certain ways and degrees, as good as the older in other ways, and worse than the older system in yet other ways. We discuss this sort of result in Section 2.1.6, below. The result itself is achieved through a process of organizational and system accommodation which constitutes a previously undefined mixture of the old and the new. One might well ask whether this precise sort of mixture should not have been attempted in the first place. A planned for and intelligent mixture of manual and automated processes should do at least as well as the haphazard or unpredicted. Costs and effectivity ought to be better determinable in advance, and the general growth pains significantly lessened. To take this route to automation is to consider various ways of putting the pieces together by forming various mixtures of old and new processes. The task becomes one of constructing blends of manual and computer processes from which to choose. This approach returns us to the tentative solution path previously mentioned. We accept the fact that we are involved in a growth process rather than an attempted ultimate solution. There is never a new system start-up simply because the system has already started and has been long since working. Transforming the system by introducing new blends of automation and human effort can be considered as just another way to keep the system working, of working better or at cheaper costs or faster or more reliably.

2.1.6 The Cycle of Organizational Changes

At some point along the path of automated progress the transformation of problems produced by automation reaches the point where, as we have said, the new system more or less works. Usually the personnel count has gone up and costs in general have increased, but the services performed are broader and sometimes better than before. Although organizational happiness is rather difficult to measure, a reasonably satisfactory state of affairs has resulted. This stems as much from organizational adaptation of goals and working processes as from the improvements resulting from more automation. However, the ripple effect of these mutually enforcing changes may continue for quite some time. Moreover, certain niceties, such as personalized information services, may have been lost in the process. The librarian or information specialist who served clients so superbly did so because these clients were known so well for so long. This same librarian may not have been able to provide the mass services now offered by the new system and may find the new environment uncongenial. The librarian may be absorbed in the new organization where the librarian's specialized talents are not appropriate or appreciated, or be cut off by new layers of hierarchy. This kind of information specialist is no longer in the position to provide for the intimate and unique informational needs of clients as in the past. On the other hand, attempting to continue to provide such specialized services apart from the new organizational structure becomes more and more difficult. Such information specialists, however valuable they may have been, become relics. They have lost status and inevitably find themselves cut off from both the existent new sources of information and the career rewards available only through the new hierarchy. Sooner or later, top management clients adjust themselves to the new system, with perhaps a touch of nostalgia for the old ways and personnel. The new system has produced its changes and it is working.

However, problems have not been solved. They have been transformed. The costs of information remain high. Information outputs are late or insufficient or still too often focused on the wrong features. New requirements have built up over the time period of system implementation. New constraints, new laws and reporting requirements, new needs for information unavailable at present, and new ways of doing business confront management. At some point or other in the ongoing process, somebody, perhaps having heard of the latest developments in information systems technology, raises once again the question of automation. The eventual decision to automate is based on a variety of spoken reasons, but in fact the grounds are few. In fact, most decisions to automate feel forced, as we observed in Section 2.1.1.

2.1.7 Some Assumptions About Which To Think

In partial summary of the preceding discussion of the implementation paradigm, some contrasting assumptions about the automation of complex information processes are worth considering. Evidence, experience, and prejudice can be found to support and contradict each of these:

Linear Assumptions	*Nonlinear Assumptions*
1. The decision to replace or abet manual processes by automation is essentially objective and settles the matter once for a long time.	1. The decision to replace or abet manual processes by automation is essentially subjective and settles very little for very long.
2. Given enough time and money, the justification of the decision to automate can be based upon rational and scientific grounds.	2. Given enough time and money, any decision concerning automation can be justified in accordance with scientific fashion and each such justification will miss or mislead about relevant costs and performance factors.
3. A meaningful fix on the system requirements can be established in a finite time for a time longer than that needed for implementation.	3. The validity of any statement of requirements is not invariant with respect to time. The variation occurs faster than the system implementation.
4. A realistic description of the state of the art (systemsware) is obtainable.	4. To be realistic, any description of the state of the art must include the statement that it will be outmoded before any system based upon it can be implemented.

Linear Assumptions	*Nonlinear Assumptions*
5. System performance and the costs of the given system performance can be determined.	5. System performance and costs can be determined only after the fact, if then, and important costs and performance factors will be indeterminable at any point in time.
6. Without being experts (information or data processing systems) themselves, management can hire a staff of such experts.	6. Management can rely upon and make use of experts only by becoming sufficiently expert in the fields involved themselves.
7. A fixed set of informational requirements can be satsified by a fixed configuration of systemsware for a fixed cost to achieve a fixed performance level.	7. Fixes are possible only for fixed organizations satisfied and able to live tomorrow with what they thought they wanted yesterday.
8. Most users of complex information systems get what they wanted, paid for, and deserve.	8. Given the surprises discovered during implementation, anything can happen including the achievement of success. But there usually is a sense in which it can be said that "all concerned get what they deserve."

It is fair to assert that whatever the truth of these contrasting assumptions may be, the preferred approach to implementation would differ in accordance with whether the linear or nonlinear assumptions are given more weight. It is also fair to state that most implementation approaches to date appear to have given far greater weight in deed if not in words to the linear assumptions.

Our discussion to this point has attempted to show that a good deal of the recent literature as well as our own views of the implementation situation tend to give far more weight than previously to the nonlinear assumptions. As such it becomes our task to describe and discuss a preferred approach to the implementation of complex information systems compatible with the greater weight given the nonlinear assumptions. Later chapters shall take on this task. First, however, let us see what we can learn from some contributed case histories. Other minds and cases should enable us to better evaluate the preceding descriptions of the way things are and help us to formulate more accurately and definitely an approach toward better implementation methods and practices.

NOTES

1. From a paper Sam Genensky and I wrote quite a long time ago, "Some Thoughts on Developing Future Command and Control Systems," S.M. Genensky and A.E. Wessel, P−2941−1, The RAND Corporation, 1964.

2. Wessel, CAIR, and Social Use.

Chapter Three

A Very Short Introduction to the Case Histories

The case histories represent a variety of viewpoints roughly equal to the number of different contributors. They share one important characteristic. All are viewpoints of individuals directly involved and on-site. This does not mean that a purely objective discussion is being offered. Given the ongoing controversies concerning historical writing about historical events, even rather recent ones, perhaps purely objective stories are impossible, and those that pretend to be objective are merely objectively misleading.

However, taken together, these various case histories offer a most useful form of evidence. Each offers a knowledgeable, although unique perspective of the same kind of event—the attempted implementation of automated information systems. For each case, the other side may be missing or neglected in the particular discussion offered by the contributor. However, the sides presented by the differing contributors are by no means the same. As such, a careful reader should be able to obtain from these case histories a rather full picture of the implementation situation exemplified and differentiated by the individual cases.

The criteria for selection of these contributions were in accordance with this attempt to present a larger and more significant portion of the total picture. The criteria were:

a. Knowledgeable, on-site experience for each case.
b. Significant information to communicate.
c. A willingness and ability to communicate it.

Lastly, there was no attempt to enforce or obtain conformity with the viewpoints of each other or with the principal author of this book. In fact there was a conscious effort in the opposite direction.

The case histories are listed in their order of presentation:

Implementation Problems in Patent Office Applications, by Patricia M. McDonnell

The Implementation of a Computer-Based Documentation System Within an International Affairs Research Institute, by Dietrich Seydel

A Credit Bureau Conversion, by Donald L. Drukey

Implementation Problems for Information Systems Within International Organizations, by Ivo Steinacker

Reflections on the Implementation Problems of Complex Documentation Systems in Industry, by Hermann J. Graml

Chapter Four

Implementation Problems in Patent Office Applications

by PATRICIA M. McDONNELL

4.1 THE SCOPE OF THE PROBLEM

Retrieval of scientific and technical information for the determination of patentability is based on requirements established by laws passed by duly constituted legislative bodies and by decisions rendered through judicial systems. The burdens placed on patent offices by the acts of these legislative and judicial authorities, the magnitude of the workload, and the way in which that workload has been handled over the years must be appreciated. These factors comprise important parts of the nature and depth of the problems encountered in attempting to introduce new, complex automated information retrieval systems into the patent office environment. This chapter emphasizes the United States Patent and Trademark Office (to be called the PTO). However, many of the problems described are common to other major patent offices in countries with examination systems.

The comments expressed in this chapter are those of the author and do not necessarily reflect those of the Patent and Trademark Office, the Department of Commerce, or the United States Government.

The United States Congress first established a patent examination system in 1790, and the task of administering patent law was given to Thomas Jefferson, then Secretary of State. Jefferson used his own extensive personal library as an information retrieval tool for the issuance of 57 patents before the examination system was dropped three years later in favor of a registration system. Search and retrieval for examination was resumed following passage of the Patent Act of 1836. This act not only prescribed certain requirements for patentability, but it also called for the establishment of a classification system to facilitate the work of patent examiners in their determinations about the patentability of claims to invention. The system consisted of 22 classes and remained substantially unchanged, officially, until 1868.

Today the United States Patent Classification System consists of 355 broad classes of technology, which are further subdivided into over 95,000 smaller subject matter groupings called subclasses. Implementation of automated information retrieval systems for patent search in recent times has been applied to previously existent search systems. Automation has been an attempt to replace processes which at least appear to have been satisfactorily meeting the diverse requirements imposed on the PTO by patent laws and practices for many years.

The statutory requirements for patentability today are set forth in Title 35 of the United States Code.

In order for a patent to be granted, an applicant must make a complete disclosure of the invention and set forth one or more claims defining the subject matter for which protection is sought. Claims can be drawn to new and useful processes, machines, manufactures, or compositions of matter or to new and useful improvements thereof. In addition to being novel and useful, the subject matter for which a patent is sought must be sufficiently different from the prior art that the subject matter as a whole would have been unobvious at the time the invention was made.

Two aspects of these requirements — prior art and unobviousness — are deserving of special comment because they impose burdens on patent offices not faced by many other organizations in solving their information retrieval problems. Prior art is considered to encompass all publications before the date of invention. Because of this fact, in developing and implementing a new search system, the system designer cannot pick a recent literature cut-off date to keep costs low if the resulting system is to be capable of meeting the users' needs. Consequently it has been nearly impossible to design and implement an automated system that is cost effective compared with the manual system already in place.

An even greater challenge, however, is presented to the system designer by the unobviousness requirement. Patentability searching entails not just looking for documents disclosing what is being claimed in the application under consideration. It includes looking for documents that would disclose something close or analogous to what is being claimed — documents which, taken singly or in combination, would enable a reader with ordinary knowledge of the art to do or make what is being claimed.

4.2 CURRENT PROCESSES AND FILE STRUCTURING

Retrieval of scientific and technical information in the PTO today consists for the most part of manually shuffling through piles of paper arranged according to the United States Patent Classification System. This classification system is a system for arranging documents (the prior art) disclosing all kinds of scientific and technical information. This document collection is structured to facilitate the selective retrieval of such information in documents both by patent examiners in the examination of patent applications and also by inventors and their agents in their investigations to determine whether a discovery is patentable or infringes a patent.

The most important aspect to note in this definition is the arrangement or structuring of the document collection. The classification system involves the filing of documents in such a manner that the desired documents can be retrieved in the shortest possible time with the least possible effort. It is basically a filing system and functions very effectively as such. It is not an indexing system, and much of the criticism is leveled at it by persons who attempt to use it for this purpose. As noted earlier, today it consists of 355 classes and over 95,000 subclasses. To facilitate identification of subclasses containing documents thought to be pertinent to the search need, a *Manual of Classification* is available containing copies of the subclass schedules (i.e., hierarchically arranged lists of subclass titles) for each of the 355 classes. There are approximately 20 volumes of definitions and search notes to aid further in selection of classes and subclasses. A single-volume alphabetic *Index to Classification* is also available.

The classification system in the PTO is used to process over 100,000 patent applications each year. Normally each application receives one complete search through the documents in several subclasses when the examiner first considers the merits of the application and one updating search when the examiner makes a final determination regarding patentability. In addition to these 200,000 searches conducted annually by examiners, at least another 50,000 are conducted in the PTO by patent attorneys, agents and other persons from the private sector. Many large industrial companies maintain patent collections for in-house searching. Frequently these collections are also arranged somewhat as they are in the PTO.

The United States Patent Classification System and other national classification systems have proven over the years to be effective, economical search tools. They have grown over a period of time to the point where the cost of replacing any of them would be staggering. The examiners' search file in the PTO is estimated to contain 22.5 million copies of documents. Fewer than 8 million of these are duplicates. Over half a million copies, representing about 350,000 different documents, are added each year. However, the cost of classifying new documents for placement in the system is estimated to be about 5−10% of what would be the cost of indexing them in depth for computerized or other automated searching.

Searching takes about 20% of the total time spent by an examiner on an application. The remainder of his time is spent primarily on the following activities:

a. Reading and understanding the application before searching.
b. Applying the prior art found during searching in his examination of the merits.
c. Drafting letters to and conducting other forms of communication with the applicant.

If the examiner and the applicant finally agree on the extent to which the latter is entitled to patent protection, certain other formalities are completed by the examiner, including classification of the new patent. If they cannot agree and the applicant files an appeal, then the examiner must prepare a brief to accompany the application at the Board of Appeals review. None of these activities are amenable to automation.

No expensive hardware is required for searching the classified file—only a large amount of filing space, most of which would probably be required for document storage and retrieval in support of an automated system. A patent examiner familiar with the classification system can identify the subclasses to be searched within a few minutes, look through them at a rate of one document per second, pausing at those which appear closely related to what is being claimed in the application, and remove those which he or she thinks will be useful in completing the examination and preparing the response. Examiners average about three or four hours search and retrieval time on each application using the manual search system. Use of an automated search system might cut the search and retrieval time spent by an examiner to one or two hours at best, but that is only 5−10% of an examiner's time required to completely process an application. This saving is probably too small to justify the high development, input, hardware, and other operational costs of automation.

A number of other important features of manual searching contribute to the viability of classification systems as technological information resources for patent examination.

First, as stated earlier, patent searching entails not only looking for documents disclosing what is being claimed, but also looking for documents disclosing something close or analogous to what is being claimed. Before filing an application, an inventor, attorney or agent makes a search to assess whether the claims being drawn are new. If the prior art retrieved during this prefiling search shows that the discovery is clearly not new or unobvious, an application is never filed. Patent examiners are faced with the burden of searching applications in which the probability of patentability is higher than one might otherwise expect but in circumstances in which the economic consequences of an inadequate search can be very great. They must be thoroughly familiar with the current state of technology in order to assess accurately the extent of novelty and unobviousness. Knowledgeably browsing through large numbers of documents, as the examiner does in manual searching, permits him to find documents disclosing subject matter close to that for which he is asking and, at the same time, enables him to maintain his knowledge of the current state of the art.

A second reason why this classification system is particularly appropriate in the patent office environment is that it fulfills the two functions of document identification and document retrieval. When an examiner browses through a subclass, he or she not only identifies those documents potentially of use in replying to the applicant but also physically removes them from the file. Thus, when the examiner finishes searching, not only have the needed documents been identified, but also they have been retrieved. On the other hand, most automated search systems produce only citation lists of potentially useful documents but do not retrieve them for study and evaluation.

A third advantage of this type of manual search is that portions of the document collection may readily be revised or rearranged in response to sudden shifts in technology. These portions may be as small as a single subclass that has suddenly grown to several thousand documents or as large as several entire classes containing hundreds of subclasses that no longer meet the search needs dictated by new technological developments, legislative acts, and judicial decisions.

Revision and updating of the search file in the PTO is the responsibility of the Documentation Organizations. Close to one million documents are reclassified each year, at a cost in the neighborhood of two to three million dollars in professional effort. Selection of art areas for reclassification is under the jurisdiction of the Classification Groups among the Documentation Organizations, but is usually done in response to requests from Examining Groups. It is based on such factors as search activity, length of search times, and availability of persons to do the work. Much of the work is done by examiners knowledgeable in the art, working under the direction of professional classifiers thoroughly knowledgeable in the principles on which the United States Patent Classification System is based. All revisions to the search file, from establishment and abolition of large classes to the transfer of a single patent copy from one subclass to another, pass through a Classification Group for technical review and through the Documentation Processing Division for clerical processing.

4.3 PROBLEMS OF THE MANUAL PROCESSES

Patent offices began investigations into the use of automation for searching over 20 years ago when punched card machines were becoming readily available and computer technology was in its infancy. Management recognized that manual access search systems were not without their inherent weaknesses and began to explore ways of using automation at the time to the extent it might be cost effective. When we look at the nature of these explorations, hindsight may emphasize the advantages of manual searching (see Sections 4.1 and 4.2) as well as the problems associated with use and maintenance of manual files. Historically, perhaps the problems of the existent manual system were predominant.

The first weakness of a classification system for searching is technical in nature. A single facet (e.g., chemical structure, biological utility, industrial process steps) must be selected as the basis for construction of a hierarchical classification schedule. Documents must be arranged according to fixed principles aimed at providing placement of a minimum number of copies in the search file while at the same time providing assurance that high recall will be obtained at search time. As a result of all these competing factors, searches for some aspect other than the facet which served as the basis for schedule development are often very difficult and, in some cases, impossible from a practical standpoint.

Another problem with the manual search file is that it requires a great deal of space. The patent examiners' search file in the PTO contains an estimated 22.5 million documents. This includes the 12 million copies of United States patents, 9.5 million patents of other countries, and 1 million nonpatent items. The PTO maintains a separate file in its Public Search Room for use by patent attorneys and agents and other persons who wish to search the patent literature. This file is not as complete as that used by examiners, since it contains only copies of United States patents based on their official classification. Nevertheless, it contains approximately 10.5 million copies. The PTO would like to make duplicates of this file available for searching at locations remote from the Washington, D.C. area, but space requirements preclude establishment of another facility.

A third, very serious problem for the United States Patent Classification System today is lack of integrity. Documents are removed from the file and taken to examiners' rooms for study. Other searchers may browse through the file and miss pertinent references. Management has been troubled by this problem for many years and is eager to find a practical means for ensuring a high degree of file integrity.

Finally, substantial clerical processing is required to refile documents, to add new documents, and to build a new paper file following the professional effort by classifiers in revising the system. Not only are the labor costs increasing for this type of work, but also it is becoming increasingly difficult to recruit sufficient numbers of persons to perform the dull, repetitive tasks required.

With this as background, one can begin to appreciate what the PTO has been trying to accomplish since it and other patent offices began to study ways in which automation might contribute to maintaining and improving the viability of patent examination system. Early efforts were based on punched technology, but the goals and discussion which follow are about equally applicable to the use of computers and micrographics today.

4.4 ATTEMPTS TO AUTOMATE

The PTO began investigations into automation for searching over 25 years ago. The earliest of these efforts to automate searching were directed primarily toward the development of coordinate indexing systems for selected groups of related subclasses, employing controlled vocabularies and concept indexing in depth. The stated aim of these early investigations was the development of systems to serve as replacements for manual search through portions of the classified file.

To the extent that these efforts were in fields of technology where the United States Patent Classification System was functioning adequately, they failed. Only in limited areas, fields in which the manual search was very long and tedious (file areas needing reclassification) did these efforts meet acceptance. Patent examiners rejected these indexing systems because they furnished only lists of citations of documents and did not deliver the full text of the documents. In addition, the systems were rejected by management because of the high indexing costs, costs which were difficult to reduce because of the lack of any statutory provision for establishment of cut-off dates.

Before abandoning the deep indexing approach, however, an effort was made to reduce the development costs through cooperation with other patent offices throughout the world. This effort was initiated by the United States in 1961 with the formation of ICIREPAT — an informal committee established for the purpose of *I*nternational *C*ooperation in *I*nformation *R*etrieval among *E*xamining *PAT*ent Offices.

From 1962 to 1964 experts from the staffs of five patent offices (Japan, Netherlands, Sweden, United Kingdom, and West Germany) were assigned as guest workers in the United States PTO. Working with the U.S. staff specialists they studied the state of the art of automated searching and began research and development activities directed toward a sharing of the workload required for introduction of automated searching. From their efforts was born the Shared Systems Program. Here the emphasis was placed on the cooperative design and development of coordinate indexing systems and on the exchange of indexing information for use within each office for searching as its own national requirements dictated.

The Shared Systems Program was not as successful as the participating offices had hoped. It is still in operation today, but its level is reduced. During the period 1971–1973, an investigation was undertaken by the organization to determine the causes of the limited acceptability of the shared systems within the various offices. This study resulted in the compilation of a list of 12 interrelated causes, linked by the irreconcilability of these coordinate indexing systems with the various manual classification systems used by the various offices. The diverse bases selected for development of the different classification systems made it difficult to define the scope of the systems in such a way to indicate precisely what part of the manual file need no longer be searched. Interestingly, three of the four causes cited as of far greater importance in the limited acceptability were equally valid for the failures of purely domestic automation efforts:

a. Delays in system development.
b. Costs.
c. Lack of ready access to documents.

After these early efforts to replace manual searching through the classified file, there was a shift toward the use of automation to overcome some of the inherent weaknesses of the classification system as a search tool while trying to capitalize on its strong points. The trend was toward supplementing rather than replacing.

The PTO undertook the development of several combined classification/coordinate index search systems. One of the problems inherent in using a classification system is that the documents are arranged according to a hierarchical schedule based on a single facet of information, and searches for any other facet are usually very time consuming, if not practically impossible. The dual system approach was evolved when the need arose to develop a new system for patents disclosing chemical compositions (mixtures) with a pharmacological or biological utility and those patents disclosing methods of using such compositions.

Two obvious bases for development of the classification schedule presented themselves to those working on the project — chemical structure and pharmacological or biological use. Both facets were significant factors in searching at that time. However, selection of one as the primary basis for schedule development would virtually preclude searching based on the other facet, if a purely conventional classification search system were presented to patent examiners or other searchers.

In response to this dilemma (the PTO was cognizant of the costs of developing a deep indexing system, especially one capable of handling mixtures of chemicals), reclassification of these patents was effected by development of a conventional manual classification search system based on the chemical structure of the active ingredients of the mixtures. Concurrently a supplementary coordinate index system was developed to provide searches based on pharmacological and other biological functions or utilities. At the time each document was considered for placement in the chemical classification segment of the dual system, a coding sheet was also prepared for the utility data only. The step of indexing the document added less than five minutes to the 15−20 minutes normally spent on the document in this phase of a reclassification project. (This was a marked contrast to the 1−2 hours spent on analyzing and coding each document for many of the deep-indexing systems.) For a relatively small expenditure of additional time and money, the retrieval capabilities of the product system were greatly expanded. Further, by using the conventional classification subclasses as chemical descriptors in the coordinate index segment, no additional expenditure was necessary for developing a chemical coding system and encoding the chemical information disclosed in the documents.

Despite the high hopes held for this approach to solving some of its information handling and retrieval problems, this system also fell victim to the lack of a suitable means for implementation which included presentation of the documents identified through the coordinate index segment to the user. In addition, the need for searches related primarily to methods of use (i.e., to pharmacological and biological effects) was diminished by court decisions regarding patents in this field of science. Thus, the system was never fully utilized as originally conceived, and it and several other similarly designed systems are today maintained only as conventional search systems.

In a further attempt to trim system development costs, in 1969 management directed that a set of experiments be undertaken in which tight controls were placed on vocabulary development and indexing costs. A mandatory feature of the first set of six such systems was that indexing times be limited to an average of five minutes per patent in the system (of the order of 2000−3000 United States patents). As was to be expected, indexing errors, particularly those of omission, were intolerably high.

A second set of systems, this time 12 in number, were initiated in which indexing times were to average 10 minutes or less. Some of these proved to be successful: those in art areas in which the classification system did not provide a convenient field of search for some types of searches, and in which well-structured information was being extracted and coded. For example, the manual search system established for the field of welding is based on process steps. As welding technology has developed, however, patent applications which used to be concerned almost entirely with claims to process steps, have begun to have more claims in which the composition of the filler material used in the process is a significant feature. The classification schedule is based on process steps, and manual searches for filler composition are very difficult. To overcome this deficiency in the manual system, an indexing scheme was developed for coding the chemical composition of the filler material, and this one facet of information was coded in an average of 5−10 minutes for each patent. These small systems were and still are implemented using desk-top tools (Termatrex optical coincidence cards for document identification and paper files of documents in accession number order for retrieval), so that the user is able to complete his or her search and retrieve the desired documents in somewhere between five and fifteen minutes. There is no waiting for 24 hours or more turnaround such as for search questions submitted for punched card or batch computer searching.

While this low level of effort in system development and implementation was proceeding, a sizeable research effort was begun in 1969 in the area of computer-aided classification (CAC) with a view toward making use for input purposes of the full-text data base which was being produced. In the late 1960s the PTO began to convert its patent printing operation from one relying on typesetting to one based on photocomposition by computer after conversion of the text to machine-readable form. Within two years of the commencement of the CAC project, the scope was expanded to include not only classification, but also search and retrieval.

At this point it became known as Project POTOMAC (*P*atent *O*ffice *T*echniques of *M*echanized *A*ccess and *C*lassification). Shortly thereafter, largely because of a sudden change in top management, work was suspended and an evaluation team from the National Bureau of Standards was brought in to conduct a thorough evaluation of the PTO requirements, the work done to date on the project, and the feasibility of the plan. The team concluded that the goals of Project POTOMAC were not achievable within the then current state of art.* As with the early automation efforts, the objectives here were too ambitious and too expensive to achieve in a cost effective way. While many of the individual components that were required to go into the implementation of a large system for storage, search, and retrieval were themselves judged to be feasible, the linking of all of them together in something as large and complex as the system required for PTO needs was to be beyond the limits of practicality in the immediate future.

*Discussion of the failure of Project POTOMAC seems to disturb certain information scientists. A statement in Computer−Aided Information Retrieval that "hard data is difficult to obtain" was pounced upon by G. Jahuda and W.A. Martin (*Information Processing and Management,* Vol. 12, No. 4, 1976, p. 296, and *The Information Scientist,* Vol. 9, No. 4, 1975, p. 158, respectively). Both translated difficult as impossible neglecting to note the citation given to a *Business Week* article where the National Bureau of Standards Report on Project POTOMAC was "leaked." The new discussion of the failure of Project POTOMAC above may continue to upset the same apple carts. Perhaps it is worth observing that pointing out one bad apple may prevent loss of some very good ones. As such, it is a bit surprising, given the public funds expended and the importance of Project POTOMAC, that this National Bureau of Standards Report remains buried. Its release could hardly be claimed to affect national security. American information scientists still disturbed by the difficulty of obtaining hard data would do well to invoke the Freedom of Information Act recently passed by The United States Congress and get this report released. It might prevent continued waste of public and private funds being expended upon similar projects following in Project POTOMAC's footsetps. And then again it might not!

A.E. Wessel

4.5 A PARTIAL SOLUTION

In 1973, in accord with the recommendations of the National Bureau of Standards team that the PTO limit its efforts to the achievement of more modest, realistic goals and attempt to overcome the deficiencies of the search tools the examiner was currently using, the PTO proposed to undertake two experiments using a combination of recent computer and micrographic technological developments, namely, minicomputers and high reduction filming. Both of these proposed experiments were directed toward seeking new methods of implementing existing classification and coordinate index search systems. One was to simulate at a computer-driven micrographic terminal what an examiner now does in searching his manual access classified paper file. The other was to use a similar terminal to combine the searching of a coordinate index data base and the display of documents identified in the search.

Funds were limited at that time, so that only one of these experiments could be undertaken. Performance specifications were prepared, and, as the result of a competitive procurement, in June 1974 a contract was signed with Image Systems, Inc., of Culver City, Calif. to develop and install a computer-controlled microform search system (CCMSS) for searching coordinate index files and displaying documents responding to the searches. This system was installed in April 1975 and has been enthusiastically received by both patent examiners and by searchers from the private sectors.

Encouraged by this initial experience with the use of the CCMSS for searching indexed files, a new contract was signed with Image Systems, Inc., to upgrade the software and to undertake the second experiment by addition of two large files for searching by the United States Patent Classification System subclass codes, enabling the user sitting at a micrographic terminal to do what he or she now does standing at a paper filing case. Delivery of the upgraded software was scheduled for late spring in 1977. The implementation of the two large files was to follow during the second half of the year.

Development of the new software package moved much more slowly than expected, primarily because of two factors. First, the contractor seriously underestimated the size and complexity of the program required to perform the tasks enumerated in the PTO specifications and had to make some fundamental design changes late in the software development process to enable the program to operate efficiently on a minicomputer (1) with only a 32K-word core memory—the maximum size for the CCMSS minicomputer purchased in 1974 with 24K words for the original implementation—and (2) serving up to 25 users on-line with no significant lags in response time. Second, because the contractor was a small business organization, he decided to subcontract much of the development of individual program modules to freelance programmers, rather than tie up his entire internal programming staff for the duration of the contract period. (This type of subcontracting is common among small organizations in the United States.) Much of their work had to be discarded, however, at least in part because of the late design changes, but also because of other problems frequently encountered when attempting to integrate various program modules into one efficient whole.

Delivery of a new search program for operational testing in the PTO at last occurred in March 1978, approximately ten months after the date originally specified in the contract. Unexpectedly, at that time a two-month series of failures of critical hardware components began causing such things as tape-read errors and communication problems between core and disk which thoroughly frustrated attempts to test the new software. Added to these were additional problems associated with integrating components (in this case printer terminals) supplied by another vendor into the CCMSS configuration.

By the end of May 1978 the PTO had gained sufficient experience with and confidence in the new software that plans were being made to begin searching the first of the two large classified files in July. The second was to follow about six weeks later. A number of cosmetic improvements in the software were still to be delivered, but, in general, the new version was considered to be a substantial improvement over the original program.

The CCMSS consists of a number of Questicon^R micrographic storage and retrieval units operating under the control of a single minicomputer. Each unit contains a set of microfiche and is equipped with a viewing means and a keyboard through which the searcher communicates with the minicomputer. This in turn, controls selection and display of micrographic images. The microfiche are clipped with binary coded metal strips and located in a carousel in the base of the Questicon unit. Images on the fiche are at 48X reduction, and each fiche can store up to 273 images. The carousel can store about 750 fiche, so that the capacity of a Questicon unit is close to 200,000 pages or 28,000 United States patents. Average accession time between patents is 2−3 seconds. Maximum is 4 seconds.

In using the system, the searcher is presented with a series of step-by-step instructions by means of a set of 'INSTRUCTION' messages displayed on the micrographic screen. Associated with each 'INSTRUCTION' message is a 'HELP' message (accessed by pressing a key labeled HELP). This contains explanatory information pertinent to the execution of the instruction to which it is related. Thus, in designing the system, an attempt was made to anticipate when a user might need assistance and to provide necessary information and instructions within each Questicon unit for those not familiar with its operation. At the same time, the CCMSS was also designed so that users thoroughly familiar with its use avoided being bogged down by extensive amounts of instructional and informational material.

One advantage that patent examiners see in CCMSS to offset the disadvantages of working at micrographic terminals, is the 'EXCLUDE' feature. Searching the paper file frequently involves browsing through several related subclasses; the same document may be located in two or more of these subclasses. In searching with the CCMSS, examiners and other searchers can choose to avoid looking again at any document they have already viewed.

One other interesting feature of the software is tagging. As a searcher browses through documents, he or she can press a key labeled TAG/UNTAG while viewing documents of particular interest. At any point the searcher can interrupt browsing to go back to review those previously tagged. Documents can be removed from the tagged list if they are no longer of interest (because a more pertinent reference has subsequently been found) by pressing the same key. There is a light on the control panel which signals to the user whether the document being viewed is currently on the tagged list. At the end of the search session the searcher can obtain a printed search report containing the questions asked (subclasses searched), the total number of documents viewed in response to each question, and a list of the documents that have been tagged.

4.6 SOME NEXT STEPS

The extent to which the CCMSS may prove suitable for implementation throughout the PTO cannot be determined until some experience is obtained with its use for searching by the United States Patent Classification System, using only the subclass codes by which the paper file is arranged. One of the evaluation elements to be studied will involve a direct comparison of the two methods of searching, both in terms of cost (including time) and of effectiveness. The PTO has a legal requirement to maintain the highest possible recall, and it is felt that this is best met for unobviousness searches by giving the examiner the capability of conveniently browsing through relatively large numbers of documents. Ideally, the searcher should also have available a means (e.g., additional codes for index terms or concepts) by which he or she can improve precision when searching for novelty, but cost-justifying such indexing in the patent office environment is well nigh impossible.

The impact of a computer system such as the CCMSS on examination time and pendency is expected to be small when used for searching by subclass codes, but, as just indicated, no attempt is planned at this time to undertake additional indexing to improve the precision the users will experience with the CCMSS over that presently obtained with the paper file. However, improvement in recall and hence in quality of search—which should necessarily follow from the file integrity inherent in such a system and so sorely lacking in the paper system—is expected to be significant.

Computer systems such as the CCMSS can have terminals located at remote locations and thus offer the opportunity to improve service to the public by making feasible the establishment of one or more search centers in places outside the PTO.

Upon installation and evaluation of the proposed system for searching classified files, if warranted, an effort will be made to obtain a software package which will enable reclassification of patents on-line at a termianl by a classifier using much the same thought processes and creative techniques that he or she now uses in creating a new classification search system.

Substantial benefits could flow both to the PTO and to the public if such an on-line capability is developed. The clerical processing to build the new paper file following the professional effort by the classifiers and technicians costs in excess of $1.50 per patent reclassified, and hundreds of thousands of patents are reclassified each year. Further, with the present procedure, large numbers of patents are unavailable in the Public Search Room for as much as two years while they are being reclassified and the new file is being prepared.

If classifiers are able to work on-line at terminals, this substantial clerical effort can be eliminated. Further, there need be no period during which files would be unavailable, other than the time required to read in a data tape and insert a few new pieces of microfilm into each terminal.

It is anticipated that classified search files implemented on the CCMSS may have supplemental index terms assigned, such as those developed for the pharmacological patents. Also, International Patent Classification symbols can be stored in the system and used for searching. Both of these additional ways of accessing documents can be employed at little cost and should contribute to improved quality; neither is practical for classified files implemented with paper.

While the CCMSS may hold promise for use extensively at the PTO, those closely associated with its design and installation recognize that there are many problems to be faced and questions answered before large investments in hardware and microfilming are justified. One of the most serious concerns is that of assuring high quality, easily readable images on the micrographic screen and on paper copies made from those micrographic images. The CCMSS is more promising than other computer-driven micrographic retrieval systems, because it has the capability of presenting to the user an image of any one of approximately 28,000 patents in 2 or 3 seconds, 4 seconds at most. This high terminal capacity is the result of recent developments which permit use of high reduction ratios through use of two-step production processes. There is, nevertheless, a price which has to be paid in the form of a slight decrease in resolving power of high reduction systems compared with low reduction systems. Extensive use of the CCMSS or any other image retrieval system will depend on the ability to obtain high quality source documents for filming. This is a significant, though not an insurmountable, problem for the processing of United States patents. Options within the PTO for obtaining good copies or, alternatively, enhancing poor copies of foreign patents and nonpatent literature items are not as readily available or apparent.

Another unknown yet to be addressed but a prerequisite for successful widespread implementation of the CCMSS is management of both the micrographic and magnetic files. The micrographic and computer technologies embodied in the present version of CCMSS point to expansion via installation of a plurality of perhaps 15 to 25 minicomputer systems, each serving a group of classes in the United States Patent Classification System. Determinations must be made about how the total search file may most effectively and efficiently be subdivided into data bases of 20,000−25,000 patents each (to permit file growth within a terminal), how much overlap there will be between data bases, how to handle large reclassification projects which may extend over several data bases, and the like.

The history of attempts to implement automated systems in the PTO is the story of a series of attempts to phase in new technologically advanced search techniques without disrupting PTO operations and to do so cost effectively. The existing manual system, simple in its initial implementation with only a few thousand documents almost 150 years ago, has grown into an extremely large, extremely complex entity. The fact that it is still functioning as well as it does is a testimony to its inherent suitability. Nevertheless, PTO management recognizes that a concerted effort must be made to find ways of overcoming its weakness to the extent that sheer necessity dictates and economics permit. As the cost of labor increases and of computers decreases, the day is rapidly approaching when searching by purely manual means through piles of paper will no longer be a viable way for patent examiners. The CCMSS probably is not the final answer, but the experiments currently undertaken with it are providing valuable ''hands on'' experience with automated searching and much needed information about the man-machine interface.

The fundamental reason for a strong patent system is to promote and foster technological developments. To maintain a strong patent system, a patent office must seek the latest in information handling technology for effective searching and retrieval. In seeking that technology, it must examine all aspects carefully to determine which aspects are applicable currently, which are gleams in the eye of some researcher or some salesman, and which will probably be feasible within a few years. In 1969 and 1970 the PTO used computers only for their much touted potential for processing full text, since the full text of patents was becoming available in machine readable form. Proposals to use computers to search existing indexed files and to display microfilm images were ignored, because human indexing was considered to be on the verge of obsolescence. As time went on, the dreams of searching based on full text processing dimmed, and computer-assisted retrieval of micrographic images is finally getting a fair test.

Chapter Five

The Implementation of a Computer-Based Documentation System Within an International Affairs Research Institute

by **DIETRICH SEYDEL**

5.1 THE IMPLEMENTATION BACKGROUND

Computer display units providing on-line access to data banks and computerized libraries could soon be as ubiquitous as the telephones now at the working places of social scientists, policy planners, and government officials. By the end of this century such means of accelerating access to information and information processing capabilities should be generally available for use within the social sciences. To bring about the implementation of these computerized capabilities no longer requires a basic technological breakthrough. What is still needed is a more consistent and selective application and further development of existing technology.

However realistic the technical potential is, meaningful applications within the social and political sciences are quasiutopian. This is primarily due to the socio-organizational framework within which the technology must be implemented.

The introduction of large-scale computerized information services and centers in the social and political sciences today is in a transitional stage. Hardware technology has not sufficiently matured. Existing computer systems are not as yet capable of satisfying all pertinent requirements. For example, current hardware still lacks inexpensive and flexible storage capacity, and expensive communications gear is often required. The terminals and displays are too small and not sufficiently adaptive and are limited in number and kind of alphanumeric characters and other symbols. Furthermore, neither a coherent list of requirements nor software satisfying known requirements exists capable of offering comfortable solutions for all of the necessary functions. These functions not only include retrieval, data acquisition and the required search processes, but also are now understood to cover indexing, classification, file description, thesauri development and maintenance, product production and printout services as well as the administrative functions for the information and documentation sector. Most existing computer program packages are just barely capable of satisfying bookkeeping and other simple requirements for these critical functions.

Concerning rationalization of the socio-organizational aspects, investigation and understanding of the organizational requirements and the new forms of organizational division of labor and task assignments required for even partial automation are by no means complete. What results we have are not consistently interpreted. What seems clear, however, is that those involved in the development of one part of the overall information system do not understand well enough the problems of those in other parts. Because of this, a coherent integration of all of the critical elements in the functional fields listed above has not been achieved. As a rule, data processing people understand too little about documentation and documentalists comprehend too little about electronic data processing, its possibilities and problems. There is a general lack of overall system comprehension and agreement about all the relevant factors of the implementation environment.

The processes involved in the exchange and processing of information within organizations not only change with time, they are themselves transformed by the introduction of new techniques and technology. The introduction of computerized services transforms most of the critical man/man and man/machine interactions. These interactions and processes in the exchange and processing of information and their transformations resultant from the introduction of technology are simply not well understood.

Whether this situation is peculiar to the social and political sciences or extends generally throughout other fields of application is not at issue here. It is sufficient to note, however, that with regard to the social sciences the technical revolution is regarded as more a subject of potential research than as a means of directly and significantly transforming the working processes within the social sciences themselves.

Given immature systemsware and a lack of clarity about requirements and the socio-organizational aspects of implementation, the current situation for the introduction of computer-aided information and documentation systems in operational social science research institutes cannot be regarded as optimal. Nonetheless, without serious attempts to implement, accepting the difficulties involved, the implementation context for the social and political sciences is hardly likely to improve. Simply hoping for technological solutions or adopting an ivory tower approach emphasizing laboratory development and simulated application, merely delays facing the necessary learning processes. Such a strategy is based on the illusion that the developmental and implementation processes are unaffected by seriously conflicting organizational goals and the general lack of comprehension of the socio-organizational environment.

On the other hand, early implementation is afflicted with the limited flexibility and capabilities of curent systemsware. These systemsware inadequacies severely restrict the ability to adapt or improve the system and use as feedback what has been learned during implementation. To proceed under such circumstances has its risks. However, without actual implementation within organizational environments, the inflexibility and limitations of the systemsware might never have been determined, and meaningful technological developments might have never occurred.

This situation of mixed possibilities and dilemmas provided the background for the implementation of a computer-aided documentation system within a German research institute for international politics and security policy. The implementation process began in 1970 and continues today. The goal of the implementation process was to provide improved and new documentation services in social sciences for use inside and outside the organization. The external services were intended to be achieved through a gradual expansion of the institutionally oriented services. How well these dual goals have been met and what has been learned from the ongoing implementation is the focus of the remainder of this chapter.

5.2 THE RESEARCH INSTITUTE OF THE STIFTUNG WISSENSCHAFT UND POLITIK (SCIENCE AND POLITICS FOUNDATION)

The research institute for international affairs of the Stiftung Wissenschaft und Politik (SWP) was established in the Federal Republic of Germany in response to an information and analysis deficit discovered by those in German parliament and the federal administration concerned with foreign and security policy. During the late President Kennedy's term of office foreign and security policy consultations with the United States required increased participation of scientists and scientific institutions for international policy planning. The small number of political science institutes established in the 1950s in German universities were not able to provide sufficient consulting backup in comparison to that available in the United States. To help narrow this gap a research institute for international affairs was established in 1964 as a foundation under German law financed under the Chancellery budget.

The primary task of the research institute was to provide scientific analyses of problems of international and security policies in a form applicable to the appropriate German ministries as a basis for their foreign political planning and decision-making. The research program was determined both by the institute's perception of problems and by the requirements of the ministries for analytic work. Although the research institute is the largest in this field in the Federal Republic, consisting of about 100 staff members, including 45 scientists, its research could not cover all of the relevant problems because of the size of the field. For quite some time, therefore, work was focused on the international relations of industrial states. Later this focus was extended to include the relationship among the industrial states and developing countries.

The actual research topics for the individual scientist continually change within their relatively broad systematic and/or regional working fields. Correspondingly the informational requirements for each scientist continually change as well. The research institute from its conception has followed an inter- and/or multidisciplinary approach. As such, the staff members come from a variety of differing disciplines, not only political science, economics, law, but also physics, mathematics, and engineering. The informational requirements for the institute are obviously complex.

Scientific research undertaken at the institute ranges from comprehensive studies on longer-range systematic and/or regional problems to working papers on current topics, colloquia, and short ad-hoc tasks. This range of research services is to be supplemented in the future by providing information to clients directly from the documentation developed for the established working fields.

5.2.1 The Research Institute's Documentation Department

The documentation department was established with the primary task of supporting the scientific work of the research institute. Given the wide range of research subjects and working fields at the institute, the variety of disciplinary approaches, and their worldwide orientation, the documentation department itself could not obtain, store, and maintain all of the information nor cover all of the information sources necessary. At the same time it proved impossible to sufficiently expand the documentation department without extending its services to

56   The Implementation of a Computer-Based System

users outside of the institute. (This was one reason for accepting the task of providing services to external clients as part of the overall goal described in Section 5.2). Furthermore, soon after the establishment of the research institute it was acknowledged that an in-house documentation department could only perform satisfactorily by also assuming external service functions which would encourage a necessary division of labor and exchange of information with other information and documentation centers or systems. In addition, the necessity for such exchanges of information in order to satisfy the requirements imposed on the documentation department as well as the broad range of services to be undertaken, lead to the conclusion that electronic data processing support was essential.

Initially the institute had developed a professional library and a press documentation service. These were gradually supplemented by the development of documentation files for journal articles. During these earlier operations, using conventional techniques, a good deal of methodological experience was obtained for determining the requirements for a computer-aided system.

5.2.2 Some Conclusions from the Conventional Operations

An important positive conclusion stemming from experience with conventional documentation operations is that a close cooperation between research experts and documentalists specialized in the corresponding informational field is essential. This close cooperation between the ultimate research user and the documentalist is required not only to select relevant literature for the documentation base, but also to prevent the relevant information in the documentation base from being lost among the mountains of information. The phrase "documentalists specialized in the corresponding informational field" means that the staff members of the documentation department are required to cover the specialists in their specific research fields. As such, a given documentalist is responsible for indexing, retrieval, collaborating in the acquisition of literature, and for keeping the scientists generally informed about available information relevant to their specialties. In order to successfully perform these services documentalists must be regularly informed about the informational requirements of the scientists they serve by participating in meetings of the research working groups and by direct personal contacts.

The basic negative conclusion obtained from conventional operations is that conventional documentation systems (i.e., not computer-aided) are inadequate where sophisticated and varied information services are required for scientific research. Conventional systems are limited and unsatisfactory because:

- The number and variety of search elements or document retrieval tags assignable to a given documentation unit are too limited and generally one-dimensional.

- As a practical matter, it is difficult, if not impossible, to store and identify items of information at some later date which originally were not recognized as being relevant or useful.
- It is practically impossible to change classification systems, search term lists, or thesauri so that older or other document files can be covered.
- Searches are very time consuming and information losses high.
- Information has to be stored several times in order to be available when needed, or time-consuming and difficult to maintain, remote storage is required.

5.3 THE CONCEPTUAL DESIGN FRAMEWORK FOR THE COMPUTER-AIDED SYSTEM

Starting in 1970 a conceptual framework for a computer-aided documentation system was established for the research institute. At that time the research institute had neither a computer programming staff nor a computer of its own. However, based on experience with conventional operations and an investigation of the existing state of the art, long-range objectives were established that could follow from the attainment of short-term solutions.

The long-term objectives were:

- All data necessary for documentation to be stored in a central computerized store were to be available for direct access retrieval.
- The system had to possess sufficient flexibility to facilitate the changing of data records.
- The system had to permit differentiated retrieval or specialized information for a variety of users.
- The system had to be capable of accepting informational inputs from information and documentation bases outside the system, and had to provide services for other external search centers, thus establishing a means of information exchange.
- The system had to be capable of supporting the broad range of documentation tasks extending beyond ''book-keeping'' functions. In particular, the system must be capable of supporting the intellectual functions of indexers and/or searchers.

The short-term objectives and constraints were:

- The development of a thesaurus to cover the specific research fields of the institute. A thesaurus appropriate for this purpose did not exist,* and

---

*The APSA Political Science Thesaurus did not exist in 1971. It might have been a basis for the institute's own thesaurus for international relations.

neither automatic indexing nor free text search appeared satisfactory for the institute's fields of research.

- Computers and systemsware capable of meeting the requirements previously discussed were not available. The first implementation phase would therefore attempt to provide computer support for a limited set of basic functions rather than attempting a "complete" solution.
- On financial grounds, hardware equipment capable of providing for a comprehensive dialogue access system using *one* central storage was not obtainable.
- Full staffing of an appropriately qualified documentation department was not available for the same financial reasons.

5.4 THE INITIAL IMPLEMENTATION PHASE, 1970–1973

Between 1970 and 1973 the following accomplishments occurred:

a. The research institute developed its own field-specific thesaurus appropriate for use with computer-aided systems and covering international politics and security policy and certain other related fields. This thesaurus became known as the Stiftung Wissenschaft und Politik Thesaurus (SWP-T).
b. The research institute participated in the further development of a software package providing for interactive, computer-aided indexing and search. The concept for this software package was originally developed in the United States and later implemented as the PRIMAS system for use with Siemens AG computers in late 1969 (1).
c. An initial concept for appropriate indexing procedures was developed.
d. Toward the close of the 1970–1973 implementation period these three accomplishments were supplemented by the development of an appropriate organizational concept for the interaction and cooperation of documentailists and scientific research specialists.

These accomplishments will be further discussed below.

5.4.1 Thesaurus Development and Test Procedures

A variety of working concepts evolved during the development of the field-specific thesaurus (SWP-T) for the research institute. The most important of these were:

- The use of keywords or selected terms from text was determined to be unsatisfactory for content analysis of the literature pertinent to the specialized research fields. For one thing, literature from the research field contained many critical terms for which there were strongly diverging definitions. At times there is a Babylonian confusion of language within the social sciences fields for which no universally accepted keyword "tower" seems constructable. In formulating search questions there can be great confusion about the meaning of terms used to tag documents for potential retrieval, and for describing the desired subject matter.

- At the same time the decision to use thesaurus descriptors for the description of subject matter in the documents for content analysis has certain drawbacks. Thesaurus descriptors are, in principle, limited in number and category fields. They can be supplemented or updated only during limited time intervals as a process of thesaurus development. Furthermore, the satisfactory description of documents requires the use of certain terms not systematically listable, such as names of persons, institutions, projects, and ephemeral descriptors, etc.

- Uniterm descriptors appear inappropriate for the content description of social science textual material, principally because of the large number of potentially erroneous combinations of such descriptors in formulating search requests. Furthermore, the degree to which precombination of such descriptors is feasible cannot be determined a priori. Useful or nonerroneous precombination of descriptors depends too much on the differentiated description required during content analysis. This in turn depends upon the variety of potential search requests, the focuses of which change with time. Another factor involved is the size of the documentation units, which will be discussed later.

These considerations led to the design of a thesaurus containing two basic descriptor sets or files. One file consisted of established thesaurus descriptors, essentially fixed, that constituted the controlled terms for the special fields. This file could be updated only periodically. A second file consisting essentially of proper names was established as a free descriptor set. It could be updated at any time. Certain terms selected from text as keywords could also be included.

The file of controlled descriptors was structured in monohierarchical form. The identification and use of additional hierarchical structures or relationships functioning as term fields was postponed to the next developmental phase. The result was a thesaurus containing systematic groups of terms and practical hierarchical structures which could be represented using an alphanumerical notation system for convenient machine entry and handling. The free descriptors were filed as they were acquired from incoming documents, and they were sorted in alphabetical fashion. Free descriptor relationships to the hierarchical structure had to be explicitly identified.

Two procedures were developed for handling relationships between free and controlled descriptors—a thesaurus-oriented procedure and an indexing-oriented procedure. The thesaurus-oriented method was applied to free terms. For each such accepted free term, the higher level terms from the list of controlled descriptors were explicitly identified. The indexing-oriented method was applied to proper names. It consists of explicit recommendations to indexers for using specified controlled descriptors in addition to the proper name. If the proper name of an institution was assigned during indexing, a searcher could directly retrieve all documents concerning this institution if so tagged.

For a more systematic search, however, a searcher would be forced to use several search descriptors. When controlled terms are associated with proper names during indexing, search may be conducted using these controlled terms without considering the proper name descriptors. For example, a document dealing with the attitude of the British Labour Party about direct elections to the European Parliament could be indexed with the free descriptor "Labour Party," supplemented by controlled descriptors such as "Political party," "United Kingdom," "Direct election," "European Parliament," and "Institutional problems of international organizations." Such an indexing method permits the retrieval of the document both under the direct search approach using "Labour Party" and "European Parliament" and using the more general search question, "Political party" and "European Parliament."

The list of free descriptiors was developed through ongoing indexing. However, during the initial phase structural development of the thesaurus was restricted to the controlled descriptors. This development was more practical than theoretical, since several years of experience obtained from conventional operations was available. Initially an attempt was made to have the scientific research staff of the institute participate in the thesaurus development. It turned out that extensive participation of the research staff proved unrealistic because of the limited time the research staff could expend for continuous advisory support of the thesaurus project. Nonetheless, it was essential to the success of the project that the research scientists were able to participate in an advisory fashion during discussions and selections of the controlled term lists. The thesaurus structural development, on the other hand, was left to the documentalists.

Research scientists tend to want to have their special terminologies and languages more or less completely represented within thesauri. Given a multidisciplinary thesaurus with differentiated fields, experts' terminology, and languages, an attempt to satisfy this wish inevitably would lead to both conceptual confusion and redundancy. The documentalists soon realized that although a thesaurus constitutes a purposeful language, the purpose of the thesaurus was to facilitate multidimensional document storage and retrieval rather than to reflect all the conceptual differentiation of the researchers and their specialized languages. The division of labor and focus between the research and the documentalists dscribed above proved useful.

A test thesaurus resulted from this initial developmental effort. Its suitability for content description of documents was next determined. During the test phase six staff members were assigned to determine the practical utility of the individual terms and their thesaurus structuring. This was accomplished over a several months period during which 60 documents with contents covering the conceptual fields of the thesaurus were simultaneously indexed by all six staff members. Summary listings of the descriptors used by the members of the test group for each document made clear where identity or similarity was realized and where not.

The experience gained during the test period extended beyond the narrower test objective. In particular, it was discovered that opinions about the importance or relevance of items and viewpoints expressed in documents diverged greatly. A significant part of the divergence over which items were worth indexing was based more on differences in indexer evaluation than on indexer knowledge. Although differences in evaluating the informational items within the documents were not profound, variation in indexing usually resulted from the use of different hierarchical choices. Some indexers selected several lower level terms, while others selected the associated upper level term.

The various insights into indexing practices obtained during the test phase were used to make changes in the design of the thesaurus. The chief result of the test phase was therefore a revised thesaurus that has been in use at SWP since 1973. The SWP-T contains about 8000 descriptors, some of which are strongly precombined. At present SWP-T remains monohierarchically structured and uses an alphanumerical notation system. A register of keywords out of context (KWOC) is available in which all character sequences appearing between blanks, with the exception of words on a stop list, are generated automatically as keywords. The keywords are sorted alphabetically and refer to the descriptors from which they have been generated.

After several years of use, the SWP-T is now being supplemented by a polyhierarchical structure. Various relationships among descriptors can be explicitly identified for each descriptor. Further supplements, such as definitions, scope notes, concordances referring to other thesauri, and translations into various languages, can also be shown. In the near future SWP-T will be available in a tri-partite representational form consisting of an alphabetical list of descriptors with term fields, a systematic list of controlled descriptors with term fields, and a keyword index (KWOC). Given the current computer programs, SWP-T is stored in its systematic form with term fields and with its KWOC register. Access to the stored thesaurus is through a dialogue mode with both a sequential and a hierarchical dialogue procedure.

5.4.2 Development of the Computer-Aided System

During the initial implementation phase financial constraints led to a lack of in-house hardware and very limited access time on external computers. As such, the input of data for the documentation effort could not be accomplished with one system. The development of the computer-aided dialogue system was focused on two functions for which conventional operations and systems have proven least effective. These were descriptive indexing of document contents and search for specified document contents. The data not entered in the dialogue mode were entered offline and transferred to disk storage by batch processing procedures.

The basic software system was a computer-aided indexing and retrieval program called PRIMAS being developed at the time by Siemens AG (2). SWP participated in this further development as a pilot user with a social/political science orientation. Program development and test were accomplished by the Central Research Laboratories at Siemens AG.

The close cooperation of users and program developers over several years was extremely useful. For one thing, the participatory development helped to overcome the preexistent disciplinary isolation among users and between users and developers. Not only did the cooperative effort support the initial creative impulses, but also it tended to avoid development failures resulting from the lack of appreciation of user requirements and user organizational problems.

As a result of the mutual effort, the conceptual framework of the computer-aided system itself was considerably transformed and broadened. For example:

- The system was transformed from one with one index file to one with two index files.
- The thesaurus was supplemented by a computer-stored KWOC register.
- Data were formatted so that console input was simplified, reducing alphanumerical input to a large degree by using the display screen output.

After the transformation of the initial system, there are now four principal computerized files. These are:

a. An index file with the thesaurus in systematic form.
b. An index file of the free terms integrated with an alphabetical file of KWOC keywords and a file of the non-descriptors.
c. A file of documentation units for search.
d. A supplementary file of calendar dates for search.

The data records of the indexing files and the document search files are mutually inverted. This means that each documentation unit contains the addresses of its assigned indexing terms and that each indexing term contains the addresses of its associated documentation units within their respective files. Free text can be stored with each of the data records in the three main files. Such textual formats can be used to enter bibliographic data, abstracts, references to other publications cited or reviewed in the document file and term relationships, scope notes, concordance references, and applicative rules for indexing for the terms in the index files.

The computer-aided system furthermore permits data input, file change, and retrieval to occur in parallel in the on-line dialogue mode. It is therefore outstandingly suited to documentation operations or networks accomplishing different functions according to a variety of division of labor tactics. Each system user can immediately gain access to newly acquired data records for search and/or file updating. With strict application of organizational rules, double-storage of data records usually can be avoided.

The interactive system provides both indexers and searchers with a combination of machine-generated and intellectually produced aids. One example is the unique suggest function. The suggest function is based on the application of mutually inverted data records in accordance with a statistical evaluation of term usage as reflected in the descriptor records. During search the suggest function permits the searcher to survey the descriptors used for indexing in conjunction with a selected limited number of other descriptors. Thus the searcher can discover which other descriptors may be available to further delineate a search request and as such define the set of documentation units to be retrieved.

During indexing the suggest function indicates which other descriptors usually have been associated by other indexers to describe similar subject matter. During interactive indexing the suggest function speeds up the discovery process of finding descriptors, which the indexer might have used anyway, listing them in a form appropriate for direct entry. Furthermore the suggest function offers the indexer descriptors he might not have otherwise found. As such the suggest function helps to improve indexing consistency among different indexers and the same indexer at different times. Indexers are advised not to rely on suggest when materials contain new facts or new combinations of facts, particularly in complex subjects.

Another example of aids to indexers consists of the variety of intellectually constructed references, indexing suggestions, term explications, and the like, not representable or accessible in a practical fashion with conventional systems.

5.4.3 Uncertainties in the Indexing Process

The decision to use a thesaurus with approximately 8000 descriptors and a supplementary file of free terms provided SWP with a framework for further development. However, this decision did not in itself resolve the large uncertainties about how the indexing processes should be accomplished for a computerized retrieval system. SWP had no previous experience with the search of differentially indexed literature during its operation of a conventional library system. Nonetheless, in order to proceed with development, a decision about the size, kinds, and scope of the system acceptable search terms was essential.

Uncertainty remained about the text size on which a documentation and/or information unit should be based for the various document types. For example, it was not clear whether it would be useful to index books by chapters or, in individual cases, to form still smaller documentation units. The degree of differentiation with which subject matter within documents should be covered was not precisely known. Nor could the number of descriptors usable without risking too low recall, relevancy, or precision rates be determined in advance.

These issues concerning the documentation unit size and the number of system acceptable descriptors are closely related. The extensive subdivision of documentation units permits the retrieval of specific subject matter with a small number of descriptors. Without such subdivision of the documentation units, the same degree of specific recall can only be achieved with high relevancy using the accumulated assignment of all of the descriptors associated with the subdivided units.

There was also uncertainty about whether relationships among individual descriptors should 'be indicated during indexing. The negative decision on this point for the SWP documentation system was influenced by the experiences of the U.S. Patent Office in using links. There the use of links in indexing had turned out to involve too much effort relative to its utility for search. This result led SWP not to include descriptor links in the design of the computerized system. This decision prevented the SWP indexing procedures from going beyond the assignment of equally weighted descriptors. However, later tests covering a sufficient number of indexed documents created new interest in the use of weighted descriptors. Our present experience indicates that relevancy of search results would be significantly increased if descriptors appropriate for the indexing of the subject matter of a document would be given a different weight than those descriptors used to index aspects under which the subject has been discussed. During search one would then be able to first form a subset of documentation units using subject related descriptors and then continue search within those documentation units using aspect related descriptors.* This procedure would apply for use in indexing and search only. Within the thesaurus, no difference would be made between descriptors for one or the other application; the same descriptor could be used for indexing the subject matter or for indexing an aspect. To counteract subjectivity factors involved in this procedure—application of descriptors to subject or aspects—search must be permitted without consideration of the weighting criterion if desired.

In this light there are three closely related factors involved in the decision about indexing prodecures. These are the size of the documentation unit, the number of descriptors per documentation unit, and the weighting during indexing based upon use for subject and aspect description related to the subject.

The SWP computer system in use now does not permit the weighting of descriptors during indexing nor the weighting of considerations during search.

*For example, in a search of literature on American West European policy it should be possible to separate documents covering the searched subject matter from such documents in which this aspect is discussed in connection with a different subject, for example, an article on French foreign policy.

Given a sufficient number of documents handled according to these refined procedures, comparative tests could be accomplished. However, investigations of the refinements possible through subdivision of documentation units and the possible change in the number of descriptors required could be useful. Nonetheless, the shortage of personnel and financial contraints previously noted meant that during the implementation phase we were not able to develop appropriate solutions to this problem by practical tests. It was not possible to split large groups of documents into many documentation units nor to index many documents intensively enough to regularly assign large numbers of descriptors.

5.5 THE TRANSITION PHASE

The transition from a documentation system with conventional storage technology at SWP to a computer-aided one was accomplished in two steps over a period of approximately 18 months. In October 1973 documentation covering periodicals (Journal articles, yearbook articles, etc.) was transferred to the computer-aided system. This process took three months. After this first step had been taken and operations stabilized, the second step transferring monographs to the computer-aided system began in October of 1974. By April 1975 this transition phase was concluded.

During the implementation of the computer-aided system a series of organizational changes took place, some of which could also have been introduced during conventional operations. However valuable these organizational changes may have been in themselves, it was only through the implementation of the computer-aided system that organizational inertia could be overcome. In short, change became imperative.

An essential change in the organization of work was the transition from a document related division of labor to one oriented toward the research disciplines for indexing and general documentation activities. Previously, individual staff members were responsible for the separate classification of journal articles and yearbook articles, monographs, and reports. For the computer-aided system professionally competent staff members handled all types of documents pertinent to their disciplines. Because the computer-aided system permitted more differentiated content indexing and multi-dimensional search, higher professional requirements were imposed upon indexers.

In the formal organization this change in the division of labor resulted in a shift of tasks from one organizational entity to another. For example, the responsibility of the library for the classification of books was transferred to the documentation department, which had already organized its content descriptive work in a manner permitting professional content analysis for its newspaper clipping system.

As a long-term objective one scientifically trained documentalist for a given field was to be responsible for each important special field or discipline and supported by qualified documentalists without specialized scientific training. For budgetary reasons, at the beginning of the implementation phase there were only a few such scientifically trained documentation staff members. Several years were required to gradually increase their number. At present each of the fundamental research fields of the information system is handled by one or two scientifically trained staff members. However, the individual special fields within these major disciplines are still handled by nonscientifically trained documentalists. This personnel problem has been a serious one. Not only had the documentation staff to be trained during the implementation phase to the new computer-aided indexing and search using a thesaurus and on-line computer terminals, but also a more profound scientific training in the specialized fields had to be required as well.

Instruction of staff members in the new indexing procedures and the thesaurus application was accomplished using methods analogous to those of the thesaurus test phase. The indexers were divided in groups, each guided by one scientific documentalist. Each group indexed identical textual material, and synoptic surveys were used to compare the individual indexing results, checking in particular for deviations in descriptor assignments. Establishing a correct comprehension and application of the thesaurus was only part of the problem. As we found during the thesaurus test, it was particularly difficult to establish agreement about the relevance of the factual information contained in the textual material, that is, which factual information was important enough to be considered for indexing. Those staff members who had already participated in the thesaurus test had faced this problem previously, and were able to provide significant help during the training of indexers.

Indexing instruction in large groups was supplemented by smaller sessions of more field-oriented groups. Furthermore, the quantity of indexing results to be checked in group discussions was gradually reduced until indexing checks could be limited to samples. However, the instruction process was complicated by the fact that the SWP system developers themselves did not have practical experience in the application of sophisticated systems. They were very much involved in the learning processes and often had to modify indexing rules in the course of the instruction process.

As a longer-range objective, it is intended to have all data for direct filing entered by the responsible staff members at terminals located near their working places. Such direct entry would then permit immediate access to all available data in the system. At the same time the individual staff members at the terminal would have access to the computer-aided and file-supported procedures and guidance. At present financial constraints limit the number of terminals and the amount of daily computer time available. This led to the requirement during the transition phase for preliminary noting of the indexing of documents on work-sheets. Such indexing was later entered at computer consoles by the respective staff member, who only then had access to machine aids and guidance. It is worth noting here that console entry was not required for a small number of the older staff members. These members simply could not get used to computer terminals, even with the comfortable dialogue language and interaction.

Early during the implementation phase a major transformation of organizational procedures occurred, permitting the more timely updating of the documentation base. The conventional documentation methods offered only a limited capability for correcting or updating files. As such, journal articles to be added to the documentation base were first read by the staff members within the appropriate research fields. Only after the initial circulation of a document had been completed was the document indexed, using whatever input may have been obtained from research staff, and entered into the documentation base. This produced time delays of up to several months for document entry, leaving significant gaps within the current literature available through the system.

For the computer-aided system, content indexing of documents occurred before initial circulation. In accordance with SWP directions the documentalists determined which documents should be indexed. Printouts of the indexing protocols were attached to the documents during circulation, enabling the research field staff members to correct or complete content indexing in addition to adding their inputs to the decision involved in the selection of documents. Since this new procedure involved a significant change of the existing circulation procedures, causing certain problems and delays in initial circulation, the new procedure raised significant controversy.

5.6 SOCIO-PSYCHOLOGICAL IMPLEMENTATION PROBLEMS

The implementation of a new system affecting the working processes throughout an organization inevitably creates a series of socio-psychological problems. The distribution of the responsibilities for decision making, however previously delegated or decentralized, had to be modified during the conceptual phase. During the implementation phase there is a significant push toward relocation and centralization of responsibilities.

Organizational regulations and procedures established for conventional operation, however successful, may not conform with the regulations and procedures appropriate for the new system. It is not just that older regulations required modification; generally the scope and requirements for regulation are considerably increased. Often the degree of operational flexibility created through informal as well as official arrangements developed over a period of years with conventional operations is starkly reduced, at least temporarily. The introduction of a new system throws a glaring light on organizational regulations that were not stringently enforced or negligently followed even when such latitude was required in order to make things work. On the psychological level a subjective fear of being found out arose for those paying lip service to the formal organizational regulations but had worked out their own informal methods of work assignment and accomplishment. The typically hidden nature of this deceit made it rather difficult for the administrators of the new system to appreciate the depth of the actual requirements for flexibility during the early implementation phases.

Such difficulties stemming from attempts to automate based on only the formal organizational structure and regulations are not new to information and documentation applications. The effect at SWP of so overturning pre-existing informal working arrangements and organizational procedures was particularly strong. It was not possible to have staff members from each of the functional sections participate in system development in a manner sufficiently comprehensive to provide their detailed inputs concerning their actual working procedures and requirements. Furthermore, the introduction of the new system necessarily involved a shift of functions among the different working fields, the full effects of which could not be completely determined in advance.

As might be expected, the staff members' attitudes toward the acceptance of the stringent system regulation necessary during implementation and their abilities to comprehend and adapt to the complex interrelationships were in flux. Where subjective or objective status problems were perceived because of the new system, difficulties with staff members became severe. This was particularly the case where some staff members perceived themselves as being better qualified for working within the new system than their superiors or vice versa.

The introduction of the computer-aided documentation system posed problems for the research staff members as well. Their future role as users of the new system and their participation in documentation activities had to change. In conventional documentation systems the description of the contents of documents is so little detailed and retrieval is so inflexible that the search for literature becomes very time-consuming. Scientists attempt to compensate for these disadvantages by maintaining their own personal or work-specific index card files. Such private files provide scientists with a limited information monopoly. Furthermore, they travel with the scientist when the working place is changed. To a significant degree, the combination of the limited efficiency of conventional documentation facilities and the availability of private files adjusted to the scientist-specific requirements and capacities protects the individual scientists from being flooded with information. Many scientists expressed their apprehension that the introduction of computer-aided documentation services would mean that they would be overwhelmed by supposedly relevant information. Many scientists also felt that computer-aided documentation would not be able to provide them with sufficiently differentiated information directly related to their research requirements. These apprehensions are partly justified, given the present information and documentation capabilities, and can be overcome only by gradual improvements in the performance of the information and documentation services. This does not happen overnight.

On the other hand, modern documentation procedures can clearly show scientists some inefficiences in their own professions. For example, the enormous amount of redundant information which scientists themselves produce becomes quite visible. Certainly this is one reason for the high level of redundancy obtained in the retrieval of ''relevant'' information. Another reason for the information flood are the very broad documentation fields covered by the individual staff member that make it difficult for even scientifically trained documentalists to distinguish between new and redundant or important and unimportant information during content indexing. A better means of handling these two redundancy-producing factors lay behind the documentalists' desire to have the research scientists support and participate in the documentation activities. In particular, scientists were to participate by indicating subject matter of interest to them and thereby highlight such subject matter for the documentalists. In an interactive computer-aided system such inputs from the scientists could aid the documentalists while indexing or could permit correction of indexing during updating.

Opposition to this form of participation by the scientists was significant. In part the opposition was based on legitimate reasons stemming from the pressures imposed on scientists by their research activities. Any increase of reading time required to cover the scientific literature could only be taken away from the time allocated for research and particularly from the periods of research report writing. The increase in literature reading time necessitated by the noting of important subject matter by scientists is trivial and more than made up for by the reduction of the time wasted by scientists in filtering irrelevant or excess search results. There is no question that the feeling that documentation is an inferior or lower-level activity persists within most research facilities. Time-consuming attempts to point out to the scientists that, regardless of whether documentation work was beneath their dignity, they were spending a significant portion of their own working time doing the documentation for their own private files were without singular success. The usual response by the scientists was that they did not believe the new system would reduce their need for their own private files. It is also quite likely that many scientists did not wish to have the need for their own private files eliminated by any documentation system.

After four years of operations using the computer-aided documentation system, the attitudes of the research staff users have become more objective and specific. Apart from personality-related and subjective factors, user valuation has become very strongly dependent on the type of research work and the specialized problems pertaining to the individual research fields. Both the documentation and the searches for information related to theoretical and/or sophisticated systematic informational requirements are more difficult to accomplish successfully than requests for information related to regional research areas. Some of the research working fields pose particularly difficult problems for evaluating information in the literature.

On the whole, the range of user reactions reflects a variety of conditions. The more important of these were the fundamental dependence on in-house documentation, the relatively rapid transition from conventional to computer-aided operations, the uniqueness of the computer-aided procedures, and the limitations imposed by financial constraints and personnel. Most important is the fact that the introduction of computerized processes for the documentation facilities does not lead immediately to the perception of improved efficiency or results for the users. Improved operations come about through evolution over a time period best described as the middle-range future. In situations where the additional personnel required for implementation must be obtained from the permanent personnel, the lack of immediate payoff can cause severe problems within the organization. As the conditions surrounding information and documentation activities and the requirements imposed change over time, this time-lag in payoff may well become a permanent feature to be lived with and prepared for.

To the extent that the participation of the research scientists is minimal, given the normal division of labor within a research organization, the staff members of the information and documentation facilities will in the long run become more professionally competent in the search for information than the scientists themselves. The consequences of this result are still unknown. However, it should lead to the subjective upgrading of the status of the more specialized and experienced documentalists. This in itself should tend to encourage more productive participation from the scientific research staff.

5.7 THE CURRENT IMPLEMENTATION EMPHASIS

After several years of computer-aided operations for SWP documentation, the emphasis of development shifted to the optimization of existing computer system components and further development of the noncomputer parts of the documentation service. New objectives were to improve existing and to develop new services. Since the SWP information base relied on in-house documentation, improved or new services required expansion of the document input capabilities.

5.7.1 Information Retrieval and Services

The services performed by the information and documentation system are based on interactive retrieval for retrospective searches. Searches are conducted through a dialogue mode at consoles by professionally specialized staff documentalists. The number of searches conducted for external users has approached the number of searches conducted for internal SWP staff over the past few years. Different working processes for the external and internal searches have been adopted. For internal users the optimal search procedure is to have the user conduct his search at the console together with the documentalist. This permits an efficient combination of computer-aided retrieval with supplementary intellectual search focusing on the user's personal information requirements and carried out in one working process. Given the user's specialized knowledge of the literature, he can directly suggest modifications of the search request formulation during the interactive retrieval process. For example, information relevant but already known to the user can be eliminated from the search result by refining the search question or by explicit selection.

Over a period of time a sufficient number of searches based on the user-documentalist combination significantly upgrades the documentalist's knowledge about user requirements and in turn upgrades the documentation services. Furthermore, this direct form of user input during search is extremely useful for document indexing, increasing the indexer's sophistication about the utility and relevance of the information to be stored. In addition, this procedure enhances the documentalist's ability to achieve higher relevancy results for searches conducted for external users who are not present during the search process.

All searches for external users and some searches for internal users are carried out at consoles in the documentation department without this significant interaction between documentalist and user. In these cases intellectual supplementary searches are accomplished separately using the initial search results and protocols.

At present the information available to the user for each documentation unit in the literature information file includes bibliographical data and the list of indexing terms (thesauri and free descriptors). Financial constraints and lack of personnel do not yet permit the production of abstracts. In the near future the amount of information so associated with documents is to be gradually increased to include the provision of externally supplied abstracts, references to further publications, references to reviews of documents and the reviews with their separate document numbers if any, references to quotations, also indicating document number, and the catalogue numbers or shelf numbers of the documents in other libraries.

In accordance with the computerized inverted files described previously, content identified search may be accomplished with:

- Subject terms from the thesaurus and from the list of free descriptors.
- Names of persons, institutions, and projects from the list of free descriptors.
- Dates concerning the temporal period of reference.

In addition, search may be conducted in accordance with the more formal characteristics stored in the inverted files as well:

- Formal terms of document descriptors concerning the type of document and its language, including the original language of translated material.
- Names of authors.
- Library shelf numbers and/or ISSN number for periodicals.
- Dates indicating time of publication.

These varieties of search elements can be used individually or in combination. The combination of search elements in search questions is accomplished by using the following operations: positive selection, negative selection, selection with Boolean logic using bracketing and notation hierarchy, and a variety of sorting routines that leave intact the subsets of retrieved target information. During interactive search, search questions obviously can be modified. Furthermore, the computer-aided suggest function provides direct machine support for the intellectual task of search question modification. Using a form of statistical analysis of the descriptor addresses associated with a given subset of retrieved target information, additional descriptors are displayed for consideration that the searcher can select for refining the search question or for resorting the target information by including additional descriptors without changing the subset. The systematic hierarchical thesaurus file has also proven extremely useful for search question formulation. These advantages could be made still more useful if it were possible to combine a given notation chain with individual additional descriptors from other notation chains in a direct manner. Supplementary search is supported by a free text search mode permitting the sequential search of titles, abstracts, and other text. This procedure requires a large amount of computer time and is therefore used only for the search of small subsets.

Finally, during the display of target information on consoles, the operator can mark relevant or important target information for selected subsequent printout.

Based on the experiences of SWP with computer-aided search, the search processes could be improved by:

- Providing for separate procedures for search according to subjects and subject aspects. Such dual search capabilities would require some new computer procedures and storage structuring as well as establishing the appropriate indexing practices.
- Subdivision of documents into more refined documentation units, individually indexed.
- Supplementing machine-generated guidance for the selection of relevant descriptors by additional intellectual development—completion of a polyhierarchical thesaurus.

Given the emphasis on the strongly interactive working processes of indexing and search as well as the primary orientation toward the requirements of the institute's staff, printout capabilities were neglected. This neglect must be eliminated during future development of the system in order to meet the requirements of external users and to provide for the production of printed catalogues, registers, and other systematically structured information.

The expansion of services for external users will also be attempted by connecting external information and documentation facilities as referral stations to the SWP computerized documentation files. The referral centers will have terminal connections to the SWP computer using dedicated lines or dial-up exchanges. Since they will be located in external facilities, the referral centers will have the advantage of being in close proximity to their users. In this manner the requested information can be more quickly supplied and supplemented by the documentary literature for external users.

A magnetic tape service with inverted data structure can be made available to external information facilities possessing their own computer systems. The magnetic tape in this form should reduce the computer time necessary for its integration with other data bases or entry into a data bank as a separate file.

Information, particularly search activities, cannot be limited to data stored in or retrieved from computer-based files. Retrieved information has to be supplemented by the use of a variety of printed output, including bibliographies, handbooks, and reference material. It should be expected that current developments in the technology of computer storage will soon permit the computer storage of a far greater share of the information required for information and documentation services. However, noncomputer-stored information will always remain necessary.

The current documentation storages of SWP permit only systematic information services covering what is called the literature. Soon to supplement the storage of literature will be a systematic documentation covering institutions. Information about institutions is obtained from a variety of files including data supplied by institutions themselves. Later files with information on persons, events, projects, and problems are to be added.

At present the documentation storage covers about 35,000 documentation units. Content description or indexing has been accomplished for:

- 1500 periodicals (journals and yearbooks).
- 25,000 journal and yearbook articles.
- 1000 other publications (speeches of politicians and texts of communiqués).
- 7800 monographs (books and reports).

5.7.2 Database Building, Indexing Procedures, and Thesaurus Maintenance

The annual rate of acquisition of literature has continually increased over the past few years. At present about 9000 documentation units are acquired annually, including about 2500 monographs. In addition, approximately 7000 individual packages of newspaper clippings and other press material are stored in the computer as documentation units. Content description indexing of these files gradually has been accomplished using thesauri descriptors. The inclusion of such newspaper clipping files within the computer-aided system essentially completed the standardization of the indexing and description of the system's files of information. Citations obtained from the newspaper clipping files are regarded as a useful supplement to the citations in the other forms of literature. In any event, the computer storage of index terms of these files was necessary to adjust their description to revised thesaurus forms using simplified technical procedures.

At the SWP expansion of the informational files will also emphasize official publications of national and international organizations. It is expected that the rate of growth of journal articles and monographs in the files will decrease.

An important means of improving retrieval quality would involve the use of more differentiated documentation units. A documentation unit is the standard unit in the file containing the set of descriptor addresses. Furthermore, it is that part or whole of the unit of literature cited during retrieval. As such, smaller or more refined documentation units per document of literature stored should improve retrieval quality and relevancy. However, the working time for content description and indexing would be significantly increased.

Today the major portion of time spent in entering documentation units is allocated to reading. Improvements of indexing procedures using machine aids and the display of thesaurus structure improve performance of those portions of the indexing task which consume the smaller amount of working time. According to SWP experience, reading of documents for purposes of document entry and indexing constitutes approximately 70% of the total effort. To increase further the reading effort seems possible only through a better division of labor distributed throughout a documentation network made up of various documentation centers or facilities. This will also require an increase of personnel. Whatever increase in indexing time may be involved, the improvement of retrieval quality should lead to a far greater saving of the time users and research scientists spend in filtering and reformulating their search requests. However, once again we are confronted with the complex situation resulting from a lack of immediate payoff. Improved retrieval can come about only after the expenditure of efforts required to improve indexing and content description. The time lag between expenditure of funds and time to improve indexing and the achievement of improved retrieval is sufficiently great that extreme constraints are often placed on expenditures for indexing (3).

Given constraints mentioned previously, a major portion of the indexing is accomplished by worksheets that are later used to complete the indexing and entry of documents. It is only in this latter process occurring at the computer console that the indexer is supported by the computer aids. Under these circumstances indexers use an average of 15 descriptors to characterize the contents of documents. The number of descriptors does vary strongly according to reading time expended, content differentiation requirements, and type of document. A binding rule about the required number of descriptors has not so far been established, since the desirable degree of content differentiation frequently cannot be achieved by the already overburdened staff members. Indexing is checked by means of a person-related procedure. Currently such indexing checks attempt to improve the performance of the individual staff members rather than correct the indexing of a larger number of documentation units.

Standardization of indexing among the individual indexers has been attempted by means of regular discussions of the thesaurus, with particular emphasis on thesaurus revision and updating. The same procedure with group discussions, which proved useful during the training of indexers, also proved useful for analyzing and improving ongoing indexing.

Given the computer aids available in support of both indexing and search, an indexer can initiate a search using a descriptor referring to his own indexing. Having done so, the indexer can obtain a list of the thesaurus vocabulary used by him in association with this descriptor and thereby discover whether he tends to use some terms from certain sections or hierarchical portions of the thesaurus while neglecting others.

To make full use of these procedures in a systematic and methodological fashion requires an increase in personnel. The computer-aided techniques used for making analyses of the indexing behavior of documentalists are still in a formative stage. Improved procedures are required to permit documentalists to apply the computer aids individually. However, procedures are required which ensure that professional advisers can help documentalists improve their performance. Improved machine aids, however important, will never in themselves be sufficient.

One critical area nonetheless strongly requiring improved computerized procedures is that of supporting thesaurus development, maintenance, and use. Conventional operations and systems fail to offer much support to this area and to the general development of system acceptable search term lists. So great an effort is necessary currently for thesaurus development that further development or revision, however necessary, is usually left undone. There is a particular shortage of machine aids to the intellectual work associated with the thesaurus development and revision and also for the thesaurus production where the thesaurus must be available not only in its stored machine version but also in a variety of printouts. For example, the current SWP-T was introduced in 1973. An expanded version was produced in 1975. However, a thorough revision of SWP-T has not been accomplished so far, primarily to avoid the necessity to produce once again its printed version. Nonetheless at present a revision is in process.

For changing the machine version of the thesaurus, a computer change program is available which reassigns document addresses in the index file, the descriptor addresses in the document file and carries out correction of the internal referential structure to the extent that this can be accomplished by machine. A batch processing program permits the production of a printout based on the revised version stored on disk. The thesaurus change program has been modified recently to permit the exchange of descriptors and their address assignments within the thesaurus and the list of free descriptors. This makes it possible to tentatively include descriptors within the thesaurus that were initially suggested from the list of free descriptors. After the determination of the utility of these tentatively accepted descriptors, they may be officially accepted within the thesaurus, left in the list of new descriptors, or deleted. This procedure now permits the regular inspection of new terms appearing in the list of free descriptors and provides an organizationally simplified method of ongoing thesaurus maintenance.

As a general rule, the thesaurus should be revised once a year. However, the decision process concerning the acceptance of new descriptors should be continuous. At SWP the suggestions for new descriptors come from many sources. Those submitted on suggest forms produced during ongoing indexing reveal that while there is a consistent trend to suggest new and differentiated descriptors, the suggestion to delete descriptors is rarely made.

In parallel with the revision and expansion of thesaurus descriptors the further development of the structure of the thesaurus is toward the production of a coherent polyhierarchical system. For this purpose, an extensive category schema (sets and groupings of descriptor classificatory categories) has been developed. This will permit the systematic and computer-processable assignment of definitions, applicative rules, concordances to other thesauri, and translations, in addition to the usual categories established as national or international standards. Preparatory work permitting the integration of data from other document stores using the new categories has begun.

Through its participation as a pilot user in the development of computer programs supporting thesauri construction and revision, SWP has attempted to focus on this critical neglected area. Computer support as well as intellectual methods are essential to enable the intellectual work of thesaurus revision, the integration of thesauri, the production of concordances among different thesauri to be accomplished, within the usual constraints of funding and manpower. National and international exchanges among information and documentation facilities can be feasibly envisaged only given the successful achievement of such methods providing support to the laborious and complex work associated with the development of thesauri and structured search term lists.

5.8 OUTLOOK

As the development of the SWP information and documentation system proceeds, a trend toward integration and cooperation with other information and documentation systems is inevitable. The expanding informational requirements of user groups can be satisfied only within a framework of efficient networks of information and documentation systems. This ideally should include the international exchange of data from advanced data banks and networks of systems.

SWP is working toward such network developments satisfying certain conditions necessary for field oriented information. These conditions are:

- The integration and standardization within networks should largely consist of standardized technology and methodology.
- The organizational units responsible for content description and other intellectual work required to create information products must continue their close interaction with the institutions of respective research fields.

From this perspective the optimal networking solution would appear to be an integration model containing both distributed and centralized elements. The information and documentation facilities for a given field could operate in concert with central storages but with the actual information and documentation working units distributed in accordance with the research activities of the institutions involved. Using standardized methods and technology and system-operational procedures, they would get support from a centralized facility for handling technological, methodological, and administrative problems.

Feasibility studies and planning for such networking solutions have been intensified over the past few years in the Federal Republic of Germany. This effort has resulted in the program "Fachinformationssysteme" (field/disciplinary information systems) established as part of the research and science policy of the Federal Republic. The SWP has participated in the planning for one of these field/disciplinary information systems covering regional research, international relations and development policy ("Länder- und Regionalforschung, Internationale Beziehungen und Entwicklungspolitik"−FIS 15). The SWP is connected to FIS 15 as a function of its research field "Area Studies," "International Relations" and "International Security Policy." A planning report for FIS 15 has been published (4). The SWP information and documentation facilities will promote a network system under FIS 15 in conjunction with two other important information and documentation facilities within the Federal Republic working in the FIS 15 area.

The first phase of such institutional cooperation will involve a gradual adjustment of existing information and documentation instruments such as thesauri, instruction manuals, formats of information products, and the like. At the same time new prototypes of these instruments will be developed. For long-range planning in this area an analysis of the national market for FIS 15 information products is urgently required.

A rough grouping of users considered in the planning phase includes:

a. Political planners and decision makers in the legislative, executive, and administrative branches of the government.
b. Research and university institutions.

c. Mass media.
d. Planners and decision makers in the economic sector.
e. Educational sector.
f. Organizations supporting foreign cultural policy and development aid, such as the Goethe-Institut or the German Development Service.

Because of interests of all such groups, priorities will have to be set about the provision of information products that can satisfy requirements without too costly an initial effort.

Analysis of the market for information and documentation in the Federal Republic indicates that the various potential user groups' informational requirements can be satisfied only in a limited fashion by currently existing information products. In particular the usual literature documentation systems will be inadequate. For many users, especially those in governmental and economic sectors, new information services are needed more appropriate to a wider range of situations. To better adjust the information products to the variety of user and institutional needs, a concept of information referral units located at the institutions served has been developed. Information referral centers can be responsible to given institutions or for covering the informational requirements of specific regional geographic areas. Documentalists and information scientists assigned to these centers should be much better able to recognize and appreciate the special information requirements of their users than information professionals functioning in a highly centralized facility serving everyone. Furthermore, the regional and institutional information referral centers should become highly responsive to their own users in a relatively short time. Where privacy or confidentiality of information is a concern, such as in government ministries, the location of information referral centers involved can enhance the protection of information.

Information referral centers could have access to the various data or documentation pools with which they are associated through communication links and terminals. Where information required is not directly accessible, the information referral centers could function as mediators arranging for external information services. Within the FIS network a more complete coverage of special fields should be obtainable. Not only must the usual types of documents such as journal literature and progress reports and in particular official publications of national and international organizations be available, but also information about institutions, organizations, projects, and events should be provided. At the same time as the information coverage is extended, the analysis and description of documents and content will have to become more accurate and differentiated. The network concept, while making document coverage and indexing more arduous, at the same time makes it possible to reduce the task load for individuals and individual institutions by distributing such intellectual work throughout the network and by making possible the exchange of already indexed information with other field/disciplinary information systems and with foreign documentation centers.

To make international exchanges of data feasible requires a significant increase in the support provided by computers to the intellectual problems involved. At a minimum, computer-aided production of concordances connecting the documentation bases to be exchanged is necessary. More attention devoted to the development of this capability is likely to have a greater payoff than the various attempts to achieve internationally standardized or even compatible thesauri by means of conventional intellectual methods. The fact that international exchanges of information must be based on mutually agreed procedures and, to a still unknown extent, generally accepted standards cannot be denied. Nonetheless the cultural diversity of national societies, particularly reflected by the variety of languages, the essential carriers of information, must not be neglected. Such cultural diversity should be preserved rather than eliminated, an attempt both futile and counterproductive. In particular for the field of social and cultural sciences, cultural and linguistic diversity must not be repressed on grounds of presumptive effectivity or efficiency. The implementation of new technologies within the social and cultural sciences should support rather than attempt to destroy their diversified cores.

NOTES

1. See Wessel, CAIR, Chapter Ten, pp. 140–168, for further discussion of the PRIMAS system. See also Chapter Eight, pp. 75–107, for an additional discussion of the SWP–T.
2. Wessel, CAIR, Chapter Ten.
3. See Dietrich Seydel and Volker Steidle, "Aufbau von Datenbasen im Realzeit-Dialogverfahren. Erfahrungen und Entwicklungsmöglichkeiten" (Database Construction in a Real-Time, Interactive Mode. Experiences and Development Possibilities), in: Rainer Kuhlen (ed.), Datenbasen - Datenbanken - Netzerke. Praxis des Informationsretrieval, Vol. 1: Inhaltserchliessung and Aufbau von Datenbasen (Databases - Databanks - Network Systems. Practice of Information Retrieval. Vol. 1: Indexing and Database Construction). Munich: K.G. Saur, 1979.
4. "Fachinformationssystem 15 Auslandskunde. Planungsbericht," Im Auftrage des Bundesministers für Forschung und Technologie, o. O., 1978 ("Field/Disciplinary Information System 15 Foreign Studies. Planning Report," prepared under the auspices of the Federal Ministry of Research and Technology).

Chapter Six

A Credit Bureau Conversion

by DONALD L. DRUKEY

6.1 INTRODUCTION

The project in this example is the conversion of a credit bureau from manual to a computer-aided operation. This credit bureau had been highly successful over a number of years, providing a very large number of inexpensive credit references every day. Most of these services were provided on-line.

As we considered the future of the credit bureau, we saw that it had grown nearly as far as it could in its present mode of operation, yet the business was growing at about 10% per year. It was foreseeable that, if the number of reports continued to grow, the amount of labor to produce each report would increase. That would mean that the cost of producing a report would increase faster than the hourly cost of labor. Our analysis showed that the elasticity of the market was not sufficient to absorb a corresponding growth in the price of reports.

The management of the manual operation had been efficient. There were no obvious ways left to reorganize the work to cope with higher volume. We, therefore, initiated a design study to see whether computerizing the system would provide the desired solution.

The goals of the automation study were to:

- Provide the same (or improved) services for the customers as the manual system.
- Break even in the total cost per report.
- Maintain that unit cost through a 60% growth in volume (five years).
- Draw upon the existing pool of credit operators to man the automated work stations.

The balance of this report is a technologist's view of that design effort and some commentaries on the design and implementation process.

6.2 THE MANUAL OPERATION

The credit bureau is located in Los Angeles and provides coverage of the entire metropolitan area. It furnishes over half of the credit reports for the region, but since its products are inexpensive, it does not account for that large a fraction of the sales dollars.

There were two principal products, and a third was introduced during the course of the analysis. The dominant one was the oral report. For that, a customer phoned the credit bureau and a credit operator searched the file and gave a report to the customer over the phone. Over 80% of the reports were of this type.

The bureau also produced written reports. These, too, were initiated by a phone call from a customer who might or might not receive an oral report at the time. In either case, a written report was also prepared and mailed to the customer that night. The management had discouraged these reports in the past since they were less profitable (even though more expensive) than the oral reports. Clearly, here was an area where computerizing might pay off unusually well.

The new third product line was mailing lists. The credit reporting industry is a conservative one, and mailing lists had not been considered a dignified product from one's credit files, but times were changing. Several other credit bureaus in the area were producing lists for old-line customers, and some of our clients were beginning to press for these services too. The first such lists were produced manually during the early phases of the automation study. Since these were profitable even when manually produced, they should be a lucrative by-product of the effort. A decision was made, however, that the revenue from this source might be jeopardized by right-of-privacy considerations and could not be included in conversion rationalization. It could, of course, be used to justify those costs associated with the hardware and software required to produce the product itself.

The credit bureau to be automated was physically arranged as shown in Figure 1. Its principal components were the credit operators (all women), their phones, and the files. As seen, the files were in the center to facilitate access by all of the credit operators. The latter were arranged in small desks around the perimeter of the file system. There were approximately 200 employees of whom about 160 worked a day shift, with the balance working on one night shift. Both the number of credit operators and the size of the files had been growing continuously over the period of operation.

The girls worked for slightly over the minimum wage, had very modest education, were mostly of minority background, and suffered a considerable turnover. While a number of them had been there for several years, the average was about a year and a half. The girls on a shift were divided into four squads, each monitored by a supervisor, as shown in Figure 1. In addition, there were a total of six executive personnel.

The credit bureau catered primarily to jewelry stores and other small merchants. The next most important set of customers included banks that utilized the credit reports in approving small loans. Then followed department stores, some of which used the bureau for an immediate credit verification to be followed up at a later date by a more extensive credit report bought elsewhere.

The characteristic of the service was that it provided access to an unusually large collection of credit histories on a very prompt basis, but the reports did not generally contain much detailed information. Since the small stores, most merchants, and the department stores operate from nine to nine, those were the hours

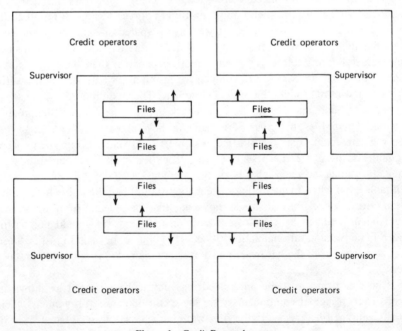

Figure 1   Credit Bureau layout.

of operation. A lunch hour and a dinner hour were rigidly enforced, with all the phones dead on those half-hour intervals.

The files with which the girls operated were maintained on 3 × 5 handwritten filing cards of which there were approximately one and a half million. These cards were alphabetically arranged by name, with one card per individual. There were approximately 2000 cards in a file drawer, and the file drawers were arranged in cabinets, with height limited by the fact that many of the credit operators were short. The file cabinets were closely packed along aisles to improve access.

The growth of the files and of the number of credit operators was beginning to limit the ability to provide prompt service. As the files increased in size, the operators had to walk further and took more time with each search. As the number of operators increased, congestion became more and more of a problem. There was already evidence of these problems at the million-and-a-half record level.

The data on the cards is shown in Figure 2. There was no way to ensure that the cards would be maintained accurately in this format. When the girls were hired, they were trained in filling out a card. To the extent that that training stuck, the cards would remain in that format. Actually, the format was surprisingly consistent. All the cards were handwritten except those which contained only legal information. The procedure will be outlined below. The data on the cards consisted of identification information by which one hoped to be able to ensure that the correct individual was being referenced, the credit data themselves, and legal information.

The identification information is familiar to most of us from filling out our own credit applications. The principal purpose of that application is to identify an individual so that his credit references can be researched in an organization such as this credit bureau. It consists of one's name (and for a woman, maiden name), address, and previous addresses, the name of spouse, if any, and children, phone number, employers, usually the date and place of birth, sometimes social secu-

LAST NAME, FIRST, MI, SPOUSE NAME MARRIED_____

    NUMBER, STREET, CITY   SINCE   SOCSECNO

    PREVIOUS ADDRESS   SINCE   DRIVER'S LICENSE

    CREDIT GRANTOR   DATE   EMPLOYED BY SINCE JOB TITLE

    CREDIT GRANTOR   DATE

    LEGAL DATA   TYPE   DATE

Figure 2 File card.

rity number, sometimes driver's license number. On a typical credit application, one also shows organizations which have granted one credit. This information also can be used as a weak confirmatory identification.

The second class of information contained on the filing cards consisted of credit references. The first and most copious of the types of credit reference information was the fact that a previous search had been made against this file. For example, the record might indicate that the X,Y,Z Jewelry store had queried an individual's file in March 1973. There was no indication about whether credit was granted and no indication about whether the researchee lived up to his credit. The second class of information was adverse information which might be provided by either a credit grantor or by a collection agency using the file as a source of information to attempt to find the individual. There were no positive credit references.

The third set of information in the files consisted of legals obtained from a legal research service. It included records of all cases in which a suit involving credit was initiated against the individual, for example, a suit initiated by a merchant to collect a bad debt. There were also records of judgments. There was no indication of the disposition of suits unless they resulted in judgments.

These were the data that were to become the data base for a semi-automated credit bureau operation.

This is how a typical credit check is carried out. The scenario begins with a credit operator seated at her desk. Her phone is on the hook and she has a 3×5 filing card on her desk which she retrieved as a result of the previous credit inquiry. The phone rings, she identifies the caller and checks to see that he has a current password. Then, she takes the credit information from the customer. Occasionally, the customer will have several references to check. Usually, however, there is only one request. She writes the identification information provided by the merchant on a filing card like those in Figure 2. When this is complete, she sets the phone on the desk and walks to the filing area. First, she refiles the card from the previous inquiry, then proceeds to the section of the files in which the new inquiry is located. She pulls the appropriate drawer and begins to search, using the last name of the individual, then the first name and any other identification information. She chooses a single card or no card if there is no record of the individual sought. She then returns to her desk, picks up the phone, and gives back to the customer credit reference information and legal information from the card. She may have nothing to report, or she may have a voluminous credit reference. If the amount of information to be given is modest, she reads it all; otherwise she summarizes it. She then hangs up the phone. In front of her she has the file card on which she took the information over the phone in the first place and the file card, if any, that she retrieved. If there is one, she either adds to the file retrieved from the files the fact that the interrogation has been made or she copies the information from the card onto new card that she has produced as the result of the inquiry. She discards one or the other of the two cards. At this point, she is ready to take another credit call. Those actions are shown in Figure 3.

In a modest number of cases, the customer desired a written report for his records. He might or might not, but usually did want an on-the-spot oral report to be followed up by the written record. The procedure in that case was the same as outlined above, except the girl segregated those cards for which written records were to be produced. At the end of the day, these cards were collected, written reports were hand prepared from the cards overnight, and the cards were refiled in time for the next morning's credit transactions.

In order to service 160 girls, there were 160 phone lines. Most of these were on a single large rotor. When an incoming call was received, the rotor searched for an idle telephone—beginning with the first phone and proceeding through the list until it found one that was not busy. Then, that phone was rung. When girls were absent from their desks, they took their phones off the hook. Those girls who had phones connected to the first part of the rotor were very busy, whereas those at the terminal end of the search might have no work at all if the lines were not heavily loaded. There was no provision for load leveling and no recording to determine those circumstances under which calls were turned away or to determine which phones were how busy. This system did not provide a call-hold service in which the phone is answered by a recording and put on hold until a phone is available. There were additional lines that were not on the main rotor. They were serviced by secondary, smaller rotors used for specially privileged customers. There were, for instance, a set of bank lines, which were more likely to be answered at rush hour than the regular lines.

A number of statistics were gathered to support the automation effort. Some of these are included here. For example, the average time spent in taking the identification information from a requestor was 1½ minutes. The time spent walking to the file, searching the file, and returning to one's desk was 2 minutes, and the time required to read the desired credit information to the requestor was 1 minute. This results in a total of 4½ minutes per transaction (the amount of time spent copying records was negligible).

Out of this 4½ minutes, an automated system could only be expected to save the 2 minutes spent walking to the file, searching the file, and walking back. Those 2 minutes have to pay for automation of the system.

Making use of the average time per transaction and the fact that there are 160 personnel on the main shift, one finds that the peak rate at which inquiries can be serviced is approximately 2000 per hour. We note that this corroborates reasonably well with total statistics for the day, in that a large day would produce 10,000−12,000 billed queries. An average day would be more like 6000. There were, of course, no records for peak inquiry rate, since there was no way in which to obtain those data.

On a day in which there were 10,000−12,000 total inquiries, 1000−2000

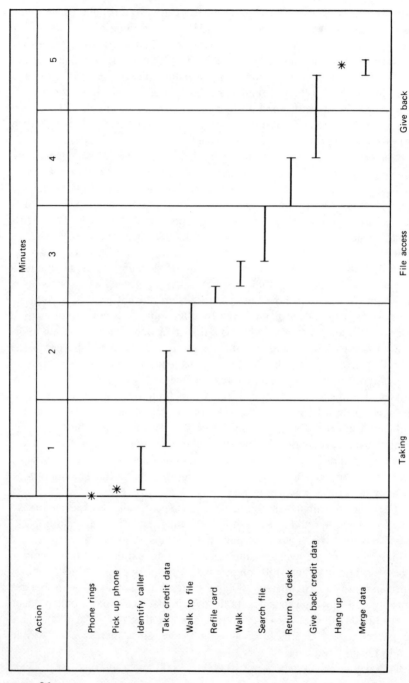

Figure 3 Query sequence.

of those would be written inquiries. Our best estimate was that a written inquiry required approximately 15 minutes to prepare. That does not include taking time or file search time, but only the preparation of the item to be mailed out to the customer.

Studies indicated that 80−90% of the credit inquiries resulted in hits. They resulted in updating a file that already existed as distinct from introducing a new record into the file. The consequence was that there were of the order of 1000 new cards a day added to the file or a total of approximately a quarter of a million each year. The file did not grow at that rate, however, because old inactive cards were purged from the file, if they had been dead long enough. The actual growth rate was more like 150,000 cards per year.

In searching for the file of a credit seeker, his current address is not a reliable means of identification. On the average, Angelenos move every three years. When credit is sought, the address the credit applicant provides will often not be the same as that contained in his file.

Although this credit bureau had been in operation for over 10 years, was well run, and the procedures had been well shaken down, there were some problems that had been recognized and from which one hoped to obtain help in the course of an automation effort. One of the problems was the performance of the credit operatives. If one of the girls was tired, had a hangover, or had sore feet, she might attempt to minimize her work load by wedging her phone off the hook. The supervisors each had 40 girls to watch, and it was very difficult to observe that some of the girls were not as busy as they should be. Clearly, an automated system with which the credit operative interacted could provide statistics on the performance of each of the girls.

Another problem with which the management was seriously concerned was the possibility of fire or vandalism resulting in destruction of those invaluable filing cards. There was no way to maintain a set of backup files in the event of destruction of the main files. Clearly, a computer-based system that could duplicate its files and where the duplicates could be stored at a remote location would provide great assurance for continued service.

A problem that came to light during the course of the study was that of potential theft or modification of credit records. Organized crime has previously attempted, and during the period of study for automation made another effort to selectively destroy records of people with known criminal patterns. The result would be that they could transiently obtain credit references to buy merchandise for which they had no intention of paying. This penetration was to be made by subverting one or several of the credit operatives. The automated system had to permit some erasures so it might not be able to prevent an operator from changing the records to a certain extent. But it could flag for supervisory or management attention those cases in which a credit operative deleted derogatory information.

The fact that the previous history of a file was available would allow reconstruction of files.

The computer operators could purge information from the files selectively and presumably without detection. There would be, however, a smaller number of such operators, they would be more highly skilled, and more highly paid. The consequence would be that screening could be more effective with such personnel. The risk would be somewhat less than with the credit operatives in the manual operation.

A problem also existing in the manual system was that of establishing positive identification for an individual, particularly in the case of legal information. Legal information was obtained from legal publications. It consisted mainly of notices of suits and judgments. Unfortunately, such records did not always provide enough unambiguous information so that the person against whom the suit or judgment was filed could be uniqutely identified. For example, the address which was referenced in the legal notice was usually that at which the process was served. This might or might not have been the residence of the individual. The consequence was that there could have been a number of records in the files for a given individual which one would like to have merged but dared not for fear that the identification was not accurate.

One of the problems which had always plagued the credit bureau was that of purging the files. In order that the file not grow without limit, it was necessary that some records be removed from the file. Removal was done on the basis of inactivity. Records that did not contain derogatory information and that had not been active for five years were to be deleted from the files. When business was light, some of the credit operators were assigned to purging files. The activity was sporadic and was not carried out systematically. The result was that large quantities of records that could have been purged were still retained. Clearly, an automated system provided the capability for purging files. If desired, the system could maintain an archive of such purged records. This would have been totally impractical in the manual system.

6.3 OBJECTIVES AND LIMITATIONS OF MECHANIZATION

A basic intent of the mechanization was to provide the same services for the same customers after mechanization as had been available before. Management conveniences or new products or services which might be derived from the mechanization were not to be considered as rationalization for the system. Moreover, the designers were to exercise caution to ensure that costs were not incurred for providing such additional services, unless they could be separately rationalized.

A second objective of the mechanization was that, after conversion to semi-automatic operation, the probability of finding a record in the file for a given credit applicant should be no less than with the manual system. There was no requirement to increase that probability over that of the manual system.

A key design parameter was that the unit cost of the credit records should be no greater after conversion than it had been before. That is to say that the savings in credit operative times would have to be adequate to pay for the expenses of operating the automated equipment and for amortizing the cost of conversion.

A difficult criterion was that there could be no significant degradation in service during conversion. That is, it was not acceptable to shut down the system while files were being converted.

The automated system was to provide a peak rate of service equal to that of the manual system, and plans were to be generated for an increase in size of the data base and increase in work load to be accommodated on an economic basis over five years. Inflation in the cost of labor at a rate greater than that of the cost of leasing the computing equipment was not an allowable rationale.

The system was to be highly reliable. While the elasticity of the market to failures to provide service because of equipment malfunction was not known, it was considered important to provide a system on which the users could count and which was up a large fraction of the time.

These considerations had a great deal to do with the eventual design of the system. These were typical examples:

- The original services concentrated heavily on the oral report and the servicing of those requirements dominated the design. In particular, since the saving of credit operative time would have to pay for conversion, it was imperative to design a system which would provide prompt response and would search the files rapidly and economically. The requirement to do this with a growing data base and with growth in the number of interrogations at about 10% a year influenced the design considerably.
- The fact that the probability of match was to be the same as with the manual system influenced the decision that the credit operative should remain a part of the decision process.
- The manual system used a logical search organized as the file was with the credit applicant's last name, then first name. The new system was designed to provide search on this basis, eliminating records that could be screened by automatic techniques and presenting the balance to the credit operative for final decision. It was an important element of the design that the final reliance was based on human judgment rather than an algorithm. It would have been highly desirable to test this approach more thoroughly than we were able during the design phase.
- The source of the material from which the query was formulated was usually written. For that reason, the coding of the individuals involved did not have to be phonetic. A number of other similar automation schemes had relied on phonetic coding, assuming that one could not rely on consistent spelling of names.

In analyzing the economics of the converted system, we assumed that the time a credit operative would expend in taking the information from her customer would be the same with the automatic system as with the manual system, but no tests were made of this. By the same token, it was assumed that the time spent in reading back the credit record to the customer would be the same in the automated as in the manual system. Therefore, the savings that were available to pay for automation were the approximately 2 minutes spent by the credit operator in traveling to the files, searching the files, and returning to her telephone, less whatever time the computer spent doing the same effort.

Since the credit operatives after automation would have to be somewhat more skilled than before, we had to base our economics on a 10% premium for the girls after conversion, relative to the wages they were making previously.

The requirement that the performance might not be degraded significantly during conversion from manual to automated operation was a severe constraint in determining how to convert the files. The file was a dynamic one. During conversion, one must either maintain duplicate (automated and manual) files, keeping track of those changes to the parts of the manual file that had already been converted, or one must operate in a dual mode, using automated search for those files that had been converted and manual search files of those that had not. At the time of conversion, it was popular to use cheap foreign labor sources for key punching large files such as this. We could find no way in which that could be accomplished in view of the dynamic nature of the file.

To meet the design goal of keeping up with peak transaction rate, the system had to be designed to accommodate approximately 2000 inquiries per hour with negligible queuing for service. That system had to be capable of increasing the rate 10% per year for five years.

Since transactions were to be shorter, the number of personnel on the main shift could be reduced significantly. We found that it took approximately 160 credit operatives spending 4½ minutes per transaction on the average to generate the 2000 inquiries per hour. The same volume could be handled at the new rate with about 90 credit operatives. That meant that the system would initially have to accommodate 90 terminals for the credit operatives, plus whatever spares would be required for out-of-service support. The number of terminals would have to increase at the rate of 10% per year. The files would initially have to accommodate approximately 1½ million credit records, averaging 250 characters each. The size of the file would increase at 125,000 records per year.

With respect to the requirement for ultra-high reliability, there was a positive factor. The company that owned and operated the credit bureau also operated two computer service bureaus in the Los Angeles area. In the interest of reliability, it was planned to provide two computer main frames, either of which could service the credit bureau. We would utilize the second main frame for a computer service bureau when it was not required for priority on-line service. It was hoped that, over a period of time, the workload of low priority traffic such as mailing lists and written reports might grow to the point where the credit bureau could be self sufficient, but this was not incorporated in the initial design.

6.4 THE CREDIT FILE STRUCTURE

As we considered the design of the automated credit bureau, it became clear that the entire system configuration would be dominated by the design of the credit file. Some of the boundary conditions on that file have been described in the preceding sections. Here, we propose to describe the way in which the file design was chosen and the characteristics with which we finally ended.

The file was to represent those 1½ million filing cards. Access to those cards was in terms of the name of the subject individual, with certain auxiliary identification information used for further screening. Since the use of the new filing system would be the same as the old, we felt that a single file organized in accordance with that same scheme would be optimal.

It might occasionally be desirable to enter the file on some basis other than the name of the individual, but there appeared to be no reason for providing such a capability if it interfered in any way with the main stream operation of the system (which was to enter by the individual's name).

In the manual system, there was a record for each individual. That record was the information contained on the 3 × 5 filing card. The information contained in those records was variable, and we chose to provide variable length records in the automated system also. That decision was reinforced by our examination of the devices on which the files would be stored. Cost was an essential ingredient in our planning. If we used our devices inefficiently, and their cost contributed significantly to the total cost of the system, we would be increasing system cost with no return.

The saving in the credit operators' time resulting from the automated system was to pay for the entire cost of designing, implementing, installing, and operating the automated system. Therefore, it was essential that the design be such that the credit operator would not spend long waiting time for access to the machine or for having her query processed once she was able to enter it. We set an upper limit of a few seconds for that operation. For that reason, we chose an indexed sequential file. In such a file, records are kept in index sequence and the location of each record can be identified from an index. In our case, the index was large enough that an index to the index (sometimes called a directory) was also required.

A key question was, "What should that index be like?" It was clear that the initial entry into the index would be by last name, and that the index information should include the first name or at least the first initial. In addition, it might include the middle name or middle initial and the current address. If one attempted to put a great deal of information in the index, the index would become as large as the file itself and would lose its value.

Some of the information to access the file provides more positive identification than the name and address. For example, the driver's license or social security number, if available, pinpoints the individual. There is a reasonable possibility of a number of people with the same name, and addresses alone may not separate them. The current address is not necessarily the one in our file, since the person may have moved. For those reasons, we contemplated maintaining cross indices of driver's license or social security numbers. An examination of the files showed that these data were not present in enough of the records to justify the difficulty of maintaining more than one index for the same file.

The design of the file was also heavily influenced by the nature of the activities to be carried on against that file. Clearly, we had to provide the on-line capability to retrieve a record promptly. There was a question of whether we needed to update the records on-line or whether updating should be done as part of a routine maintenance operation. The decision was based on the practical experience of the managers of the credit bureau. Many people, particularly those one is most interested in identifying, do their credit seeking in bursts. If someone is attempting to obtain credit with no intention of paying, he is liable to go to all the stores in an area as rapidly as possible. Therefore, prompt recording of current activity is important, and updating should be done on-line.

This leads to the questions of how much updating does one have to do, and how is it to be done? Almost every credit check results in adding a query to a record. In many cases, one adds a query and changes an address. Occasionally, a query is made by a collection agency or by a credit grantor who was seeking to find a skip. In that case, derogatory information must be entered in the files at the same time. Legal information can be added as an off-line process.

On the basis of these facts and an examination of how frequently these various items occurred, we determined that our design should make it possible to easily add a query or a change of address on any record in the file. We wanted to be able to do that updating in place. If more extensive changes were required, then an alternative method might be required.

These factors and estimates of volume and query rate led to a file design which is schematized in Figure 4. Consider the sequence of actions which occurs in the course of retrieving a record from the file. When the credit operative completes taking the credit check information, the computer examines the entry table which is maintained in core in the computer. It searches (binary search) the table to find the track on the directory file that will point to the desired credit record. Actually, it searches for the largest index value in the table that is less than or equal to the index value computed from the search information. The table provides the address of the track, which is then retrieved from magnetic disk.

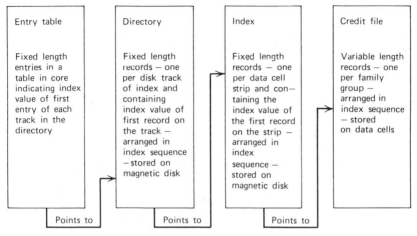

Figure 4 File design.

The data from this access is a complete track of information. The track contains the beginning index values of tracks in the index file and their addresses. The index is also maintained on magnetic disk and occupies the equivalent of an entire magnetic disk drive.

The directory track is then searched to identify the track on the index disk containing the first records which may be the identification of the individual desired. For common names such as Smith and Garcia, there may be more than one entry associated with the same name. There are a surprisingly large number of common names in a city the size of Los Angeles. The track or tracks identified by this process are next retrieved. These are searched in the same way to identify locations in the file itself. At the same time, the identification of all of the additional tracks which may contain the desired information are also obtained.

Then, the track that contains the first record is retrieved, records are compared with the search data, and if a probable match is found, the information is presented to the credit operative. If there is more than one candidate, the identifying material from as many as possible will be presented on the screen, possibly with an indication that there are still more. The credit operator can choose one, select one or more for pending status and ask to see more, or simply ask to see more. When she finally decides on one, she can request the entire record and give back the data to the customer. If candidates are found on more than one track, reads from the file will continue this until she finds the desired record or decides it is not present. Most of the time, a single retrieval from the data cell is adequate to satisfy her needs.

The information from the record was to be presented to the credit operator on a cathode ray tube terminal where she would see, in formated order; last name, first name, middle initial, current address, previous addresses, and other identification data. The display would also show the information that she entered. The search algorithm provided for making a positive match (using social security number, etc.) if that were possible. Where it was not, the data were to be presented to the operator with the most likely candidate first.

When the operator found a record that she needed, she could read the information back to the customer and indicate to the computer that she had made a match. The computer would then input the change information for the record.

In order to make this easy, records were organized as shown in Figure 5. Each record contained enough white space so that one address and three credit queries could be added without moving the adjacent records. In addition, at the end of each track, white space was provided so that the track could be reorganized to make space for records with more updates than this or to incorporate one additional record of normal length. Each track contained a flag to show that its white space had been used up and a pointer to the overflow area.

The overflow was to be maintained on magnetic disk so that it could be accessed rapidly. It was to be organized in arrival sequence so that it would have to be serially searched. It was not anticipated that there would be very much information in the overflow. The updating cycle was such that the entire file was to be reorganized at intervals of not longer than seven days.

6.5 HARDWARE SELECTION CONSIDERATIONS

The initial consideration in hardware selection arose primarily from our concern for system reliability. We, therefore, looked first at those manufacturers who had an excellent reputation for being able to keep their hardware operating. We wanted equipment that had significant numbers of the items in use, preferably in our area, and where experience had shown that the manufacturers maintenance resulted in very high equipment availability. While we considered several other suppliers, we chose to confine the majority of our analysis to IBM equipment.

We also knew that we were going to have a very large file and that the equipment to store those data files would be a dominant element in system cost. We made what in retrospect seems to be a poor decision in that matter. There were, at the time, only two realistic options for storing the file. One was to use magnetic disk. This was proven, reliable technology, but the disks did not store very large quantities of information, so that it would have been necessary to provide a very large number of them. The much cheaper alternative was a bulk storage device known as the data cell. There were two equivalent equipments available from other manufacturers, but they appeared to be less reliable.

The problem with the data cell was that it was a very complex mechanical device. It involved the storage of large numbers of strips of magnetic material

- LENGTH OF RECORD
- LENGTH OF NAME
- LAST NAME
- LENGTH OF FIRST NAME
- FIRST NAME
- LENGTH OF MIDDLE NAME
- MIDDLE NAME
- LENGTH OF SPOUSE NAME
- SPOUSE NAME
- SOCIAL SECURITY NO.
- DRIVERS LICENSE NO.
- LENGTH OF THIS ADDRESS
- STREET NUMBER
- LENGTH OF STREET NAME
- STREET NAME
- STREET TYPE (*E.G.*, ST., RD.)
- DIRECTION (*E.G.*, E., W.)

REPEATED AS MANY TIMES AS THERE ARE ADDRESSES LAST ENTRY LENGTH = 0

SIMILAR FOR EMPLOYMENT

SIMILAR FOR NAMES AND AGES OF CHILDREN

- NUMBER OF CREDIT CHECKS
- CREDIT GRANTOR CODE
- DATA OF QUERY
- ADVERSE INFORMATION?

REPEATED AS OFTEN AS RE-QUIRED

- NUMBER OF LEGALS
- TYPE OF ENTRY
- LENGTH OF PLAINTIFF'S NAME
- PLAINTIFF'S NAME
- LENGTH OF PLAINTIFF'S ADDRESS
- PLAINTIFF'S ADDRESS
- DATE
- DATE RECORD UPDATED LAST
- WHITE SPACE

REPEATED AS OFTEN AS RE-QUIRED

Figure 5 Record format.

contained in a set of so-called wedges. A mechanical device rotated a bank of wedges into position, selected one of the magnetic strips from the wedge, and caused it to be wrapped around a drum. Once there, the records could be read at high speed. Because of the complexity of the equipment, we suspected that there would be maintenance problems. We found that there were relatively few users of the data cells. The Oregon Department of Motor Vehicles had an installation with three of the devices and had had excellent maintenance results. We visited that data center and spent some time discussing the maintenance problems and came to the conclusion that we could live with the amount of down time that they were experiencing. In fact, we could stand considerably more than that without serious problems. As we look back we see that the Oregon experience probably resulted from having a specially talented maintenance man who understood and was able to make the equipment perform (as maintenance men elsewhere could not).

We were pleased to find what appeared to be a satisfactory bulk storage device from IBM. We wanted our equipment to be homogenous, from the same manufacturer. We had experienced problems when the equipment of several manufacturers was combined in a single installation. When there are failures, there is a tendency for each organization to look to another for the source of the problem. With homogenous equipment and a reliable maintenance organization, we did not expect this to be a problem.

Since we were deeply concerned with availability, our plan included a duplex computer installation and spare equipment for all of the key elements. These were to be interconnected with switches so that the equipment could be reconfigured in the event of failure of either computer or key peripheral equipment.

The choice of a computer main frame, as will be seen in the next section, was dictated by the requirement for parallel paths between the computer and the file storage. We analyzed the flow of data and determined that we needed a minimum of two parallel paths to get data between the computer main frame and the storage devices, if we were to prevent the buildup of excessive queues for resources. We also determined that the instruction time of the computer was not a serious consideration. The IBM machines available at that time were in the 360 family, and the requirement for two parallel paths to the file dictated the need for an IBM 360/40.

The next key consideration was the choice of a terminal to support the credit analyst. The cheapest alternative would have been to use a teleprinter, but we felt that input of data and output would be much more effectively accomplished using a cathode-ray type alpha-numeric display device. Some preliminary experiments confirmed this, and we decided on the IBM 2260 terminal. This affords several display formats, and we chose the format with the maximum available characters per screen. After the selection of the display device and the screen format, the choice of control units for the terminals and their interconnection to the computers were a routine matter.

The remainder of the requirements were straightforward. We configured the system to provide the number of filing devices that we required, using data cells for the credit files themselves and disk for the two layers of index leading to those data cell files. Disk was also used for the operating system and for miscellaneous logs. Magnetic tape was provided for backup logs, to support off-line printing, and for intercompatibility with other systems. In addition, since we would have a spare processor most ot the time, we planned to support our normal computer service bureau operations and provide additional peripherals for that purpose. The end configuration is shown in Figure 6.

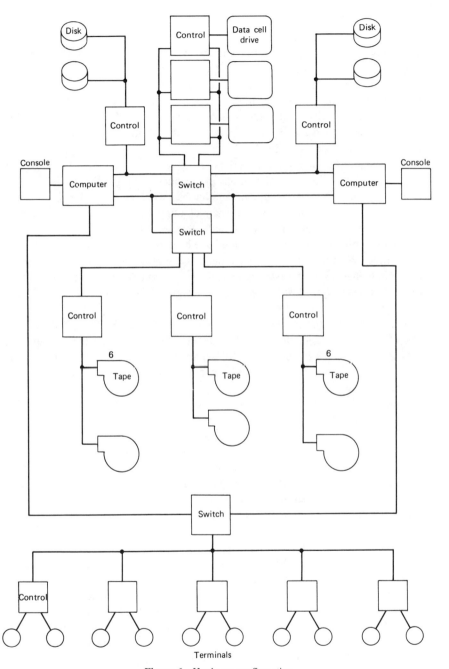

Figure 6 Hardware configuration.

6.6 ANALYSIS

The analysis carried out in configuring the system included much that has been indicated before. In sizing the file and determining the activity against it to select equipment, we found that it was necessary to weigh the constraints caused by the large number of transactions against each of the devices on which the file and its indices were stored, as well as the constraints imposed by the size of the file. We, therefore, performed a queueing analysis which was then confirmed by simulations carried out for us by IBM.

It is interesting to note that we did our own analysis first, and then asked the manufacturer to verify our calculations independently by simulation. We uncovered a trap into which we would have fallen had we done otherwise. The technical representative misunderstood certain of our requirements. The simulation called for less equipment than we actually needed. Had we simply checked the externals of his calculations, we would have been in serious trouble at implementation time. We are firmly convinced that it is essential for the system designer to do enough analysis to at least roughly size his system before he turns the problem over to someone else, lest he get serious design errors from the failure of communication.

The basis for the queueing analysis is illustrated in Figure 7. It is the time line of the flow of a single transaction against the file through the system. One sees that it involves large numbers of separate steps and that there are several devices which have to be explored for congestion before one can produce a balanced design.

Figure 7 provides a way to estimate the average time spent in satisfying a query. This number, together with the rate at which inquiries may occur, determines the number of queries that need to be simultaneously in process. As will be seen in Section 6.7, our design of the software establishes a maximum number of queries that can be in process at any given time. When that number is actually in process, all other queries are frozen out of the system at the terminals awaiting service. This is an important consideration in guaranteeing that the system will not lock up because of the inability to complete any of the processes because of conflict for services.

In Figure 7 we note that each query requires two disk reads, a data cell read, and a data cell write. On the basis of this fact and the peak rate of searches to be serviced and the time span in each of these, we were able to determine the total service requirements for disks and data cells. When one spreads these requirements over the number of devices to be used, one obtains an estimate of duty cycle. Simple queueing theory shows us that when the duty cycle exceeds 50% we begin to develop significant queues for the devices and thus begin to increase search times. Our design philosophy was to hold all of the duty cycles below 50% for that reason.

o FORMULATE QUERY – CREDIT OPERATOR FILLS IN BLANK
   FORM – INTERACTION IS WITH TERMINAL CONTROLLER – ENDS
   BY PRESSING ENTER KEY
o COMPUTER FIELDS INQUIRY INITIATES DIRECTORY SEARCH
o POSSIBLE WAIT FOR SELECTOR CHANNEL
o DIRECTORY SEARCH (DISK)
   o POSSIBLE WAIT FOR DISK CONTROL (POSITION)
   o POSITION TIME
   o LATENCY TIME
   o POSSIBLE CONTENTION FOR CHANNEL
   o READ TIME
o COMPUTER INTERPRETS AND INITIATES INDEX SEARCH
o POSSIBLE WAIT FOR CHANNEL
o INDEX SEARCH (DISK)
   o POSSIBLE WAIT FOR DISK CONTROL
   o POSITION TIME
   o LATENCY TIME
   o POSSIBLE CONTENTION FOR CHANNEL
   o READ TIME
o COMPUTER INTERPRETS AND PRESENTS INDEX MATERIAL TO CREDIT
   OPERATOR
o CREDIT OPERATOR SELECTS RECORDS – INTERACTION WITH TERMINAL
   CONTROL FOR EACH SCREENFUL OF DATA – TERMINATE BY
   PRESSING ENTER KEY
o COMPUTER INTERPRETS AND INITIATES DATA CELL SEARCH (IF THERE
   IS A CANDIDATE RECORD – HIGH PROBABILITY)
o POSSIBLE WAIT FOR CHANNEL
o DATA CELL SEARCH
   o POSSIBLE WAIT FOR CONTROL
   o RECORD ACCESS TIME
   o LATENCY TIME
   o POSSIBLE CONTENTION FOR CHANNEL
   o READ TIME
o COMPUTER PRESENTS SELECTED RECORDS TO CREDIT OPERATOR
o CREDIT ANALYST SELECTS RECORD TO MATCH QUERY, READS BACK
   CREDIT DATA TO CUSTOMER
o COMPUTER MERGES DATA FROM CREDIT QUERY WITH SELECTED
   RECORD INITIATES RECORD UPDATE
o POSSIBLE WAIT FOR CHANNEL
o DATA CELL UPDATE
   o POSSIBLE WAIT FOR CONTROL
   o RECORD ACCESS TIME
   o LATENCY TIME
   o POSSIBLE CONTENTION FOR CHANNEL
   o WRITE TIME
   o WRITE CHECK TIME

Figure 7 Transaction time line.

As we proceeded with the analysis we found that the duty cycle for index
searches (on disk) was not a problem and that a single disk could service the

maximum expected rate of request without a serious problem. Moreover, the index fit on a single disk. The actual files were spread over several data cells. The nature of the search process is such that the search tends to spread more or less uniformly across the file. For that reason, we could expect uniform loads on the data files. As long as they were all approximately equally full, the service time would divide more or less uniformly between them.

Examination of the interaction between the selector channel and the devices did indicate a problem. For each transaction, the selector channel is busy for a very brief period of time while the instructions are being given to the device controller. Then, the channel is busy full time for the actual transfer of data from either the disk or data cell. Analysis of this factor indicated duty cycles in excess of 75% and in some cases 100% for the channel. This is an unacceptable number and implies that the channel will be busy a significant fraction of the time when one wants to use it. In servicing either disk or data cell, this is a serious concern because the channel must be available within a single character time of the time that the data transfer is to be effected or an entire revolution of the disk or drum will be lost. For that reason, it was necessary to provide at least two channels and to divide the devices among them in such a way that the duty cycle on each channel would be well below 50%. This meant that we required two channels and dictated the computer main frame to be used.

We had earlier determined that an IBM 360/30 could accommodate the calculational load for the system. That computer provides a maximum of one selector channel. It was therefore necessary to upgrade to the 360/40 (which provided two selector channels) in order to get the selector channel duty cycle down to an acceptable level. Once that was done the analysis was repeated, and we determined that a transaction could be completed in approximately 2 seconds (on the average). Allowing for a margin of safety, this fact combined with our peak number of inquiries per second, 0.6, we determined that the system had to be capable of processing three queries at one time.

This number was used for sizing the master tables on which the control of the software was predicated. It also enabled us to determine the number of buffers required to handle the disk and/or data cell records and terminal inputs. We had earlier determined that since access time was a serious problem, we would always transfer a full track of data from either disk or data cell for processing. That factor allowed us to size the buffers needed for that purpose. A buffer capable of handling a full screen of data was required for each query in process. There could be as many of these as there were terminals. This permitted sizing the amount of computer core required to support the operation.

Another consideration undertaken was the analysis of how the updating of the files was to be accommodated. Both the index and directory entry could change as a result of query, since the index contained the address of the individual as well as the name. An on-line update would result in a change of the data cell record to indicate the new transaction, change of address, and any other new data. In addition, a few transactions would result in a change to the record index to reflect the change of address of the first record on a track. The directory was not expected to change.

We planned to provide for these changes by inserting white space in all of the files. Within each credit record, we provided enough white space to permit one address change and three credit inquiries. In addition, the records were to be written on the data cell tracks with 25% of each track reserved for white space at the end (where that was feasible because of record length) to provide for insertion of new records. We also provided a spill-over capability in case the white space became exhausted. Spill-over records would be written on a disk drive, and a pointer at the end of the data cell track would indicate the location of the spillover record, but, with files containing so much white space, we expected spill-over would be rare.

The index file contained formatted information. Each record consisted of the address of a data cell track and the index value of the first record on that track. An index record would change only when the first record of the track was updated or replaced so that the index value changed. This change could be accommodated in place. No white space was required.

The organization and white space requirements of the directory were the same.

The number of data cell drives was set by the combination of the space required for the records and the duty cycle of the drives. Our analysis showed that the credit file required at least 1.2 drives. In addition, our duty cycle analysis showed that the duty cycle of each drive would be (at system initiation) $0.74/N$, where N is the number of drives over which the file is spread. Both parameters showed that two drives would be required. Moreover, by spreading the file over three drives, and writing it twice, the system would support operations with any one drive inoperative. The file was spread as follows:

- First drive—first 2/3 of file.
- Second drive—first and last thirds of file.
- Third drive—last 2/3 of file.

In the event of failure, the busiest remaining drive would have a duty cycle of 0.49—acceptable.

6.7 DESIGN OF ON-LINE SOFTWARE

The software for a system such as the credit bureau normally consists of an operating system, ancillary services, and a variety of application programs. In our case, during on-line operation, only one function was to be served, that of servicing the credit operators. As a result, there was really only a single application program to be served during this time. In addition, many of the functions an operating system normally provides would not be required. Obviously, for instance, there would be no need for those facilities that support the ability to write and execute programs. Consequently, we planned for a minimal operating system and a single integrated application program.

The principal requirement of the operating system was to provide facilities for handling peripheral devices—terminals, magnetic disks, the data cell drives, and magnetic tapes. A rudimentary scheduler and dispatcher were required, and a file handling system was to be used, but it was to be customized to the operation and was considered a part of the application program rather than the operating system.

The system was characterized by its ability to service peak rate transactions of 1200 to 2500 queries per hour. That meant an approximate average arrival rate of one every 1½ seconds. Since a transaction was to be treated as an entity from the moment that the credit operator began to enter credit data until she terminated the transaction and hung up the phone, transactions would be in process for an average of 2½ minutes. The consequence was that the system had to be capable of handling at least 90 transactions in parallel (87 of these would be inactive as far as the file was concerned, while three would be in search stage).

Each of the transactions would go through the same steps outlined in Figure 7, and any one might be at any stage in that process. We chose a table driven structure for the application programs. The progress of each transaction through the system and control of the buffers in which the results of file searches were maintained were kept in central tables. The basic application programs were to be reentrant, so that they could be used several times in parallel, depending only on data in the tables.

We were greatly concerned lest the system lock up because of interactions between the credit searches which were progressing. To prevent this, we designed within a philosophy that said, "In the event that contention for resources results in filling the system, users should be frozen out at the terminals." In other words, the service that would be degraded first in the event of a busy system would be the initial response to a terminal when a transaction was to be initiated. The table-driven structure is ideal for this purpose, since a new table entry is initiated at the beginning of each transaction. The basic software modules upon which we decided are shown in Figure 8.

6.8 FILE CONVERSION

We stated earlier that the conversion of the credit files was a difficult problem, because it was necessary to convert them without interfering significantly with

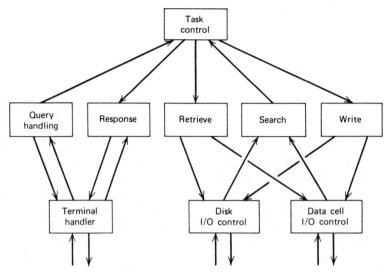

Figure 8   On-line software packages.

the credit operation and to take into account the dynamic nature of the files. This meant that they were being changed while they were in the process of conversion. With a file of this size, the conversion would occupy a very significant amount of time. In fact, we planned a period of six months to a year for conversion, so that a great many changes would have occurred in the file during the course of that conversion.

We considered a number of possibilities for converting. They were divided into two groups. In the first, we would photocopy the files, a relatively rapid process, and then convert them in a facility outside the credit bureau. The other alternative would be to carry on the conversion during third shift when the credit bureau was not in operation but when the third-shift personnel were using the credit bureau facilities and the actual credit records themselves as inputs to the conversion process. In the latter case the credit records could be returned to their normal status in time for the morning shift.

The process for converting the files outside the center involved either microfilming the records or using a Xerox machine or some corresponding full-scale reproduction method. In either case, the problem was compounded by the fact that some of the 3 × 5 cards had writing on both sides and some had some blue ink (reproduction is not guaranteed with either of the processes). In the case of the off-line conversion of records it would be necessary to keep track of changes occurring during the course of the conversion term and merge these changes with the records in their converted form. As we studied this problem, we found that we would need to maintain almost all the capabilities at the credit bureau that we needed to do the conversion, in order to keep track of changes, although not in the same quantities.

We, therefore, chose to do conversion on the credit bureau facilities. Having made that decision, the question was then, "What mechanism would we use for conversion?" The options we considered at that time were: key punching, off-line terminal conversion in which a terminal was used to produce magnetic tape or other computer readable records, or on-line conversion in which the terminal interacts directly with the computer to file the records. As we examined these possibilities, we considered the possibility of errors in transcription. In key punch operations, such errors are frequent enough that, for critical data, one enters the data twice, using the second entry for verification. We did not consider this practical in the credit operation, because of problems in sequencing the cards through the process and the necessity to be ready for operation the next morning. We, therefore, decided on the terminal operation.

We interviewed a number of people who had converted significant files using terminals (this was not too common at that time) and determined that the conversion process had been generally satisfactory and that it had not been necessary to verify the inputs. This reinforced our determination to use terminal input for the conversion. As we studied the distinction between off-line and on-line, we found that while the former required less expensive equipment, on-line conversion would provide us with a good many editing aids during the conversion process itself. This meant that we would reduce the amount of recycle of improperly transcribed cards and could prompt the operators to provide inputs in the desired formats. This latter consideration also led us to consider the use of cathode-ray type terminals rather than keyboard printers, such as the teletype machines.

This still did not solve the problem of how to handle the question of updating the file as changes occurred. We knew that conversion would have to be carried out in parallel with normal operation. While we would be systematic in choosing records for conversion, there was no real way to start at one end and go to the other so that one knew exactly where we were with respect to all of the data. As a practical matter, a drawer of cards would be removed from the file and handed to a conversion operator, who would then work her way through that drawer. When the time came to ready for the next day's business, conversion would stop with a number of drawers only partly converted at the end of the day. There was, therefore, no clean demarcation between processed and unprocessed records. To distinguish converted from unconverted, we determined that each converted card would be marked. The marking was to be done with a pressure-sensitive colored label. The credit operators would be instructed that whenever they had a credit check on a converted card, they were to mark the second card that was produced and update both at the end of the transaction. Then there would be an updated card in the file with the appropriate color code on it, and a copy of the updating information to be passed that evening to the conversion staff.

We planned that when the file was about three quarters converted, we would begin on-line operation with the incomplete file. The credit operators would obtain data from the computers for the part of the file that was converted and would walk to the manual file for unconverted records. Although this was not as efficient as one would like, it would provide for keeping the already converted files current. Transactions against the unconverted file would be recorded and could be used for converting those records or as a cross check at conversion. The break point at which this would be done was not determined.

We put a great deal of thought into the conversion format, because we wanted it to be similar to the format in which the data would be presented on the cathode ray tube screens in the ultimate system. We anticipated that we would use credit operatives from the credit staff for the conversion process. They were familiar with the records, and this would provide transition training for them. A surprising number of the credit operators had minimal typing skills, and many were eager to participate in the program.

We made arrangements with the company that captured legal records for us so that they would record them on magnetic tape. Then, they could be entered directly into the system. We planned to print out cards from that magnetic tape daily for insertion into the manual system.

In summary, we developed and did some testing on a conversion process. Our tests indicated that the production rate from cathode ray terminals would be quite adequate for the task and that the members of the present credit staff could carry out the conversion. We felt that this demonstrated their potential to function as automated credit operators.

6.9 OFF-LINE FUNCTIONS

In addition to on-line credit reporting, a number of other computerized functions were planned. These would be conducted during third shift, when the credit bureau was not active. They would be supported with DOS 360 and a regular IBM 360 operating system. They could also be handled on the backup (second) computer during the first and second shifts.

The most important of these functions was file maintenance and backup. During the course of operations, white space in the files would be used up, and it would be necessary to reorganize the file. At the same time, we would purge the old, inactive records and add data received in machine processable form, such as new legals. This was planned for a weekly cycle in which one-seventh of the file would be restructured each day. The data cells were to be reorganized one wedge at a time. When the data in a wedge would no longer fit on a single wedge, a new wedge would be inserted in the sequence and left almost empty. As the next wedge was maintained, its data would be added to the nearly empty wedge, spilling over onto a new wedge. This meant that there would be one (or more) only partially filled wedges in the file when each day's operation began. As the wedges were updated, new index entries were generated. The last task of each day's maintenance was to regenerate the index and then the directory disk records to reflect the new organization.

In the process of file maintenance, we would generate backup files planned in three echelons. The first echelon would be the file from the day before (in the form of the backup wedges) plus a log tape of the transactions that had occurred since that time. An additional generation of backup was to be preserved on magnetic tape at another off-site location in the event that fire or riot caused damage to the credit bureau facility.

A product to be produced off-line was the written reports. The data for these would be accumulated during the course of the day in the form of DLO printer tapes which would be printed over night. In this way, written reports for each day would be produced and mailed within 24 hours of the time that the request was received.

Our analysis of the privacy issue suggested that a credit seeker might have to be sent a copy of the credit report that was produced about him or receive notice that his credit had been checked whenever his credit was checked. With a manual system, the production of such reports, particularly from orals, would have been prohibitively expensive. One of the factors in the decision to convert to an automated system was the possibility of having to produce such notifications. They could, of course, be produced on the overnight cycle for nominal cost.

We mentioned earlier that mailing lists were potential products of the system. The lists provided names and addresses and perhaps other data about people satisfying certain screening criteria. The customer community had found such lists valuable, and the credit bureau had produced some manually. The production of such lists would involve a serial search of the file, matching each record against the screening criteria and extracting the desired information from each match record. Since this would interfere with on-line credit checking, mailing lists were to be produced off-line. It could be done at the same time as the file maintenance process, since that also involved serial processing of the files.

There were also a number of less frequent operations, such as the monthly billing cycle and the production of management data reports. The most interesting of these would detect credit operative productivity. It was planned that these functions would be carried out once a month.

6.10 ECONOMICS AND GROWTH

The design of this system was dominated by the necessity not to exceed the cost of the manual operation. Since the system was to service what appeared to be an expanding market and to service an expanding file, we had to consider the future to ensure that it would remain economical. Actually, we were confident that if we could design it carefully with growth in mind, we could achieve not only cost matching but also cost saving. To accommodate the future as we then saw it, we laid out a five-year growth plan. This predicted the growth of the file and the increased number of the credit operators with time. We used this to establish a machine expansion plan. It indicated that it would be necessary to expand from the 360/40 to the 360/50 at the end of three years to accommodate the volume of credit transactions.

The machine plan permitted us to predict machine cost (based on the present rental cost of equipment). Our analysis showed that the unit machine cost of a credit check would decrease over the period (as a result of increased volume of transactions). Of course, rental costs would suffer inflation, but not as rapidly as labor costs. Our analysis indicated that the unit cost of a record would actually increase slightly over five years, but not as rapidly as the cost of labor. The cost plan was complex. Cost would increase in steps as equipment was added. The steps for additional terminals were small, larger for additional data cell drives, still larger when a new data cell drive controller would have to be added along with the data cell drive, and very large at the time of conversion from the 360/40 to the 360/50.

6.11 FRINGE BENEFITS

The most important fringe benefit was protection against fire and riot. The manual credit bureau, with its very sizeable investment in the files, was completely vulnerable to these elements. Even though one could insure the file and facility against fire, the credit bureau would be out of business in the event of the destruction of the files. Once the system was computerized, the backup files would have permitted an orderly return to business, even after a catastrophe.

The theft and subversion problem appeared to us to be much improved as a result of conversion to an automated system. The possibility of major theft, such as production of a copy of the file which could be sold to some other credit bureau, was actually greater with an automated system, but that risk appeared negligible. Fortunately, the credit industry is a very responsible one, so that it is unlikely that anybody would buy such a file even if it were available. Also, the number of individuals to be controlled is small, and it is possible to do substantial background checking of those few people. The real risk was subversion, where credit operators could be induced to remove records of key individuals from the files. As we mentioned earlier, an automated system can control deletion and provide ways to determine whether files or adverse information are being deleted. We planned to introduce this capability secretly so that if deletions occurred, management would receive prompt reports of the fact. Such reports were to be by exception rather than standard products.

The credit records could be modified by computer personnel. The number of people who would be in a position to do this would be much smaller, but they would be more highly paid and thus less subject to temptation. If we considered this a serious hazard, we could do some file cross-checking at another location using backup files.

Management control capabilities were mentioned earlier. These had never been available before. There was no way of knowing the peak rate of production of credit reports or getting any but the most general-trend information. It was very difficult to determine diurnal patterns or usage patterns of our customers. We anticipated that as we grew to understand the operation better, we could manage it more effectively and that greater statistical information could be derived.

It was mentioned earlier that production of written reports would be much less expensive with the automated system and that, if it became necessary to provide notice to the credit seekers that a check had been made, the cost of providing notice would be much less than with the manual system.

We mentioned that the cost of equipment rental goes up less rapidly than the cost of labor. As inflation occurred, we expected to produce a relatively cheaper product with the automated system than we would have with the manual system. As volume increased, the cost would go up linearly or perhaps even less rapidly with the automated system, whereas in the manual system, we expected costs to go up almost quadratically, because of the interference of operators with one another.

Also, we were exploring the acquisition of additional credit bureaus and, in fact, we did acquire one credit bureau during the course of the study. We planned eventually to build a national network of credit bureaus. An automated system is desirable for such a network. It provides a basis for communicating between credit bureaus. In addition, we anticipated obtaining credit data in bulk from new sources and introducing them directly into the files. This could not have been assimilated in the manual system. For example, negotiations were in process with some of the major department stores to obtain key credit history information about their customers. This was particularly important for this credit bureau, since it represented the kind of data that had not been available in the past. It would provide positive credit information, distinct from our previous almost purely negative information content. This in turn led to new products.

6.12 CONCERNS AND SECOND GUESSING

The credit bureau we have been discussing here was never automated in this way. The company that owned the credit bureau acquired another conventional system, and the automation of the two was combined. Since that other file was greatly different from the file described here, the design of the automation system for the composite bureau was different in enough aspects that it is not possible to compare the two experiences. Here, however, we can look back from the standpoint of theory at what has been learned since and examine the decisions we made in the process of designing that automation system.

The most obvious case where our judgment was probably wrong was in the choice of the data cell as the vehicle for file storage. This is a very complex mechanical device. In service very few centers were able to match the results obtained at the Oregon Department of Motor Vehicles on which we based our decision. Ten years later, there is hardly any one left who even remembers the data cell. It is almost impossible to get any literature which describes it. It is clear, therefore, that it was not a success. This no doubt would have been a serious problem for us.

The second flaw in our planning would have been aggravated by bad data cell performance. While we had a general scheme outlined for backup, we had not really thought through the question of file backup. This would have become of crucial importance with on-line failures of the data cells. We might have solved those problems, but our plan had not really been adequate at the time that the decision to automate was made.

One of the things we did well was the study of file conversion. The study showed that the credit operators could indeed convert the file efficiently, and it is our understanding that the conversion of the file itself did go well.

As we look back, we see that we did not give enough study to the structure of the index for the records. We relied heavily on the experience of the Associated Credit Bureaus of America and other credit agencies, but we did not carry out the experiments we should have to verify that the girls could make use of that index information for search. In particular, we were not able to ensure that their success in retrieval with an automated system would be the same or better than with a manual system.

Our studies of the theft and accidental destruction were superficial. We believe that the basic philosophy was correct, but we did not carefully examine our vulnerability to computer operators and system programmers or how we could have controlled them. Finally, we did not analyze system availability, and we did not carry out experiments to check our response time calculations.

Chapter Seven

Implementation Problems for Information Systems Within International Organizations

by IVO STEINACKER

7.1 INTRODUCTION

This chapter is devoted to a discussion of the problems encountered in the planning, development, and operation of information systems in international organizations. One may ask about the special problems that arise in such an environment: Are the problems of goal-setting, justification, analysis, and implementation sufficiently different from those encountered in other environments?

The comparison here is between international organizations and the environment in business or industry. This chapter aims less at the technicalities of information systems itself—the methods of analysis, choice of system structure, selection of hardware, and so forth. It has become increasingly clear that when attention is focused only on these aspects, other, much more important factors about implementation are overlooked. Ignoring these factors may, however, lead to complete failure of the system in spite of the fact that the work done in system analysis, definition of system structure, selection of hardware, and the like, was fully up to the technical standards of the profession.

Business or industry is essentially governed by the principle of making profit. The implementation and operation of information systems can be measured in accordance with the degree to which they contribute to the economic performance of the enterprise. Do the new systems reduce stock-on-hand by permitting better control of inventories, obtain more rapid insight into the development of the market through rapid sales statistics, clarify the financial situation of the company, and the like?

Although answers to such questions in the commercial world are not so simple or straightforward that measurement of efficiency and justification of the use of an information system are easy, it is at least not unreasonable to assume that such answers are obtainable by rational procedures. However, even in corporate structures, there is accumulation of power in a single individual or in a small group of executives, and this tends to promote special interests. The study of the implementation of information systems could therefore best start by assuming two extreme cases: one where business is run by purely rational criteria and the other where it is not run by rational criteria. It is remarkable that most treatises on systems analysis assume that systems analysis can be done under the hypothesis of a purely rational environment.

In reality, this is never true, and the question is only to what degree a rational environment can be assumed. For international organizations, the assumption of pure rationality is manifestly wrong. This may be most unexpected to the information systems professional experienced in other application environments. In order to understand the differences in context, we must first consider the types and structures of international organizations and highlight the pertinent factors influencing the implementation of information systems.

7.2 TYPES OF INTERNATIONAL ORGANIZATIONS

According to their political or legal status, international organizations fall into two main classes, into governmental and nongovernmental.

Intergovernmental international organizations are established by agreement among national governments. Their operating funds come largely from the contributions of the participating governments. The organizations usually are governed by a general assembly in which the representatives of governments have a seat, and where, somewhat similar to a national parliament, the general policy, the budget, and the like, are discussed. Such a general assembly can be supplemented by one or more councils in which only representatives of a few governments sit and which may deal with special policy or administrative questions.

An intergovernmental organization may be a purely political body or political and economic, or it may specialize in a particular field of technical activity (technical must be understood in a broad sense). Depending on the generality of the terms of reference of such an organization, the governmental representatives in the assembly and/or council(s) may be delegated to represent the overall policy of their governments, or that of the respective ministerial departments within their governments.

In the case of specialized agencies carrying out technical operations, the funding for these operations may be voted by their own international assembly or may come from any other kind of national contributions. In such cases, the budget of an organization comes from two sources which impose differing constraints and create varying degrees of dependency.

Nongovernmental international organizations are established by agreement among any type of private or semi-official institutions that share a common interest, or need an international office for conducting activities, harmonization, or establishment of general rules of procedure and conduct. They usually also have a general assembly and/or a council to establish their policy. However, in these bodies the representatives of their respective member bodies are in general not government representatives, although there are some exceptions.

International organizations can also be distinguished by their field of activity. We have already mentioned the distinction between general political or economic organizations and more specialized organizations. Specialized organizations have an additional interesting feature. They generally promote a common activity for their member countries (or member bodies, if nongovernmental), presumably in the interest of all their members. They may also have goals oriented toward activities to the direct benefit of only certain of their members. This is normally the case with organizations engaged in providing development aid on an international level. However, there may be no connection between the composition of the membership and the actual recipients of their activities and aid.

7.2.1 Some Examples of the Variety

There is a rich variety of international organizations and, no doubt, an equally rich vocabulary for their description. Given the general distinction just made, more detail about the more general and political organizations and the more specialized or technical ones is useful.

7.2.1.1 *Example of an International Intergovernmental Organization with Largely Political Orientation.* The United Nations is a political organization with almost all governments on the globe represented. The budget for running offices and administration is from national budgets according to agreed percentages.

However, the U.N. is interleaved with specialized agencies, such as UNESCO, FAO, the IAEA, and others. In total, there are some 20 specialized agencies within the structure of the U.N. This relationship is evident in the mandate of the General Assembly of the U.N. to discuss matters of the specialized agencies and to recommend actions by these agencies. This is true in spite of the fact that each of these specialized agencies has its own general assembly (1).

7.2.1.2 *Examples of International Intergovernmental Organizations with Largely Specialized Orientation Directed in Their Activities Toward Development Aid.* Many of the specialized agencies of the U.N. fall into this category. UNESCO (United Nations Educational, Scientific, and Cultural Organization, Paris) and FAO (Food and Agricultural Organization, Rome) are examples. These organizations, largely designed to promote development in the third world, are financed from two sources: their regular budget, which is voted by their own assembly and which is accumulated from contributions of member states, and special funds or donations. Such donations may come from many sources. However, there is one source of primary importance, UNDP (United Nations Development Programme, New York). This agency was established to receive contributions, primarily from member states, on a voluntary basis. This arrangement was made because member states, guarding their national sovereignty, wished to avoid paying taxes to an international body, beyond what was required to run the U.N. proper as a political organization.

UNDP accounts for almost 50% of the budget for the development work of many of the specialized agencies. Agencies compete for these funds, and UNDP tries to exert some control over the activities of the specialized agencies.

In summary, it can be said that in this type of organization there is split authority on the political or management level and a double source of funds. We shall see later how this influences the corporate structure and the substantive activities of such organizations when dealing with information systems.

7.2.1.3 *Examples of International Intergovernmental Organizations Specializing in a Technical Activity and Oriented Toward Working for the Benefit of Their Member Countries.* CERN (Centre Européen de la Recherche Nucléaire, Geneva, Switzerland), EURATOM, ESA (European Space Agency, Paris) represent organizations of this type. In Europe such organizations have been established mainly to promote high technology or advanced fundamental research activities (or both), which are much too expensive to be carried out separately by individual member states. The technological infrastructure for such activities requires a minimum investment that is beyond the reasonable budget capabilities of most, if not all, of the European member states.

CERN maintains and operates large particle accelerators in which researchers from member countries can carry out their experiments. ESA was established because the development of spacecraft and/or launchers is a very large technological project. Also the exploitation of meteorological, telecommunication, or navigation satellites is only cost efficient if shared by several countries. EURATOM was conceived as a joint venture to develop nuclear energy. Although necessary on economic grounds, political divergencies have brought about grave difficulties in establishing a coherent work program for this organization.

7.2.1.4 Example of a Nongovernmental International Organization Engaged in a Technical Field, but also Engaged in Development Aid. ISO (International Standards Organization, Geneva, Switzerland) is a specialized organization of this type. ISO has been established to promote the international standardization of basic engineering dimensions, the properties of raw products or semi-finished products, and of test methods and measurements. Its member organizations are, for countries with a free market economy, the national standardization offices which in their turn are financed by private industry. However, in socialist countries, where standardization is the concern of a ministry of standardization, metrology, and quality control, the contribution comes from government sources. This organization has a general assembly and a council to run its affairs.

7.2.1.5 Example of an International Nongovernmental Organization Engaged in Establishing General Rules in Conduct of Business. IATA (International Air Transport Agency) with its participating national airlines establishes pricing, schedules, service rules, and so forth, and serves in the homogenization of, for example, freight service administration.

7.2.2 Some Basic Similarities

Although international organizations differ widely in their legal characteristics, their financial support, and their fields of activity, there are essential features that are common to most of them. These essential features often determine the factors to be taken into account when considering the problems encountered in the implementation of information systems within such organizations.

7.2.2.1 Influence of Member Bodies. Regardless of whether member bodies are national governments or their ministries, or semi-private or private institutions, it is a basic fact that these bodies, either individually or in groups, want to pursue their special goals within international organizations. They function as lobbies within the organization. Their goals may not be completely divergent from those of the international organization, but they do attempt to promote their own influence on decision making, distribution of funds, political attitudes, and policy statements of the organization as a whole.

The management of such an organization, for this reason, is confronted with the conflicting purposes of such lobbies. As such, organizations are seen as secretariats, that is, offices of execution of tasks given to them, and often must laboriously steer an undulating course through the various forces trying to influence their destiny.

7.2.3 Environmental Constraints on the Implementation of Information Systems

The conditions briefly described above have led in most international organizations to an internal atmosphere which is difficult to understand from outside.

In these organizations, management, in general, strives to survive on the political level, dealing primarily with the influences of the various member bodies. There is rarely enough force or intent left to deal effectively with questions of running the organization. Running any organization has two aspects. The first is administrative, which includes employment policy and personnel selection, and all the basic tasks, such as financial administration. The second is substantive, including the selection of work projects, the assignment of personnel to these projects, the advance planning, and the execution of projects. Projects may be anything from development projects in the third world to the setting up of a new group of staff to deal with a specific, in-house task.

We shall only deal with the substantive part. It is in the substantive sector that the peculiarity of planning and management in international organizations becomes clearest. In most business enterprises there is one final yardstick for measuring success or failure—profit or loss. However, it is extremely difficult to assess the success or failure of projects in international organizations, and even more difficult to find any final yardstick by which the performance of international organizations can be measured.

The existence of many such organizations has come about in the hope of promoting and supporting a variety of interests and goals. Such ethical urges cannot easily be denied their justification, nor can they easily be measured. In fact, however, when it comes to practical implementation, the mere creation of an international organization often is an excuse for inaction and sometimes retrograde policy.

One example of the latter is the now defunct ELDO (European Launcher Development Organization). When Europe went into space it needed, apart from satellites, vehicles to shoot them. For satellite development, another organization was set up (ESRO, European Space Research Organization, now ESA). As this organization was at least initially oriented toward research satellites, there were no heavy political or military implications. However, when it came to launch rockets, there were such implications.

ESRO consisted of an integrated vertical structure, including centers of technical competence, apart from management, planning, and scientific research. ELDO was conceived as a pure planning secretariat that had to interface with national efforts to produce a multistage rocket. It was evident that national military and political establishments did not want to give away the national technology in the field. The result is known. Whereas ESRO has had a rather high rate of success, ELDO has misfired every test shot for ten years.

These factors influencing management within international organizations—contrasting interests and power of the member bodies, orientation of the management toward the external political scene, and the difficulty of defining and measuring success or failure—have their consequences. Where the definition and measurement of success or failure is difficult, people tend to avoid accountability. The avoidance of accountability is made easier when data and information are not readily available, written down, or stored in a compatible format—where evaluation is made more difficult.

This situation results in a rather hesitant advance through projects. A clear and consistent course of planning cannot be held for long. Because of the various changing influences, management is politically oriented. As such, result oriented people are in the minority in international organizations. Either such people are rejected when applying for a position, or, if accepted, are thrown off centrifugally after a certain time. Then, too, they may succumb to the general atmosphere. The survivors flounder in an intricate, rickety structure that nobody can depend on or comprehend clearly. Under these conditions, management in international organizations cannot complain of the low level of intellectual capabilities, professional competence, and motivation when it is found in their staff. This is simply the natural environment in which the implementation of complex information systems must be considered.

7.2.3.1 *The Introduction of Computers.* Any effort to handle information through computers must deal with one fundamental fact: a computer is a mechanism, nothing but a mechanism. In places, one used to see in shop windows a moving figure playing a violin. Usually, the arm with the bow moved back and forth, always executing the same motion. Such a toy is fairly simple; an electric motor and some mechanical gear. However, imagine that such a fiddler was really playing a very simple tune on his violin. The mechanical complexity would become enormous, although the result would appear more human, and hence, simpler to the uninitiated. This common error is made in lay attitudes toward computers. The more flexible a computer system is, the more it responds in a reasonable way to human stimulus, the more natural, and hence, less complicated the system appears to be. In fact, such computers are, as with the mechanical violin player, far more complex.

Just as it would take a large engineering effort to convert the fiddler into a pianist, any change or modification of a complex computer system requires a large effort. This is not said to defend the view that a computer system, once set up, should immutably remain the same for years or decades. Every computer system dealing with information derived from some part of the real world is, in the mathematical sense, a mapping of this part of reality. Reality changes constantly, and hence computer systems dealing with real-world information must change with it.

However, the question is whether planning for such inevitable changes takes place in an open environment where problems are clearly defined, criteria for acceptable solutions established, and possible solutions weighed in the light of these criteria. Or is it that secret motivations, camouflaged by other arguments, are the driving forces of such decisionmaking?

Unfortunately, it is much more the second kind of environment for decisionmaking that prevails in international organizations. This is counterproductive to the efficient development and operation of information systems.

A computerized information system can be viewed as a flywheel. It takes some time and energy to accelerate, but once rotating, it cannot be stopped abruptly or be reversed. If this is attempted, something breaks in the gears of the organization. Because management is conscious of the ever-shifting political conditions under which an international organization must operate, it is reluctant to take long-term decisions that might engage its responsibility, funds, and manpower for extended periods of time. This is particularly true with systems that, once initiated, continue on their unpredictable courses, little subject to directed change.

7.2.3.2 *Establishment of System Configurations.* At the beginning of planning and implementation for complex information systems, it is difficult to foresee the reactions of the directing management within international organizations. Very often a green light is given initially, because nobody realizes what the implications of implementing a computer information system are. They are essentially:

- Such a system can only be built in a corporate environment where goals are (fairly) rationally defined, and definitions are based on preceding analyses of the relevant factors.
- Time scales and targets for achieving system completion must be realistic. It must be understood that any such information system, however good initial analysis may be, will go through several stages of prototype development. This requires that time and funds be available to rework earlier prototypes. It may take three or more prototypes before the system is established.

In this context, it is erroneous to believe that a careful initial analysis will reveal all the requirements to be met, all the functions to be executed, and all the data elements to be taken into consideration.

During the required analytic stages, people are still reticent about accepting a computer and do not divulge all their knowledge, all their problems and wishes. Very often staff members are not even aware of what they may get out of the new information system if it is properly used: that the capabilities of a computer to rearrange and select data rapidly and to carry out various kinds of surveys, such as statistical ones, are the real justifications for such a system.

7.2.3.3 *Considerations Pertinent to Project Staff.* Computer experts confronted with the circumstances surrounding the development of information systems within international organizations may well conclude that they face the "mission impossible." An impossible task can be defined as a project where even the best efforts will invariably fail. Failure of information systems is encountered in international organizations quite frequently. This should constitute a warning to anyone embarking on such an enterprise to be extremely careful in checking the conditions surrounding the project and to take the above description quite seriously.

In our present world, there are few people who can claim a significant degree of independence from the constraints of income and the place where they live. Whoever works for international organizations will rarely have the resources to say, "If I wish, I can quit this job any time." In particular, people working in advanced fields of technology or in management often do not reside in the country of their nationality and may be restricted in relocation by regulations concerning residence permits and the like. Finally, at a given location, there may not always be a job available within the appropriate field and seniority level to permit transfer if the conditions become impossible.

One must be prepared to encounter impossible conditions, however disquieting this may be. Furthermore, there is no regular way, at present, within international organizations to upgrade one's skills and be supported by funding. Because of the acceleration of technological change, the computer professionals must take it upon themselves, personally, to continue their education while on the job. This constitutes very often a heavy additional burden on the individual. One hopes the time will come when the necessity for permitting paid leaves for extending skills and knowledge is generally understood and correspondingly facilities are established for this purpose within international organizations.

The general constraints that information system experts must expect to find in international organizations are not insignificant. Because of this, it has been thought worthwhile to include these observations and not limit the discourse to discussing the purely technical factors relevant to the development of information systems. The case histories to follow will further explore these factors.

7.3 CASE HISTORIES

The case histories described below are abstracted from the unessential details of a particular organization. However, they are based on detailed evidence which makes them sufficiently realistic. There is no intention to criticize or extol any particular organization. Rather, the aim is to present the facts as they were experienced.

7.3.1 Intergovernmental International Organization (With a Technical Activity in High-Technology Research)

This organization is distinguished by a high degree of success in its substantive activities. Technical projects are built and developed within the foreseen time limits and fall—grosso modo—within their budget limits. The projects are then operated successfully and provide the kind of results they were intended to yield.

The organization established a special service to provide technology data for research and development in its member countries not only in those domains of research which would be closely related to the main activity of the organization, but also for research in general.

The service began its work by scanning a large computer file containing the technology data stored on an external machine for individual researchers or laboratory groups. Selective listings were produced to satisfy the requirements of the users. Potential users were informed of the existence of this service by a group of advisers who traveled to introduce the service directly. They also collected questions relating to research topics of users or user groups.

These advisers worked with the users to establish a combination of search keys. If the result of the computer search was bad, the adviser could share the responsibility with the user, based on their agreement concerning the search formulation. However, this advisory service was a minor activity of the organization as a whole. It was justified more or less under the flag of direct assistance to research closely related to the objective of the organization.

Matters changed when the external computer system was transferred to the computer center of the organization and on-line interrogation by the advisers became possible. This meant that the "editing" of user questions—using certain search keys from a list of such terms—could no longer be jointly accomplished through a user-adviser agreement. At that time the advisers at the computer center had to decide whether the user formulation of the initial question was appropriate to retrieve the proper answer.

To be capable of doing this, advisers not only had to have a broad and very solid background in the scientific specialties concerned but they also had to have a good understanding of the computer system and of the way search keys were to be combined to formulate search questions fed into the computer.

When the on-line system was installed, some capable staff were hired. Because they could, on a significant level, satisfy the need of users, they rapidly increased the turnover in number of questions answered. For such a system, a measure of effectiveness is the number of questions answered (per adviser). Another factor, more difficult to measure, is quality of answers. However, unless the service attempts to give one printout of technological information to an unending row of new customers rather than establishing a satisfied customer base, the quality is reflected by the number of users coming back to the service after an initial try. This number was also, for successful advisers, fairly high.

At this point serious problems arose. In principle, a successful operation of this international advisory service would have brought revenue to the service (services were "sold" for a charge), the image of the organization would have been boosted, and R&D in the respective countries would have benefited. However, one backfire effect was that national groups in the technology transfer business feared a loss of their influence and importance. At that point no member country was in possession of a computer retrieval system comparable in ability to that of this international organization. Simultaneously with attempts to launch a similar national service, the activity of the advisory staff was restricted and assailed by national powers. As a result, the international organization decided to reduce this direct advisory activity and finally to abolish it. Instead, the installation of remote terminals was promoted in the users' localities to permit each user to search the technology file(s) without on-site contact with advisers.*

This must be seen in the light of the following facts: To search, in on-line mode, large files of technological data, requires highly skilled staff with an excellent scientific or technical background. Moreover, it needs a large number of searches until such a person achieves mastery of the system. These capabilities were not always available at user terminals (even after short training). Also, the operational costs of a remote terminal at any location in the member countries of this organization were high because of the high costs of European telephone links.

For these reasons, the new direct, on-line access to this technology information system was expensive. Moreover, it took more than five years to persuade a substantial number of customers to link up with the central computer. Five years, however, is the average lifetime of computer hardware and, to a certain extent, also of computer software. At the time such retrieval systems were developed, the respective programs could only be served by large computers where core was at a premium. Furthermore, special control machinery was required to monitor the signal traffic over the telephone lines. For almost every action taken at the remote terminal (pressing a key) the central machine had to respond. This made overhead very heavy, increased response time to the limit of the users' patience, and made the system difficult to maintain and expand. During this period in fact the system developed from a file of some 300,000 records, each about 1000 bytes long, to over 6 million records of the same size. To maintain such files with multi-user direct access from remote terminals is quite a task.

In the meantime, computer technology advanced a significant step towards small, inexpensive computers, many of them with on-line (dialogue) terminals.

*The decision to opt for remote on-line interrogation of the central files by providing terminals at user sites was not solely a political decision. Although this shifts the difficult search formulation tasks to the users, it does avoid the problems involved in the use of middlemen, however successful the advisers may have been in establishing contact with sensitive users. At the time of this decision, direct interrogation of central files by users at remote sites had long been established as technically feasible and usually being the preferred approach where communications problems and costs were not regarded as excessive. However, the fact that decisions based on political reasons sometimes conform to or are justified on technological grounds does not indicate that the political grounds for this decision discussed above were not present nor important. The particular emphasis found in any of the various contributed sections of this book is a function of the specific on-site experiences of the contributor and, as such, of interest. In this case the difficulties of introducing on-line remote consoles discussed here are very real and caused the same problems elsewhere.   A.E. Wessel

This development, comparable to Ford's tin lizzy of the 1920s, has brought computer power within the reach of financially less powerful users—whose requirements are also less embracing.

It could have been seen, when this technology emerged, that the old concept of large central system and unintelligent remote terminals was obsolete. A different system concept is possible now for such systems. Each user installs his own machine (answering some interface requirements with the general system specifications). In this local system, information is stored which is useful specifically to the local user. At any point in time, it is possible to access a central host system to run special inquiries in a dialogue mode or to retrieve stipulated sections of whole files for transfer to the local user's files.

Needless to say, such a system would dramatically reduce costs for users. There would be less line costs, less machine time in the central machine, and a fairly inexpensive local installation. Another benefit would be that, by a suitable data capture program, users could establish their own private files (protected or unprotected) to support their own work.

Why was this not done? Whether the direct management of this service was not sufficiently farsighted to understand the potential of new technology and its implementation(s) is not at issue. The direct management had to defend, with difficulty, the existence of the system as it was, to the top management of its international body and commissions composed of member states interested in their own national developments. Political factors could be said to force a delay in appreciating technical breakthroughs. The result was that this system was essentially frozen in a state from which it would be very difficult and costly to emerge. It is remarkable, then, that other information transfer systems planned by other international organizations and some nations are not only based on the same (outmoded) concept, but also that, in one case, the present system is intended to serve as an initial building block!

The original dialogue program system used by this organization has remained rather static during the last eight years. It is true that some of the functions of disk file management and access have been improved. It is characteristic, however, that the system was originally designed to work with IBM data cells as mass storage. Although these have been obsolete for a long time, they have only been removed at a very late date in the life of the system.

No essential logical function has been added on an operative level, such as high-level, computer-aided indexing or user aids to the build-up and improvement of query profiles. Not even some very basic improvements were made. For example, the system permits, in one search, the use of 98 query statements. This is enough if one has to search only one file. If several files are to be searched for one topic and one does not want to constitute separate output listings, this number is far too low.

However, this sort of result is more typical than not within organizations functioning under the conditions previously outlined. If anything, the results are more favorable than those usually obtained for the implementation of information systems within international organizations, as the next case history demonstrates.

7.3.2 Intergovernmental International Organization (Superstructure Organization with Technical Sub-Bodies)

This case history describes a project operated with the aim of solving problems in the collaboration and coordination between several international organizations rather than being embedded in one organization alone. All organizations involved are of the intergovernmental international organization type, and they are all engaged in substantive work in a special technical field. These technical organizations are connected through a central agency, an international political organization. However, this central agency cannot directly control the operations of the technical agencies. It exercises influence through consultation and coordination.

The technical agencies are all planning, funding, and executing technical projects in the third world countries within the limits of their specific missions. However, in such enterprises it is evidently impossible to delineate clearly the fields of activity. This naturally will lead to:

- The same type of project being started in the same geographical area by two different agencies.
- Overlap between projects.
- Countereffects produced by the differing projects. (As an example, in the same country, one agency was drying swamps in order to fight mosquitoes and other pests, and hence to improve health of the population, whereas another agency undertook to build power dams, creating new water surfaces on which the pests could flourish.)

Funding of all these projects comes essentially from two sources: from the regular budgets of the individual agencies as managed by their general assemblies and from a central funding agency which administers voluntary contributions. At any point in time, about 20,000 projects are in existence, and there is practically no cross-checking being done to assure good coordination among them.

It must be added that each executing technical agency competes for influence in the receiving countries, trying to place as many projects as possible in a certain country or region. These technical agencies also compete for funding from the independent funding agency distributing voluntary contributions.

The lack of project coordination was clearly unsatisfactory. The general assembly of the central political agency therefore passed a resolution calling for the establishment of an interagency committee to harmonize project planning and distribution. Its terms of reference contained a request to study the use of information systems for this purpose. The committee was to be supported by a secretariat, a small study group composed of experts in the relevant fields. The study group was to carry out analyses and studies. Based on the findings of these initial analyses, a structure or structures for information systems which were capable of monitoring the multitude of projects planned or under way was to emerge.

From the purely technical aspect of data processing, an information system is essentially centered around a computer, and habitually consists of (a) data base(s) and processing programs. This is a very narrow conception of the term information system. Any entity that functions to create, register, administrate, select, and output information is an information system. With this in mind, it is clear that a committee itself can be considered an information system, and the same is true, in fact, for any administration in the general sense.

Under the given political and administrative circumstances, the analysis, conception, and design of one or several information systems appear to be a gigantic task, not to speak of actual implementation and day-to-day operation of such a system. The major problems were certainly not in the design of the central (computer) information system but in interfacing with the local information systems of the agencies involved—always provided that these systems themselves could supply the right kind of information.

The other alternative, namely, to impose a single type of information system on the participating agencies, might be deceptively attractive. However, each of the agencies, in spite of the fact that they all operated within the same general framework, political structure, and task execution, had developed their own methods of handling their information which later appeared to be highly divergent and sometimes incompatible with each other. This is due to historical and political reasons:

- The agencies were not created at the same time and were dispersed in many places around the world.
- They were built according to the style of their period of creation and influenced by the local national environment in which they grew.
- Up to the creation of the interagency committee, they had little formal information exchange contacts among themselves. There was no opportunity for the process of gradual adaptation and conformation to each other.

Any intervention in the information handling of an agency is seen by the agency to be a major intrusion on its autonomy. This defense reflex is augmented by the fact that agencies work administratively in a very antiquated and inflexible way. In typical bureaucracies, no one wants to take the initiative or responsibility, and hence nothing changes. The job of aligning the local agency information systems to enable them to interact with or feed a central information system, under the political circumstances, is almost equivalent to the job of implementing a military intelligence service that would work at the same time for the Americans and the Russians.

The intention behind the resolution of the general assembly to set up a committee and a secretariat was certainly motivated by the insight that coordination was long overdue. However, as in many other projects, some initial errors were made which passed unnoticed at the time they were committed. Anything that was attempted afterward had a high chance of going wrong. And it did.

The first error was to establish a committee with officials from the agencies, principally their respective secretary generals. It should have been clear from the outset that it was exactly these people who would defend the interest of their own agencies. The common interests of the nations or governments that intended to improve the services given to them (for the recipients) or to reduce the waste of funds (for the donor countries) would tend to be deemphasized.

The interagency committee operated within a web of similar institutions maintained by the agencies and the central political agency. There was already a Committee for Inter-Agency Affairs. The inter-agency committee to deal with information systems reported to a higher administrative committee, which again reported to a subgroup of representatives from the general assembly forming one of the councils existing in the organization. It was evident that this became a situation where those who were to be controlled could decide how much they wanted to be controlled. The agencies could thus very well avoid any measures for change that were perceived as an infringement of their autonomy.

This was the starting situation. Now, a second initial error was made. The secretariat which was to carry out the substantive work of study, analysis, and design of the information system was to be managed by a director to be newly appointed. Such a post required very special talents. The holder would need to be accepted by the top executives on international management, diplomatic, or political levels. He needed to be a man of profound analytical powers with a dynamic approach to problem solving but one who would rigorously adhere to the framework supplied by rational analysis of the given circumstances.

This post could only be filled successfully from a very select group of candidates. Needless to say, the qualifications as outlined above are almost mutually exclusive. A person who is accredited with the top officials of essentially bureaucratic organizations will most probably not have—or fully exercise—profound analytical capabilities. He would also very probably not be a dynamic manager.

This post was advertised in major newspapers with a job description that put emphasis on the managerial and technical capabilities in developing complex information systems. Over 800 applications were received, most of which were eliminated in an initial screening process. However, with such a number of applications, initial screening had to be handled by lower grade personnel in the personnel department. This created the danger that suitable candidates might be lost during screening and not be interviewed by top management. Finally, three candidates were selected and asked to present themselves to the committee. Of those, one backed out. The person selected was a man who came from a major multinational commercial company. In his presentation, he obviously overwhelmed the members of the committee with a grand vision of a comprehensive computerized information system which he had sketched on paper.

The operation seemed to start well. The creation of this new body intended to combat the inefficiency of this multi-agency system was welcomed in many quarters, in particular in government-aid agencies which operated bilateral aid projects. The newly appointed director was able to select, without much interference from the committee or the administration, a team of competent people with a total spectrum of skills that matched well and covered the areas of interest— general management, principles and structure of high-level computerized information systems, general administration in the multi-agency system, and system analysis and programming of information systems.

From the beginning, this group of highly motivated and efficient people was prevented from doing the necessary. Obviously, the first step would have been to go to the agencies and to study the ways of information handling used there. However, the travel budget of the group was severely limited, and the unwillingness of the agencies to make appointments for visits made this situation worse. When, even under these restrictions, the study group began to understand the obstacles and the basic nature of the difficulties that would be encountered in the development of an information system, the committee began to use what might be called the rabbit technique. When rabbits flee from danger, they react unpredictably, because phylogenetically, they are conditioned to evade birds of prey striking down on them. The rabbit technique in this case consisted in never fully discussing the findings presented by the study group or their director, respectively, but to level general and random criticism at them. Then upper management continually brought up new problems and defined new tasks so that work could not proceed in a long-range, orderly fashion. Finally the agencies that were supposed to finance the operation of the secretariat through contributions from their budgets appeared always to be having financial difficulties and hence tried to cut and limit the funding.

One of the main projects was to establish a register of development projects fed by data from all agencies. In spite of many difficulties, an initial pilot project was created using a file originating from the central funding agency administering voluntary contributions. This was about the only success achieved.

The main committee meetings were held rarely, only once or twice a year. A subcommittee, called a review panel, met more often to ensure continuous and close contact between the secretariat and the committee. These meetings turned out to be increasingly controversial. After a fairly brief period of less than two years, such controversies triggered a crisis in the secretariat. Staff members either decided to leave or to go back to their previous work in the agencies, or their contracts were not renewed. This finally happened to the director selected initially with much fanfare, and the study group disintegrated. Three members of the group collaborated, even after two of them had left the study group, to produce a critical but constructive report on the whole exercise. This report is the basis of Section 7.3.2.1.

7.3.2.1 *A Critical Appraisal of Committee Activities.* The present structure of the system of agencies in this organization has its origin in the developmental course pursued in the past by each individual agency. Over the years, every agency had elaborated its own independent operating procedures and information systems and tended to ignore efforts aimed at the introduction of harmonized, coordinated services. Yet such coordination is becoming increasingly important for the family of agencies as a whole in order to avoid unnecessary overlapping, make maximum use of available resources, and most especially, to expedite projects with a common aim.

Recognizing that the development of compatible information systems on the inter-agency level represents an elementary prerequisite to more effective cooperation, the general assembly passed a resolution calling for the setting up of this inter-agency committee for information systems.

Nearly five years later it is widely recognized that this committee has, in the results it achieved, fallen short of its stated terms of reference. This chapter suggests the reasons for this failure and offers some recommendations for improving the implementation of future projects.

The resolution of the general assembly was passed in the hope of bringing about a reversal of the diverging trends in information handling, and securing the development of compatible information systems on the interagency level as well as ensuring the proper utilization of available resources.

In reality this problem goes far deeper. The management concepts of the various agencies were not compatible, and clearly defined goals were lacking. The introduction of a meaningful inter-agency information system would require that autonomous information systems achieve compatibility. This in turn is contingent on the existence of related management systems. It is possible to introduce compatible, mutually accepted conventions that will respect the autonomy of agencies yet secure the compatibility of information-handling procedures among the agencies. This, however, implies that close working relationships among agencies must be established.

The failure of the committee to develop a consulting function with the agencies for a joint assessment of management information needs has brought about a crisis of confidence between the concerned parties. As a result, all work has been reduced to technicalities in the field of electronic data processing which is only of peripheral importance within the established terms of reference. Consequently, the goals set for the committee to improve the effectiveness of information systems within the family of agencies have not been achieved.

A lack of relevant professional knowledge within the policy and executive levels resulted in the failure to identify the role and objectives of the committee. Hence it was incapable of preparing a meaningful work program jointly with the director of the Secretariat. Unfortunately, the appointment of the director of the Secretariat was the result of a misconception of the substantive requirements of this post by those responsible for the selection process. The director selected was an expert in electronic data processing, but he was not equipped to respond effectively to the broader problems which were basically of a management and policy nature. Thus attention was given incorrectly to computer and information technology rather than to the development of conventions for securing the compatibility of management concepts.

This would have been best promoted by the strengthening of intra-agency information handling. Only when information is readily available within agencies can it be transferred to an inter-agency system. For this reason, the efforts of the secretariat should have been concentrated on consulting with the agencies on the improvement of their internal information systems.

It can be expected that such an approach would bring about the following:

- A better way of recording and maintaining information at its various sources in the agencies.
- An easier flow of this information within and among agencies. Increased clarity of the planning process and thus a better consolidation of policy of agencies in matters of development work or administration.

Summarizing, the failure of the committee to improve information handling in the system of the organization was due to the following factors:

- The inability of the committee to define its role and objectives which made it impossible to develop a meaningful work program.
- The failure to carry out a fundamental analysis of the information handling procedures and information requirements of the agencies.
- As a result of these circumstances, the preoccupation of the secretariat with the technicalities of the computerized systems, without being given clear guidelines about their applications.

It becomes clear from this study that an improvement in the exchange of information among agencies will be possible only in an environment of trust and cooperation. The agencies must realize that the benefits to be derived from compatible systems that do not infringe on the autonomy of agencies are much greater than the inconveniences resulting from adhering to a set of mutually binding management conventions.

7.3.3 Nongovernmental International Organization with a Technical Mission

This organization is a nongovernmental international organization with a technical mission. Its member bodies are the corresponding technical agencies in many countries which, through the international agency, harmonize their technical regulations within their field of activity.

Regulatory documents are produced by international agreement (among the technical agencies in each country, which are not necessarily linked with the government administration). The preparation of these documents is a process that sometimes takes several years. They are approved by going through a carefully designed sequence of voting and approval, after which they can be published as an international regulatory document. Elaboration of these documents does not take place at the seat of the international coordinating agency (or only rarely) but in committee meetings that may be convened in any part of the world. Only the results of this committee work are communicated to the central agency. These may take the form of results of voting or of the preliminary, more advanced, or final text of the regulatory documents. These documents, after final approval, are then printed at the central agency and officially announced.

At any point in time, there are about 5,000 documents under preparation. The number of approved and published documents reaches about the same number but is increasing steadily. However, approved and published regulatory documents are revised in a five-year cycle in order to adapt regulations to the state of the art as it evolves.

The agency has developed an administrative control system known and accepted by the many thousands of experts engaged in elaborating regulatory documents all over the world. The administrative control system monitors the progress of work on documents under preparation and controls documents approved and published. Reflecting the complicated voting and approval process, the control system is complicated in itself. Further, it must permit a certain latitude to be able to accommodate special cases.

When the project to be discussed here was started, the agency was already using a computerized control system for the documents. This was located in a service center. The programs had been written by staff otherwise engaged in purely commercial programming. The system had more drawbacks than advantages. Filling in the input sheets required a high degree of skill. Many purely logical decisions based on the requirements for the ultimate processing by program were required. The turnaround time after runs generating the error listings was of the order of one week. However, because of the official nature of approved documents, there were rigid deadlines for the production, printing, and distribution of the approved document announcement lists.

Under these circumstances, it was not surprising that two parallel systems were operated—the computerized system, and a manual control system which proved to be faster, although not error free either. The computer system accepted only upper case text for the titles of the documents and printed only upper case as well. However, the announcement list published every January, had to be in full alphabet, including French characters with accents, for reasons of prestige and legibility. Even if the computer listings would have been ready on time, they could have been used only as a manuscript for composing, thus creating a source of printing errors and, of course, further delay.

The designer of the original computer program system was believed to have devoted too much time to this task (the directorate obviously did not accept this design effort as a full-time job). He was forced to step aside, and left behind a system that could only be regarded as a first prototype. The central agency, without any analytical capability left, functioned with this system for about four more years. Then with the start of a new project, the old system was analyzed again.

At this point there was general disillusionment among the staff with the performance of the old computer system. In fact, each department more or less ran its own document control system which it preferred. The analysis for the new system was conducted over an eight-month period by one staff member. It resulted in conclusions of which the essentials were:

- The system had to accept and print full alphabet (upper and lower case) for better printouts or photocomposition.
- It would require on-line data keyboarding under real-time program control to check for errors immediately at input time.
- It would need close control but also permit easy modification of program structure.

These requirements excluded the use of the existing service computing facilities. It was proposed, and accepted, to install a minicomputer in the offices of the central agency. The minicomputer would have a disk capacity of about 14 megabyte, backup storage on diskettes, a CRT display, a printer with 132 positions, and a typewriter keyboard. It was also foreseen that staff programming capacity would be increased to meet the workload of developing the system.

The system design was made very carefully. It allowed for reserve space in record formats and a general flexibility to be able to adapt the system to future changes which were seen as inevitable, given the administrative structure of the organization. For controlling input data, a real-time check approach was used, basing itself largely on the comparison, at keyboarding time, of related data elements which, strictly speaking, introduced redundancy into the system. However, by checking correct correspondence between data elements, logical and even content errors could be eliminated to a large extent, and production runs could be started without prior error-check runs.

After the machine had been delivered, the on-site EDP staff started to program with the expectation that the promised help in programming would be available soon. It was at this point that an initial error was made by management which made its effects felt through the following years. Management failed to support the highly motivated and efficient effort it had initially authorized. Moreover, combined with this lack of support, critical deadlines were arbitrarily advanced. Up to this point the development of the system had proceeded fairly well. Then the deadline for the production of a major register of regulatory documents was advanced by several months without consultation with the EDP section. The time for this accomplishment was now reduced to a few weeks. Pressures began to build up, but it was possible to produce this new listing within the new deadline. However, there was a price to be paid. By such tactics the system was forced into an increasingly disorderly state. The operation turned into a positive-feedback cycle; the more work was spent on it, the more incoherent it became.

Staff possessing a modicum of professional integrity cannot accept or acquiesce to restrictions or demands imposed on systems that unbalance or destroy the system. The EDP manager therefore submitted several reports in which he criticized existing methods and actions of management pertaining to the system. Instead of acknowledging these criticisms in a constructive fashion, the directorate slowly began to eliminate this factor of perturbation and unrest. More programming staff was hired, and one person presumably qualified for the EDP managerial post was hired as a convenient tool of pressure during the absence of the existing EDP manager.

Some edited extracts from the reports which produced this situation are provided in Section 7.3.3.1.

7.3.3.1 *Future of Computer Operations in the Central Agency.* It is an established fact that the introduction of in-house data processing facilities in any commercial company or administrative organization does not only add another executing function to an existing organization but also in fact adds a new factor of management.

Rarely does the introduction of computers significantly save cost or personnel. Justification of computers lies in the fact that they provide services that cannot be provided by manual work (rapid selection of a small subset of information from a large collection, flexible statistics or control information for production, etc.). However, in order to achieve such services, the use of computers must be understood properly. Otherwise a computer may become nothing but an expensive typewriter.

Computer operations require careful analysis, both for single problems and for multiple problems. Analysis must take into account all factors involved (usually there are more factors than anticipated), decide on the kinds and presentations of printed output, and establish the methods of interacting with the administrative (human) environment. Significant human work under this concept remains to be done. Pressing a button will not substitute computer work for human work.

Programming for the processing of data may take man-weeks, man-months, or man-years. When new services or new ways of accomplishing existing services are introduced, computer operations are different from manual ones. With manual operations many changes are feasible by giving instructions to personnel. It may require only a few hours to introduce a new working procedure. Of course, much depends upon the particular changes introduced. But computers are, in any case, different from people.

The basic fact is that usually only after long preparation and programming can anything be done with a computer. As such:

- If there is no long-term planning and no clear-cut perception of how and for what a computer is to be used, the computer operation will never effectively contribute (or contribute negatively) to the work of the organization. This situation arises when:
  a. Decisions are taken without careful analysis of the factors and consequences involved.
  b. Decisions are rescinded frequently, which is equivalent to saying that there is no long-term planning. Programming and analysis efforts will then be wasted, and staff will have to work under conditions of stress and under constant uncertainty further degrading the system.

A computer in house will produce more than listings and statistics; it is essentially a tool to achieve accountability for the work of the organization. This applies to management:

- If planning is incoherent, computer operations will reflect this state of affairs and will achieve valuable output only by chance.

This basic fact applies as well to the substantive work of the organization:

- If data are not quickly available, any lag or deviations from planned workloads in the departments will be difficult to detect by monitoring through the computer system.

The establishment of long-term objectives for computer operations is not just a matter of sitting down for a while and writing up a statement. It is a question of adopting a fundamental attitude toward management functions. This is generally regarded as the systems approach. For any decision taken, it must be assumed that many factors are involved and/or influenced. In fact, with a computer in house, management's own functions should become still more rationalized.

Deviation from rationalization will be felt automatically in the performance of computer operations, and hence can be easily detected.

Up to now (and for many years) almost all the substantive tasks of the organization were carried out by human work. The computer operations at the external service center were not regarded as an integral part of the work in the organization or believed capable of providing essentially correct output. As such, the potential of computer operations in the agency was not clearly understood nor defined.

From the time of the arrival of in-house computer facilities, management proceeded by a series of unconnected ad-hoc decisions.

- Decisions were often taken through convening the individual departments concerned but without joint discussion and evaluating all relevant factors involved.
- Decisions affecting one department were often taken without consulting that department to find out beforehand what work effort or changes would be required to implement the decision.
- The agency was organized as a vertical hierarchy. Departments were not always well informed about what was going on in other departments. Each department clung to control of as much information as it could get, because each department was not convinced that information from elsewhere was correct.

Under these conditions, it is unavoidable that management decisions are taken which ignore facts and conditions known in the departments. As a consequence,

- Departments tend to modify or ignore management decisions in order to make them match—as much or as little as desired—with the real conditions in the departments.
- There is rarely a clearly defined line of responsibility for a particular item of work.
- Hence everybody does a little bit of everything.

In view of this situation, a few basic questions need to be answered:

- Is the agency to be seen as a service organization with a certain pilot or guiding function for its member bodies, or is it to be seen as an institution which may follow its own course of expediency according to the situation of the moment?
- Is accountability for the work of the agency desired or not?
- Is it accepted that management must take into account the basic requirements imposed upon them by the use of an in-house computer?

If these three questions can be answered in the affirmative, what would be the benefits?

- In managing the organization, an explicit and rational reference system could be relied on to show factors involved in decisions, effects (and maybe remote after-effects), and the actual workload created by any decision.
- Information flow within and between departments could be improved, thus creating an atmosphere of credibility and confidence in collaborating.
- The computer operations section could be capable of substantially supporting day-to-day work of the organization and high-level management functions by supplying accurate and timely data.
- Many unnecessary tensions and misunderstandings could disappear making work more productive.

7.3.3.2 *End Game*. The report as stated above was virtually ignored, and more contradictory demands were imposed on the EDP section. The EDP manager decided to accept another job, feeling forced to leave the project he had conceived before it was completed. This was the second time that the individual responsible for data processing left the organization under such circumstances.

NOTE

1. An excellent description of the U.N. system is found in Mahdi Elmandrja, *The United Nations System: An Analysis,* Faber and Faber, London, 1973, ISBN 0 571 10227 1.

Chapter Eight

Reflections on the Implementation Problems of Complex Documentation Systems in Industry

by HERMANN J. GRAML

8.1. INTRODUCTION

The reflections and ideas presented below stem from years of experience in the field of information and documentation (I&D). The experience was gained from three points of view, as a user, a developer, and a systems manager.

As a user, the main I&D problems were first in overcoming certain technological barriers in initially unfamiliar services, then finding out how to make optimal use of the different services offered, and, at the same time, learning to exercise patience in dealing with still unsatisfactory systems.

As a system developer, one was forced to start with manually operated card files in 1960 before ending with an on-line dialogue system with microfiche backup files by 1972. During this period the main problems essentially consisted of communication difficulties between I&D people and development people. Such communication problems overshadowed the technical problems, as one had to deal with forms of outspoken opposition against any change of existing operations and often vivid disagreement about the importance of selfevident system features.

Since 1973, as a manager responsible for the operation of an integrated I&D system, the problem has been mainly to identify and meet user needs optimally while at the same time taking into account the limits set by a tight budget. The I&D system itself consists of nine technical libraries and an on-line literature search service with six remote offices serving the clientele within a very large industrial enterprise.

Certain basic phenomena and problems seem to emerge repeatedly over the years about the implementation of complex information systems, when seen from these three different perspectives (user, developer, manager). Their persistence calls for both comment and action, so that we can learn from rather than simply repeat previous implementation experiences within an industrial framework.

8.2 BACKGROUND

It is generally estimated that about 40 million documents with scientific and technical contents are published each year. This includes books, journal articles, patents, conference and research reports. The amount of published material in this area appears to grow at least 10% annually. This is a rough indication of the portion of the information explosion with which modern industry is concerned.

Contemporary industrial enterprises have a vital need for technical and scientific information. Information and its utilization and communication are their "life's blood." Without sufficient information, a company lags behind its competitors, is run inefficiently, and often goes out of business. This is especially true for companies with substantial research and development operations relying on adequate I&D support.

The rate at which new products are developed and brought to market is still accelerating. For example, in a progressive company with a typical rate of innovation, 40% of the products marketed are no older than five years.

Norbert Wiener, the well-known mathematician and father of cybernetics, used to stress the importance of I&D by calling information one of the basic phenomena like matter and energy.

At this point responsible individuals in industry have learned to appreciate the significance of I&D. A generally accepted principle states, "To get information is expensive, but to have no information can be much more expensive."

Thus industry people, often in contrast to people in other areas, tend to recognize the necessity of I&D and are willing to pay a fair price for it. Once industry has decided to establish an I&D operation, it usually will plan and set up these operations in much the same manner and with much the same means as other corporate functions. There will be a long-range plan, a tight budget, and frequent control of results. From time to time, depending on the economic situation, I&D will find itself obliged to justify its existence. One drawback, perhaps not unique to I&D, is the unfortunate fact that there is no reliable way of measuring exactly the efficiency or the return on the investment for the I&D function.

Another factor of particular relevance to I&D in industry is that larger companies are not concentrated in one place. Corporate branches, both in the home country and abroad, produce a quite complex corporate structure. This in turn affects the I&D function. I&D services must then cope with long distances and language barriers, even though they usually operate only within the corporate structure, including subsidiaries, and do not render services to outside organizations.

A further characteristic complicating the evaluation of current I&D services is that most of the I&D systems are not capable of delivering exactly the information requested but rather provide citations to documents that presumably have a high probability of containing the wanted information. This situation is particularly unsatisfactory because of the failure of most I&D systems to provide aids that might better facilitate the formulation of search requests.

The prime purpose of the I&D function is to provide the information required within acceptable periods of time and cost ranges. In most cases this is achieved in a two-step process. The first step results in the information requestor receiving document references, citations, or abstracts in response to his search request. At this point, the requestor of the information then decides which of these cited documents seem worth while to actually order and read—the second step. Most I&D systems as such consist of at least two main parts: (a) some kind of access system, and (b) a file of the original documents (or copies) proper. In a library, for example, the first part (access) is the library catalogues with keywords, authors' names, and the like. The second part is the shelves with the books.

Normally, only after reading through the documents delivered, the result of the two-step process, will the requestor be able to find out whether the journal articles or books in fact contain the information desired. To our knowledge, at the moment, there is no system installed in industry that can determine the utility of the delivered information directly (by analyzing the contents of the documents) without making the requestor browse through the documents and search for the information desired.

Although there are various kinds of people requesting information, users of I&D systems in industry come from an industrial environment. Their informational requirements therefore arise from problems or assignments like:

- Modifying or improving products
- Finding already existent solutions (in order to avoid double work)

- Switching to new fields of research and development
- Investigating the state of the art in a certain field (for a patent application)
- Collecting data pertinent to research and development projects
- Collecting data for the publication of a scientific or technical report, paper, or book.

The individual I&D system is prepared to cope primarily with these kinds of questions. The size, number, and kinds of services the system offers naturally depend to a large degree on the size and the kind of the company in which it operates. In general, the users of the I&D system in industry—obvious from the preceding list—come primarily from research and development. This means that small companies with normally small research and development work of their own have only a very rudimentary I&D operation, if any. Such an operation often consists of a small, understaffed service office constantly fighting for its survival. In order to stay in existence, such rudimentary I&D services tend to deliver all kinds of individual and highly appreciated services, such as looking up train schedules, hotels, and restaurants, and providing theater tickets for important buyers or guests. The services are often associated with or integrated into the patent department of the company. Usually this sort of I&D function is handled by an older individual supported by some part-time help. In providing normal I&D services, these small I&D offices are heavily dependent on external public or institutional information services.

Only a very limited number of larger companies is able to fund and support an internal I&D operation of a sufficient scope to rely essentially on their own independent services and operations. Most of these I&D systems began long ago as manually operated systems at a time when management recognized that an individual service tailored to the needs of the company would bring decided advantages compared with complete dependence on outside systems.

Over a period of time those systems, because of the increasing amounts of material to be processed and the growing demands for information imposed, were forced to adapt themselves to technological progress. Inevitably this led to the introduction of automated systems. I&D operations changed from providing relatively simple and straightforward services to complex information systems. Let us take a detailed look at this transformation.

What are the essential differences between the simple and the complex information systems? One is inclined to think the use of mechanization, especially the use of a computer, would be the indication of a progressive, complex information system. But, if these means are used only to speed up the process formerly executed manually, possession of a computer system alone may be misleading.

Simple documentation systems employ classification systems for the filing and retrieving of documents. Classification systems (e.g., UDC or Library of

Congress Classification) have been an important tool for both small and large document collections. They still play an essential role for the one-dimensional shelving of and access to books in libraries. For patent documentation, the International Patent Classification has maintained its key position surprisingly well. But, for most of the other applications, especially for the documentation of journal articles, one-dimensional systems such as the classification used for books or patents are not sufficient. Here multidimensional access had to be introduced by the use of descriptors taken from a controlled vocabulary in the form of a thesaurus. Only by assigning more than one descriptor to a document is it possible to retrieve the document from more than one point of view.

Thus one of the characteristics of the transition process from simple to complex information systems is the step from classifying to indexing the documents. This step requires the development and use of thesauri and an indexing language more powerful for facilitating multidimensional retrieval than a list of classification headings. On the search side this means the substitution of linear look-up in lists by the formulation of search requests with descriptors in mathematically defined combinations (e.g., Boolean algebra).

Closely connected with these processes is the change of methods brought about mainly by the exploding number of publications. I&D offices with their individual ways of working and resources no longer could keep abreast of the information flood. Cooperation and standardization (rules, vocabulary, data formats, etc.) became inevitable. This was required for the whole information storage and retrieval field but especially so for the applications in industry. Keeping up with the rapid technological progress made access to the equally rapidly growing amounts of information more important than in slower growth areas. As such it is quite common now in industry to conduct a thorough literature search before the initiation of any important development work.

There has also been a change in the philosophy concerning the selection of personnel for the I&D office. Management had a tendency of recruiting people whose jobs had become obsolete and who were not regarded as being the more flexible and active individuals in the company. Now the importance of employing active and competent people is better recognized. At the same time, I&D, through its use of modern equipment, operations, and procedures, has become a more and more attractive profession.

8.3 CONSIDERATIONS FOR THE CONVERSION TO AUTOMATED SYSTEMS

It has been observed that the introduction of an automated complex information system in industry seldom means that there has been no functioning information system before. Only occasionally does one start from scratch. In general, there was already a system which had been outgrown; a critical mass of activities had been reached which necessitated a step upward. User analyses conducted before any decisions concerning the introduction or extension of automation show a strong reluctance to change the information procedures to which the users are accustomed. Such opposition to change, however, does not lessen the user tendency to criticize the quality of the existing information services.

In any event, even changes that are supposed to upgrade quality cannot be introduced without significant effort devoted to the preparation of the users of the new system. Such preparation is not only necessary for the users. The operators of the system have to be prepared and often retrained for the change. With the new complex system, the old separation of information people into librarians and documentalists gradually vanishes. This trend is clearly visible already. Another trend that has been borne out by experience is to refrain from attempting full automation. To aim at solutions with computer-assisted procedures now appears a better choice. The reasons for this will be discussed below.

Once user studies and system analyses have been completed, the difficult process of system selection begins. By system in this connection we mean the data processing system—the computer and the accompanying software. The hardware for most of the information systems in industrial enterprises is seldom selected for I&D operations alone. In most cases already existing computers have to be shared with already existing users in the company. Furthermore, most available hardware is adequate. The main problem lies with the programs or software. At present, software selection remains an unsolved problem. In part, this is a direct result of the incompatibility of data processing (DP) people on one side and I&D people on the other.

If one scans the software market for computer programs suited for the automation of complex information systems, one finds that there are not very many available from which to choose. However, it is almost impossible for an information office in industry to have its system tailored exactly to its needs, mainly because of programming costs. Consequently, most installations in industry are forced to take one of the available software packages that meet their specifications only to a limited extent. Why is the available software less than satisfactory?

Most I&D software systems have been developed by DP experts under the assumption that nearly any problem could be solved by the use of a computer, the only limitations being storage capacity and command execution time. This view was strengthened by the initially successful computer applications in areas more suited than I&D for computerization. However, a data bank with fixed information concerning products, wage accounts, price or address lists, and the like is different from a data bank with document subject or content descriptions. The items of the first kind of data bank can be described, identified, and retrieved by means of exactly defined ''hard,'' descriptional data. For I&D data banks not only is it necessary to identify the stored items but it must be possible also to retrieve them according to descriptions of their contents. Retrieval of documents using content description depends on highly sophisticated intellectual processes every bit as important as the machine programmable functions.

There is a difference between the retrieval of facts and ideas, and this difference is reflected in the distinction between mechanical and intellectual operations. Most DP experts have failed to appreciate these differences sufficiently to affect their approach to developing an effective information retrieval dialogue between users and machines. Further, ideas and working processes of the potential users were not properly understood or appreciated. DP people and I&D people did not find it easy to communicate with each other. There were persistent problems in understanding each other. For example, a library for a DP man is a collection of programs on magnetic tapes, whereas for the I&D specialist it means catalogued books on shelves. A file may be regarded as a collection of data in core storage or a drawer of catalogue cards. For their part, I&D specialists seldom had experience in developing or producing complicated computer programs and had little inclination to learn this new trade. Nonetheless, there is only one way to arrive at somewhat satisfactory results. A very intensive communication between the DP and I&D people must be established during the whole development process.

Such a participatory development of software was attempted for the PRIMAS program system (1). The idea for PRIMAS (*P*rogram for *R*etrieval and *I*ndexing with *MA*chine *S*upport) was conceived by A.E. Wessel in 1967–1968 at The RAND Corporation. The conceptual framework and a primitive version of the computer program (then unnamed) for experimental purposes was brought to Siemens AG in late 1969. With this material as a basis, an initial version of the PRIMAS program was developed at the Central Research Laboratories of Siemens AG in Munich under the direction of H. J. Graml, with A.E. Wessel as consultant. This version was tested thoroughly in cooperation with patent examiners of the German Patent Office in 1970.

Subsequently, the further development—because of the prolonged hospitalization of Mr. Wessel and the transfer of the responsibility for the program to a primarily DP-oriented section within the company—took a direction different from the initial plan. Thus the system as it stands today contains certain elements of the original concept but also shows clearly the result of the more typical approach that favored programming efficiency over the active participation of experienced users. Despite these drawbacks, the system has been in successful operation since 1972 in several institutions.

Given the circumstances and despite good intentions, user input was only reluctantly accepted by the DP experts later in charge of the PRIMAS development. Since the DP staff had possession or at least the control of the computer facilities, the user-programmer disagreements were resolved in favor of the programmers. These same programmers did not feel it necessary to attempt to index or retrieve even a single document themselves in order to better appreciate the problems associated with the critical I&D operations.

The lack of identity of concept and interest between developers and users, combined with the fact that the developer is not the user of the information system, results in an underuse or misuse of the system. The system is seldom used in the ways intended by the developer. Devious ways of operation evolve, often as a kind of suboptimation of a partial process, because users tend to choose the way of least effort, even though this way might cost far more in the long run. These tendencies are merely underlined by typically inadequate (from the user perspective) system documentation, the preparation of which is regarded as a low priority task by DP personnel.

Under the best of circumstances, one of the most important problems for the implementation of information systems is the control of the vocabulary for indexing and the indexing process proper. Information systems of any real size must resolve the problem of accepting outside data for inclusion in the system's data base. It is too expensive to index and enter in-house all documents of potential value to a large company. Yet even if this could be done within one organization covering data from only one source, tight control of the vocabulary used for indexing, preferably a thesaurus, is needed. This problem becomes more complicated if different data bases are to be handled within one system. There are a lot of "false prophets" in the area, so-called thesaurus experts who specialize in academic structuring principles and have never themselves conducted a single real-world literature search based on their principles. Nor have such "experts" devoted a single thought to the special problems of an information system's purpose in industry. Yet all agree that the ultimate object of a thesaurus is guidance in finding wanted information or documents.

The search and indexing vocabulary control problem within industry has a special aspect which makes it more complicated. This is the dependence on continuous and rapid technological changes which in turn create the need for changes of vocabulary. Since the constant updating of very large thesauri is both difficult and expensive, many industrial applications solve this dilemma by keeping separate files for certain coherent periods of time with smaller file-associated thesauri or separable thesauri parts. However, this solution leads to complications during indexing and search.

There are many different indexing procedures in use, three of which are very often found in technical I&D.

The best type of indexing, according to an often-expressed opinion, is that produced by the authors of the publications. This method is applicable where sufficient influence can be exerted on the author. This type of indexing is often used for the indexing of internal technical reports in industry. It is not often used for journal articles, although there are exceptions. The "Communications of the

ACM'' advises its authors to assign category numbers (taken from a classification schedule) and keywords and phrases (preferably taken from a technical thesaurus) as content indicators in addition to the informative abstract.

If the publication is to be indexed by a person other than the author, this often will be done by an expert in the same field to which the publication belongs. In industry this is often accomplished by a senior engineer who would normally also have experience in searching. In practice, most of the people who do the indexing for industrial I&D systems are part-time indexers, who do their indexing work after office hours at home to earn some extra income. The disadvantage of this procedure lies in the fact that it is practically impossible to support such indexers with on-line computer aids.

Bibliographic files purchased from external sources normally pose few problems about their inclusion in an existing data base, despite the different vocabulary used for indexing. Purely bibliographic data can be entered automatically by means of existing computer programs. Most of the keywords and some of the descriptors are translatable automatically through concordance lists stored in the computer. However, there always remains a significant portion that has to be reindexed intellectually. Fully automated content analysis and descriptor assignment to date has been attempted for small and experimental data bases. For most applications in industrial I&D installations, the resultant quality and especially the difficulty of formulating and conducting accurate searches have not proven acceptable. This fully automated easy way in reality turned out to be more expensive and time consuming in the overall process of information retrieval than it first appeared.

Another characteristic of the transition to a complex automated I&D system in an industrial environment is that there is always a very cautious attitude of the institution concerned toward the new system. The reason for this is the evident risk of introducing an incompletely developed or tested system and the danger of a system breakdown after the old system is taken out of operation. Therefore, there will be parallel operations for a certain period, lasting from several months to more than a year. Before and during that period all people concerned with the operation and the use of the system have to be retrained in accordance with the new system's operations, functions, and philosophy.

The first period of system usage is often a period of experimentation. At this point people discover what the initial system analyses failed to disclose. Potential users then learn that they had not known what they could or should expect from the new system as a functioning reality.

Finally, one last and quite interesting fact should be noted in connection with I&D systems in industry. Individual scientists and engineers maintain private files of information in their offices. In small companies without an I&D operation of their own, this is necessary, of course, but such private files exist also in companies with a central information service. Certain information-oriented people keep card files of material of interest only to them and ordered one-dimensional by the classification or indexing provided by the central system. These private and partially duplicate files should be supported by the I&D center. This is desirable because it helps these individuals, who show a high motivation for using and maintaining information files related to their work. These private files also aid in reducing the workload of the information center and can function as emergency files if the central system or the transmission lines break down.

8.4 THE OPERATIONAL STAGE

The transition stages can be said to have resulted in an operational system when at least four principal processes become functional. These are:

a. Data recording and storage. Here the use of new equipment should have resulted in lower costs and higher efficiency. Punched paper cards or paper tape, direct input on magnetic tape, direct on-line input through optical character recognition typewriters combined with improved error detection and correction procedures characterize this operation.

b. Indexing (including vocabulary control). The problems previously discussed must have reached solutions offering enhanced quality control of indexing along with improvement in indexing accuracy and consistency. Improved means of thesauri maintenance should be available.

c. Information retrieval. By this point system operators must have obtained sufficient experience with the system to have developed a variety of short-cut and efficient search processes. Means to achieve high-quality search results, or at the least, to filter search results prior to delivering them to clients should have been attained. Furthermore, adapting to changes in user requirements in speed, quality, range, and volume of search request should have become a familiar and routinely accepted process.

d. Procurement of document texts. The last of these functions often is given too little consideration during the conversion to a complex information system. The new system, by offering its superior services, automatically creates an increased demand for the document texts cited as search results. There must be provision for an effective capability for the production of copies of the original documents. The originals in turn have to be kept in readily accessible form. In many cases not all of the documents or journals can be accessed and stored within the system, because of space limitations and the costs of subscriptions. Therefore, I&D systems must rely on outside sources (cooperation with other libraries in the industry or public libraries, e.g., British

Library Lending Division) for the procurement of the copies wanted by the system users.

As to the overall operations, success depends to a very high degree on the skills of the people operating the system, whatever its sophisticated mechanisms. Experience in industry shows that senior engineers with good scientific and technological backgrounds as well as a thorough knowledge of the internal corporate structure are suited best for this job. The basic I&D group should consist of people with such backgrounds. Through the ongoing operation and use of the system, I&D staff become a new form of experts, those called variously information engineers, information scientists, or information specialists. However, only through practical experience with searching and indexing can such experts become adequately familiar with the state of the art, the condition of the stored material, and the services required by users and organization. In this sense the successful operation of the I&D system depends on maintaining the close contact with the actual users of the information services. Direct personal contacts are best.

In a large company, however, it is impossible for the relatively small group of information specialists to know all its clientele and their environments well enough. Therefore, all of these systems employ some more or less formalized way of obtaining feedback from their users. Thus they are able to react positively to justified wishes of the users and build up a clientele of satisfied customers. In this sense, the situation of the I&D system in the company resembles the situation of an enterprise in the free market. It serves a market, it advertises its services, it seeks new customers, and attempts to keep its users better served (informed) than they could themselves by means of outside sources. Success means the existence of the in-house system is continually justified.

As such, I&D systems are continually forced to monitor the quality and quantity of their answers. However, this is not enough. In order to offer reliable services, the services must be maintained, even during system breakdown. One way to do this is to keep the complete files on microfilm or microfiche parallel to the computer files. With modern COM (Computer Output Microfilm) equipment this can be achieved without great problems. Microfilm files, though accessible only one-dimensionally, can be very helpful in emergency situations. In addition, such files can be used in subsidiaries of the main I&D operation, where full system services are not required nor economically justified or where an on-line operation is not feasible.

Modern, complex I&D systems must be kept up to date by adapting to changes in technology. System improvement and the always necessary maintenance represent a substantial cost factor which is often underestimated. A similarly important problem is the fluctuation of personnel which can endanger the satisfactory operation of the system.

In the course of normal operations of the system, one inevitably is faced also with the problem of continuously increasing files. Since the system must be set up with a certain upper limit of file size, many systems split their data base into a readily accessible active file, and an inactive file that is accessible only under certain conditions, for instance during night hours or on special demand. The cut-off date for entry into the active file often coincides with fundamental changes in technology, informational requirements, and/or changes in the controlled vocabulary used for indexing and search.

Technological change to date has led to a major switchover in systems hardware and software about every five years for large, centralized systems. At the moment, however, there are extensive reports on the trend toward the application of small decentralized computers connected in networks for I&D applications.

Should such continuing technological progress offer the possibility of cost reduction or a significant improvement in services (speed, convenience, reliability, security), its application to industrial I&D will have to be considered. Both the continued transformation of technology and the requirements of users and industrial organizations imposed upon I&D systems indicate that the operational stage is but one more step in an ongoing process of permanent transition.

NOTE

1. See Wessel, CAIR, Chapter 10.7.

Chapter Nine

Toward Better Implementation Methods

Given the depth and range of the problems and the difficulties of achieving even the partial solutions described in the case histories, attempts to change matters may appear hopeless. The issue is not, however, whether pessimism is warranted but rather where pessimism may justifiably be directed. The problems associated with the implementation of complex information systems are not going to disappear as long as the same kinds of methods are used to implement the same kinds of systems. Further, the claim that new and different systems are now or soon will be available and will be capable of solving or avoiding the problems of implementation has not, to date, solved or reduced the problems, no matter how often and regularly such claims have been announced.

Chapter Two provided a general discussion of the problems confronting us. In light of the case histories, the themes there explored should take on more meaning. In particular, a closer look at what were called "The Nonlinear Assumptions" is worthwhile. The nonlinear assumptions (Section 2.1.7) are taken more seriously than in past years. However, significant changes in managerial perspectives and in the information system technology itself are called for by these nonlinear assumptions. These changes have not yet taken place. This is not to claim that managerial methods and the technologies relevant to complex information systems have remained static over the years. Both have changed, often in radical ways and in many ways for the better. However, the implementation problems illustrated by the case histories clearly reiterate the statement, "the more things change, the more they remain the same."

The required transformation of the pertinent management policies and the technologies associated with the implementation of complex information systems are long overdue. They involve profound adjustments in attitudes of managers and technologists toward one another and toward system users. The place of users and their roles in the development and implementation processes need clarification, redefinition, and more than verbal acceptance by all concerned. The specific transformations in methods, technologies, user roles, and the need for their more general acceptance are the topics addressed in the remainder of this book.

9.1 THE FUNDAMENTAL TRANSFORMATIONS

A brief statement of the fundamental transformations required can be put in terms of a rather specific and interrelated set of tasks respectively confronting technology, management, and users. The basic technological accomplishment is to provide the systemsware that permits and aids users and system operators to get at the data bases and files. Much better means and the options to change the better means of activating the system functions and to create, adapt, and search files than are now available must be provided. Technology will have to offer greatly improved interface functions connecting the information stored in system files with the users of that information. However technology may provide these better interface options, emphasis must be placed on producing feasible (from the user perspective) methods for adapting and transforming all the means of getting at the system and system files. System-aided procedures are needed that make it easy to carry out and accommodate continual changes in files and in interface options. The systemsware must be capable of satisfying the time-dependent requirements, since these are transformed through user experience with the system. Furthermore, "adaptability" of the system must be achieved within cost and workload ranges acceptable to users and managers.

The basic problem for management is how to provide an environment and the working means that encourage and take advantage of the new technology. This requires management to accept the fact that final fixes are not deliverable and that they must structure their organizational environment for information systems accordingly. Verbal acceptance of the nonlinear assumptions combined with organizational structures and management policies suited only to the fixed or linear assumptions has not worked out well in the past. It will not work tomorrow. In addition, management must educate itself sufficiently as to the new technology. The ultimate-solution "snow job" must be seen for what it is: a blueprint for costly failures. Management must be knowledgeable enough to demand the appropriate systemsware and be willing to pay for the development necessary to produce the flexible systems capable of meeting rather than multiplying their specific organizational problems. At some point in the future, there may be reliable and useful off-shelf systemsware. At present what exists might better be left on the shelf.

The basic problem for users and potential users of complex information systems is to learn how to accept the system as an adaptive organization. Users must be willing to interact with the system in a positive manner. They must not expect merely to be passive observers pushing buttons and obtaining canned products. Users must be taught how to approach complex information systems using their own skills and intelligence. Machine-like adaptation to machines will not work and should not be required. In fact, users should refuse to be reduced to machine-like behavior. Users should not be as resistant to change itself, as are machines. Users must be willing to learn the new ways to use their skills and intelligence made possible by the interactive supporting functions of the system. Naturally, this sort of user attitude will not flourish in an environment constructed by management that rewards passive acceptance. Management will have to adjust to a long period of living with fluid job descriptions where performance ratings and rewards must be adjusted frequently.

These are somewhat radical adjustments required for technology, management, and users in the approach, interaction with, and attitude toward the systemsware for complex information systems. Furthermore, these transformations have to be accomplished in the operational world, not merely in some academic environment. One very difficult bottleneck preventing their accomplishment is the persistent myth that such transformations in technology and management have already been accomplished. Surely we have learned how to live with change over the last few decades. A glance back at the case histories should indicate that living with change has not been accomplished all that well. Rather, it appears that not all of the problems of information system implementation are resolvable for all application contexts and organizations.

Nonetheless, we assume that a significantly better and generally applicable approach to the implementation of complex information systems can be based on the nonlinear assumptions. To describe this better approach means to spell out the more detailed and specific implications of the basic transformations posited as required for technology, management, and users.

What are the specific adjustments to be made? They essentially involve the interface areas, those critical points of contact between people and computer files; people and the system functions and options to produce, transform, store, and retrieve information; and, of course, people and people at all levels within the new information system environment. These points of contact within complex information systems are where most of the implementation problems and their solutions begin and end.

9.2 INTERFACE AREAS

In the late 1950s, early in the development of computer systems, significant efforts were devoted to producing so-called friendly terminals as a solution to the interface problem. This was before computer capacities grew sufficient to permit the storage of very large files of information and to permit as well on-line interaction with these files. Nonetheless the development of input-output terminals and a variety of on-line cathode ray tube (CRT) display consoles was accepted as a vital technological goal quite early. These pioneering efforts, perhaps best characterized by the term "intellectronics" coined by Simon Ramo, constituted one technological answer to the then not clearly understood question about the role of the coming generations of computers. Were the computers under development to be viewed as means to enhance or to replace human capabilities?

The term "intellectronics" was itself somewhat ambiguous on this issue. Did it mean that machines were going to be developed that could take on the significant anthropomorphic functions involving the exercise of human intelligence or its machine-like equivalent? Or were the machines to be developed to provide significant machine support for the enhancement of human functions?

This old ambiguity is still with us. Then as now, technology followed both directions of computer development often simultaneously and confusedly. And now as then, this ambiguity lies at the heart of the implementation problems. To put the issue in blunt, if oversimple terms, are we to implement systems providing us with varieties of artificial intelligence within our organizations, or are we to implement systems providing us with varieties of computer support for people exercising their human functions in accomplishing their organizational work?

This question is still very much open. Furthermore, as it stands, the question is probably more confusing than enlightening. A reformulation of this question in terms of our concern for the implementation problems would be useful. We can focus on the interface areas by asking some rather specific questions concerning just what we are attempting to automate. For any given implementation of computer technology, we can ask which functions and processes now being performed by humans within the organization:

a. Are to be replaced by machine functions.
b. Are to be aided by machine functions.

And perhaps more relevantly for most applications we can ask which functions or processes not being performed within the organization:

a. Are to be performed by machines.
b. Are to be performed by humans aided by machines.

However these questions are answered for any given case, further questions must be raised. Precisely:

a. What human support or work not now being performed will be required in support of any of the machine functions being implemented?
b. What human support or work now being performed within the organization will be increased, decreased, or eliminated?

These questions lead us directly to the interface problems. Without a clear and detailed set of answers to all these questions, no implementation plan can be said to exist.

The nonlinear assumptions tell us that any set of answers to these interface questions is dependent not only on the type and place of implementation and the technology to be implemented but also is very much dependent on time. To take the relatively simple case of the credit bureau (Chapter Six), very few of the tasks then being performed by humans were to be replaced by machine processes. Essentially, the computer was to replace manual files with computerized files. Then the routine look-up and search of these files in fixed predetermined ways would be automated. The basic variable in the formulation of search questions would be the name of the individual whose credit rating was being checked. File construction, the addition or deletion of items of information pertaining to individual names in the files, and the individual names as well, remained a manual process. However, sundry aids to the manual file updating process could be made available in the forms of selected computer printouts of file portions or the files in their entirety. The interfaces to the automated files remained essentially the same as those existing with the manual files. Customers, the clients of the credit bureau, would make telephone contact with the credit bureau clerical staff. The staff would then initiate the search keyed to the individual name(s) for which credit checks were requested. In most cases, search results obtained through the computer would be conveyed to customers by the clerks during the initial telephone call. When written credit reports were requested, the computer would replace the typist by producing the requested computer printout, providing that the requested report could be satisfied by a predetermined output format(s).

Given this particular framework for the interface details of the credit bureau, a reasonable system design was produced. Its goal was to increase output, the number of credit requests handled per unit of time per clerk, while maintaining if not reducing cost levels involved in handling the requested credit checks. In addition and within acceptable cost levels, subsidiary products—such as name and address lists, specially requested written reports, or other file printouts— could be more speedily obtained through the automated system. Nonetheless, the system was not implemented. During the time required for system design both the technology and the requirements changed. The data cell chosen was later found inadequate compared with disk storage systems, and the credit bureau was merged with an organization already possessing its own functioning system. The more pertinent issue, however, was whether much more important factors changed, factors concerning the definition of the interface framework.

Without going into the problem of whether the specific design for the credit bureau system was cost effective in comparison with other potential or competing designs, a more important question must be faced. Were the answers to the interface questions assumed by the credit bureau system design correct? Further, if these interface answers were correct at the time of the system design, how long a time period could be assumed for their validity? Are they correct today?

The system design for the credit bureau represented a relatively conservative approach toward automation. Except for machine search itself, the existing manual processes were left essentially unchanged. Let us consider a more radical approach. Suppose we answer the interface questions by tending toward the extreme of replacement of most if not all of the manual processes and clerical functions. The entire process, as described in Chapter Six from customer call for credit data through the resultant file look-up and subsequent provision of the requested data, involved little significantly human intelligence. If the means to construct the necessary automated files could be assumed, why not automate the entire process? This would involve the design of a system that would permit direct customer dial-up and initiation of the search request for credit data about the specified individuals or entities listed in the files. This would not only save clerical time, it would also reduce customer waiting time, a factor given little weight in the original design. Even many written reports could be made available via customer dial-up using predetermined request formats for predefined reports. Billing could be equally automatic. Control monitoring by the credit bureau could be incorporated with manual override when necessary or when indicated by control stops built into the automated procedures. Left unautomated in such a system would be the file input, correction, and maintenance processes, for which a variety of aids and special file printouts could be provided. While these manual operations remain highly expensive, if not the most expensive areas for credit bureau operations, software development has not as yet provided feasible means to automate or to aid directly these file construction tasks requiring significant human intelligence.

Leaving this limitation aside, perhaps our suggested approach to automation is not radical enough to make efficient use of today's technology. Given developments within the microprocessor and micromemory areas, major customers could consider having their own automated credit checking systems in house. With the expected cost reductions coming in the next few years, if not already present, perhaps almost all customers for credit bureau information could purchase or lease their own hardware for their credit checking systems.* Credit bureaus might then be reduced to supplying and maintaining the computerized files and updating these at regular intervals. The design effort applied to credit bureaus would then appropriately shift toward providing automated aids for the expensive tasks of file construction, correction, updating, and general maintenance. Perhaps this is precisely where the design efforts should have been focused from the start.

Of course, such a radical distributed system was not economically feasible a few years ago, nor is it without question the way to go today. The point of this discussion is to show clearly that differing answers to the interface questions are

---

*To a significant degree this form of distributed network simplifies the security problems which create the need for complicated controls in a centralized direct dial-up solution.

in fact quite feasible. Further, such differing interface question answers call for quite distinct applications of and perspectives toward the available technology. This interdependence is bidirectional. New technological developments, as we have just illustrated, call for and make possible very different answers to the interface questions.

By using another of our case histories, we can raise a different point concerning the interface areas. Strangely enough, the simplicity or complexity of the application has played an almost inverse role to what would be expected when answering the interface questions. One might have expected that the simpler applications of computers, such as the credit bureau case, would tend toward a more radical set of interface answers. The technology required to achieve more automated interfaces is equally simple. But as we have seen in the case just discussed, the credit bureau design in this sense was conservative. However, when we return to the Patent Office case (Chapter Four), we find that conservative answers to the interface questions come about only after years of radical attempts to replace, at least in part, human intelligence by artificial intelligence. If we posit the framework for answers to the interface questions implied by Project Potomac, we can see that some rather significant tasks involving human intelligence were to be automated. These included the classification of patent documents by machine analyses of text as well as various forms of search based on terms taken from patent document texts. The development of machine aids to indexers and patent searchers and for the very expensive tasks of term list and thesauri development was neglected in order to attempt a more direct replacement of the human functions by machine functions. As we have noted, the technology was lacking to accomplish either the direct replacement of patent office staff who performed these difficult intellectual tasks or to provide the patent office staff with machine aids. The direction of technological development actually attempted was somewhat unclear, perhaps consciously so. The choice to replace rather than aid the human functions was not greeted very cheerfully by patent office staff members who were well able to sense the kind of answers to the interface questions implied.

The many attempts to automate Patent Office processes over the years remain of interest, since they highlight the cyclic nature of the implementation approach. There is a fluctuation between the extremes of leaving the manual interfaces pretty much as they may have been, perhaps supporting them in minor ways, and the attempted elimination of the manual interfaces by automation. Between these two extremes there is seldom a prolonged effort attempting to provide significant supporting aids to the intellectual tasks necessary to any functioning information system. The political atmosphere within which major organizations subsist has much to do with this phenomenon. Each change in the political winds in Washington, each change of Patent Commissioner, tends to produce a radical change in direction. The situation need not be as black as painted in Chapter Seven to ensure disappointment if not failure. It takes longer than the four-year cycles in Washington to accomplish very much successfully, as Chapter Five demonstrates and as the difficulties in meeting the schedule for CCMS operations at the Patent Office specifically illustrate. At the same time, Chapter Five shows that adopting an interface framework intended to provide machine support to the intellectual work of the staff is not without its own vicissitudes.

Three possible interface frameworks have been mentioned. One, illustrated by the credit bureau design, essentially automates the routine search and look-up functions, leaving the more intellectual tasks presumably undisturbed. The other extreme is to attempt the automation of as much as possible of the intellectual tasks that must be accomplished in order to transform data into information for someone's use. Both of these frameworks, however advanced or conventional the technology required may be, are conservative in one important sense. They tend to avoid, neglect, or simply automate away the more critical aspects of the interface areas. In one case this is attempted by providing a system which separates the routine machine functions from the intellectual, passing on only machine results to the human work force. The interface areas are reduced to printing out or otherwise displaying the machine results. There is little if any interaction between people and machines during the processing. In the case where automation attempts to perform rather than to support some of the more intellectual tasks, again the interface areas are reduced to output of results. What human interaction may take place is determined, essentially, by machine requirements. In both cases a more or less fixed system has been created singularly resistant to significant change. Human intervention in such cases generally produces system breakdown. The system can be forced to adapt only within stringent limitations. The introduction of such systems, however, creates changes and transformations within the organization, whether desired and beneficial or not. Such adaptation essentially is one way. People and organizations adapt to the system under the threat of system failure if such adaptations do not take place. However, the organizational requirements have not remained fixed. The transformations within the organization and the work force, however extensive, remain tied to a relatively fixed system. Adaptations necessary to meet the current organizational goals and requirements that have developed over a period of time may have become impossible without producing system breakdown. Once this occurs, a new cycle of software production is necessary at the least. The center of the problem cannot usually be resolved in any event. The new software must be integrated with the old. The system is forced into a new fix, one too often outdated by the time of completion.

Whether such approaches eventually work is not at issue. The more interesting aspect of both of these typical interface area frameworks is that the more expensive and critical tasks requiring human intelligence remain expensive and critical. In fact, for most applications the very tasks requiring extensive human effort are increased in scope and difficulty merely in order to permit the automated system to work. This result is the inevitable price to be paid for downgrading the interface areas or attempting to avoid them through automation.

The case history of the Stiftung Wissenschaft und Politik (Chapter Five) provides us with an example of a third approach to the interface areas. Furthermore, it represents a case of the introduction of automated processes with the user organization acting as a direct participant in the development of the technology to be introduced. Let us take a closer look at this different approach and what it entails.

9.2.1 An Interface Framework for Supporting Intellectual Activities

Any attempt to provide direct technological support to the intellectual work necessary to the documentation processes of a research oriented or multidisciplinary institution is confronted with a most serious initial problem. Beyond the automation of the more routine aspects, proven technology capable of providing systems which can participate interactively with the staff performing the intellectual tasks does not exist.

If the choice is made to attempt more than existing technology permits, development is required. The question then is the direction of the technological development and the means by which the development is to occur. The interface framework where the intellectual work of people is to be replaced by machine functions establishes one of the possible directions for the technological development. This option usually has meant calling in the engineers to replace manual by automated processes. An interface framework where the intellectual work of people is to be supported interactively with machines establishes quite another direction for technological development. Furthermore, it usually means that one cannot simply call in the engineers. One has to rely very extensively on the people performing the intellectual tasks as well. The user organization has to participate directly with the engineers during the development process. Neither the engineers nor the users find this participatory development too congenial. Nor are there any reliable textbooks covering this process showing how participatory technological development should take place.

Nonetheless, if there is anything we have learned over the last decade of information system implementation, it is that user-technologist participatory development is essential and that the participation must be more than passive. This means that computer specialists who have never taken the trouble to conduct searches to satisfy actual requests for information or attempted document indexing and classification or tried to use the thesaurus or term lists or attempted to construct them, cannot be relied on to develop realistically useful systems. (See Chapter Eight for further discussion of this point.) At the same time, users who have never taken the trouble to find out what goes on behind the buttons to be pushed cannot be very useful participants in technological development. These are two further facts we have learned about the implementation of complex information systems. One advantage of the interface framework that opts for the interactive accomplishment of intellectual work with machines directly supporting human workers is that users and computer specialists are forced into an equally direct and active participatory framework in order to accomplish the required technological development. Verbal acceptance of the interactive interface framework combined with technological development without active user participation results in systemsware merely perpetuating the separation. Choosing the interactive interface framework means choosing participatory development of technology. The failure to accept this basic principle has meant that users have not obtained the systems they wanted, and computer technologists have not been able to deliver systems that, when implemented, satisfy the actual organizational requirements.

In the case of the Stiftung Wissenschaft und Politik (Chapter Five), the stringent funding limitations which produced difficulties in other areas had the advantage of forcing SWP into the role of participant developers of the system. One most useful way ''to participate a user'' is to limit funds available for system automation so that the user can only buy into the new system by functioning as an active participant in the development and as a subsequent pilot user of the system. However, limited funds do not endear user organizations to primary developers, in this case a major hardware manufacturer. And active user participation instead of noninterference in development is seldom appreciated sufficiently by engineering divisions as a substitute for greater funds. Here again the fortuitous circumstance of limited funding worked its magic. The technology involved, the PRIMAS system, was developed at the central research laboratories of the major manufacturer and not within the data processing division. Operating divisions prefer to have a large share of the available research funds allocated to themselves and to keep them under their control. The research funds allocated to PRIMAS development were accordingly something on the order of 10% of the funds allocated to another system, GOLEM, which was taken over by the data processing division. Because of this the PRIMAS developer was forced to make up for the lack of funding by accepting the participation of users during the developmental process. However, this advantageous state of affairs led to difficulties later on. Despite the clear preference of many users for the PRIMAS system, the data processing division has not to this date seen fit to support or to accept the PRIMAS system. Some of the problems SWP had to deal with, such as the lack of available computer time and programmer support described in Chapter Five, stem directly from the very situation that encouraged user participation in the first place. It is not only the management of international organizations (Chapter Seven) who make strange decisions and create difficult conditions for useful development. Under these conditions, whatever success SWP had in the implementation of systemsware based on the choice of an interactive interface framework cannot be explained by pointing to a more favorable condition surrounding the system development than that normally to be expected!

That the kind of interface framework chosen by SWP was in fact interactive can be shown by the specific answers given to the interface questions. Initially there were two principal areas in which the interface between human beings doing their intellectual work and the new computer system required definition. These were:

a. Document indexing and classification, including the description of document contents.
b. Search question formulation and reformulation, including the selection of content descriptors used for search.

These two areas involved the input of documents to the computerized files and the means of specifying the output of search results to be obtained from those files. There were obviously other interface areas involved, as with any other large-scale documentation system. These covered the range of tasks associated with term list and thesauri construction, the printing of catalogues, reports, and other listings. Most of these were handled in conventional ways, at least initially. That is, computer support in these areas consisted essentially of routine batch-processing-produced listings and the like. The one exception for the initial phase were the computer aids for both the construction of free term lists and their incorporation within or connection to the SWP thesaurus. Yet even here the role of the computer was to produce results according to programmed routines. These results would then be made available for intellectual use and analysis. Items a and b above, however, represent interfaces with unique features. Here the man-machine interaction is more extensive and far deeper than it might appear at first.

9.2.2 The Intellectual Description of Documents as a Man–Machine Interface Area

The description of documents and their contents is not only a task for document indexing, classification, and input, but it is also required in formulating search requests. To formulate a search request is to describe the information desired in a manner that permits the retrieval of the required information. To classify, index, and input documents for storage (or storage of the document identifying formulas) is also to describe information in a manner that facilitates the retrieval of information in response to later search requests. Accomplishing the reasonably appropriate and accurate description of the information in order to facilitate its retrieval in response to search requests is an intensely intellectual process. The choice of the roles both people and machines are to fulfill in accomplishing the information description processes is the critical determinant of the information system. Equally important, but too often ignored, is the fact that the choice of these system roles for information description (what machines are to accomplish, what people, what interactions between people and machines are to occur) determines the organizational approach to the implementation of the system as much as the system technology chosen.

In practice, document and document contents description for both search question formulation and indexing has been left as an essentially manual process. This has been the result of the repeated failure of technology to replace manual description by machine analyses to most users' satisfaction. Few have attempted to answer this interface question by stipulating that the process of describing information for search and indexing and entry must be an interactive, man-machine process. SWP chose, however, precisely this course. The automation of the subsequent search or look-up processes alone were not deemed sufficient to enable SWP to obtain and offer improved documentation services. Furthermore, SWP management was knowledgeable enough to evaluate the technical feasibility of fully automated processes of information description. The choice of an interactive interface for the description of information (both indexing and search question formulation) by SWP was the principal reason for SWP to offer themselves as pilot users during the development, test, and operation of the PRIMAS system. PRIMAS provided such an interface. The PRIMAS SUGGEST mode offers additional descriptors for either search question formulation or indexing keyed by the intellectual initial choice of descriptors by indexers or searchers. This is accomplished not merely through one form or other of frequency analysis relating the descriptors but is itself based on a series of man-machine interactions, a fact not only ignored by certain commentators on the system but also forgotten by some of the primary developers later responsible for the system (see Chapter Eight). As such, PRIMAS as it stands provides far less computer support to the various steps of the interactive process behind its SUGGEST mode than is potentially there, a drawback recognized early on by SWP which they attempted to have corrected through further development of the system, as described in Chapter Five. The lack of support by the primary developer mentioned earlier in this chapter permitted only limited improvements to be made. Nonetheless, the SUGGEST mode and the various interactions between men and machine behind it are of interest to show in some detail precisely how involved and interrelated this interface area can be.

The process starts with people and the accomplishment of intellectual work. This consists of:

a. The production of the documents—their authorship and publication—to be entered into the files.
b. The production of various term lists and thesauri used for manual operations in a documentation service.
c. The indexing, classification, and formal documentation description assigned to the documents available with the manual documentation service.
d. Records, if any, of search requests and search questions acted upon by the manual documentation service.
e. Various forms of user informational requirement descriptions available with the manual documentation service.

A thorough intellectual analysis and evaluation of all of these (and other related) items is required for the PRIMAS SUGGEST mode to function as originally conceived. It is just as relevant to note that an equally thorough analysis and evaluation of these items is an essential precondition for the successful implementation of any automated documentation system. Here is still another critical fact we have learned through our experiences with the implementation of complex information systems. Only by undertaking this comprehensive analysis and evaluation can the information or documentation services within the organization be understood. These items tell us much about how the organization's documentation service works and with what and for whom it works. This is where the man-machine interface begins and where computer support should be made available. These analytic and evaluative processes covering the essentials of the organized documentation services are not only a most important precondition for successful implementation, but also themselves constitute one of the essential focuses to which the system to be implemented needs to be addressed. Existing technology can in many significant ways provide the required computer support. Chapter Ten provides a detailed example of the kinds of computer support now available and the ways such computer support can be used in combination with intellectual analyses to provide the groundwork for further computer support. Management and users, as indicated by the SWP case history, will have to become more knowledgeable about this area. The tendency to date has been either to ignore these critical areas or to presume to do away with the requirement for support by attempting a fully automated replacement of the analytic and evaluative staffs (1). Unfortunately, ignoring or attempting to avoid a precondition for successful implementation leads directly to the more serious implementation problems the case histories amply illustrate.

Once this first step has been taken, the results of the analytic and evaluative work are stored within the computer in support of the PRIMAS SUGGEST mode. As specific and relevant examples, the patterns of indexing terms or descriptors as established by any or all of the following items influence the descriptors offered by SUGGEST:

a. The results of consensus indexing by experts in committee
b. The results of less trained indexers or less field-expert documentalists
c. The results of indexing accomplished in coordination with search requestors selected generally or by field or expertise
d. Intercorrelations among terms or descriptors appearing as keywords or terms in titles, abstracts, or keywords out of context (KWOC) listings
e. Structural relationships among terms or descriptors established within the thesaurus
f. Weighting or priority values for terms or descriptors, if any, and negative stop lists.

The SWP case history describes the steps by which many of these indexing relationships and the initial consensus or group indexing were accomplished. Once fed into the computer, such information becomes part of the SUGGEST algorithms which continue to learn and transform the computer-suggested descriptors during on-line operations. Although not accomplished within the SWP framework, similar patterns and relationships among terms and descriptors based on analyses of search formulation practices could also have been introduced and used to affect the PRIMAS SUGGEST mode. Further, the descriptor relationships established by intellectual analysis supported by the computer along the lines previously discussed will often be a function of the particular document set, disciplinary field, or areas of interest of the search requestors. The variations and interrelationships of descriptor patterns so determined could also be introduced and influence the SUGGEST mode.

The direct on-line interface between computer and indexer or searcher relies next on two elements. The first is the initial human choice of descriptors or terms for either document indexing or for search question formulation. The second is the capability of the computer rapidly to process many thousands of descriptor correlations using the previously described, stored information and to determine further the frequency of such correlations and their strengths, considering all stipulated descriptor or term sets in relation to those initially selected. The result of such computer processing is then displayed to the indexer or searcher for consideration in further indexing or search question formulation. Each round of descriptor selection then becomes the new basis by which the relative strengths of correlations to all other stipulated descriptors are related. Each subsequent result constitutes a further list of suggested descriptors for indexer or searcher consideration. The stipulated boundaries for the descriptors or terms to be considered during machine processing can be the entire set of thesaurus descriptors or some subset, the entire list of free-text terms or some subset, and in fact any subset or the whole of the system-acceptable search or indexing descriptors or terms. Lastly, the document basis on which the processing takes place (i.e., from which are obtained the associated descriptors or terms to be processed as stipulated) can be the entire set of documents in files or any subsets thereof, including the subset obtained on-line as determined by the search question as it was at that moment formulated. During this process, the choices of indexers and searchers in selecting or rejecting terms from the displays of suggested lists influence over a period of time the correlations determined by the computer when composing further SUGGEST lists.

An extremely direct, iterative, and intensive interactive process occurs with the PRIMAS SUGGEST mode. Or does it, as implemented? The answer to that question is determined in part by the environment within which the PRIMAS SUGGEST mode is implemented. It is also determined in great part by the systemsware within which the PRIMAS SUGGEST mode is embedded. Both of these factors seriously affected the implementation process at SWP. The lack of computer time limited the use of the SUGGEST mode to the search formulation process and a check of the indexing sheets manually prepared in advance for documents to be entered. For indexing, the SUGGEST mode was used only during subsequent on-line entry and then not always.

During search, the SUGGEST mode was used to offer computer guidance for the analysis of the search results obtained for a given search request formulation. Here the interactive process provided computer support to search question formulation and reformulation. However, in the ultimate analyses of the literature cited at the close of any search process, computer support was lacking. Beyond the capability to offer the descriptors assigned to any or all of the documents cited in a given search result, the basis for the SUGGEST mode analysis, further information about these documents had not been stored in the computer. An example of the kind of information potentially useful to help determine the utility of the cited documents would be abstracts or other means to indicate document content and relevancy to a given search request. Nonetheless, the degree of interaction between man and machine available with the system implemented by SWP was significant and not normally available in most operational systems. That any form of this type of interaction was available was due to the choice made initially by SWP about the kind of interface desired with the new system. The primary developer's lack of support, including failure to produce user-oriented documentation for the systemsware provided and the lack of computer time because of funding constraints, limited but did not vitiate SWP's initial interface choice. The SWP case represents the partial transformations in technology, management, and user attitudes implied by the nonlinear assumptions briefly sketched in Section 9.1. All the case histories underline the need for the same significant changes in technology, management, and roles and attitudes of the users. Let us explore what these changes involve in more detail.

9.3 REQUIREMENTS FOR TECHNOLOGY

A detailed conceptual framework and technical description of the software capable of satisfying the requirements to be discussed here can be found in *Computer-Aided Information Retrieval* (Wiley, New York, 1975) and Chapters two and six of *The Social Use of Information* (Wiley, New York, 1976). Among other things such software was intended to provide the means to permit almost continuous file changes. This one characteristic, permitting frequent, on-line file changes, is the prerequisite for meeting successfully all the other technical requirements described in this section.

Current systemsware does not facilitate making frequent changes in computer files in timely or acceptable fashion. Even for simpler systems, such as credit bureau billing or subscription applications, correction of errors or the mere change of addresses can take months. Of course, the computer specialist can find fault with the human work force for the delays in making necessary file changes. But this is somewhat like blaming the sinking of the ship on the water that pours through holes left in a hull.

Currently the file structures developed for the more complex information systems are not built to accommodate frequent, on-line changes to files. Existing files are structured for the efficient storage of the information to be retrieved, whether this be directly retrieved information such as that in data banks or the citations to information externally stored such as with most documentation systems. The various means of obtaining access to the computer-stored information must also be stored. Descriptors, bibliographic information that includes titles and authors or other means to identify the desired information, must be stored in a manner permitting their association with the information described or identified. This includes the storage of the relevant parts of thesauri and various listings of the system-acceptable search terms. To permit efficient processing and very fast search response times, these types of stored information must be handled by highly interrelated and complex file structures usually requiring an architecture of file superstructures containing and keeping track of the keys to the elements stored in other files. However efficient such file structures may be, a trivial change in one file tends to disturb the structured arrangement of elements in all files. Repeated trivial changes cannot be admitted without an elaborate protective process that preserves the structural integrity of the files. To date this is why most systems batch changes to files and process these only at certain times under the control of file protective maintenance, update, or error-correction programs. Since it is uneconomic to run these often lengthy batch processing programs to accommodate very few changes, it can and does take months to change one address or to correct one error. To permit repeated on-line changes to files, entirely new file structuring concepts are required. We have shown elsewhere that this task is as feasible as its accomplishment is necessary (2).

Systemsware capable of accommodating repeated on-line and extensive changes to computer files is required in order to:

a. Handle and store computerized files prepared and offered by the various source suppliers and other information service centers. Changes in files are not merely due to the addition of such externally produced document or information collections to the files. In order to be more useful informational resources, such external collections usually require reclassification and often reindexing in order to be retrievable in accordance with the system-acceptable search terms. Although the mere addition to the files of external collections could be accomplished (and generally is) by batch processing programs, the required reclassification or indexing should be accomplished with interactive computer support. Otherwise the costs become excessive and the workload too heavy for most organizations. Interactive computer support of these functions means that the computer acceptance of repeated, on-line file changes must be made feasible.

b. Support the creation and handling of new files from own organizational informational sources. The same remarks under (a) apply here. In addition such new collections of information must go through the input processes for computer entry or be put in machine readable forms. To the extent that external collections are not provided by source suppliers in machine readable forms or as computerized files already on tape, the input or computer entry problem applies to (a) also.

c. Support term list and thesauri construction and revision, including the production of aids for term list and thesauri usage for indexing and search. A variety of batch processing and on-line aids have been described in *Computer-Aided Information Retrieval* and *The Social Use of Information*, as has the technical feasibility of better supporting this highly expensive and time consuming process. Chapter Ten covers rather thoroughly one major attempt to provide and use better methods for this area in combination with relatively normal forms of computer support. Transformations within term lists and thesauri involve both the terms themselves and their interrelationships as established within thesauri or structured term lists. It may be an unresolvable issue as to whether the type of changes occurring under item (c) can be introduced into the computer files in cyclic batch processing fashion or, alternatively, whether they require more continuous updating procedures. However, the on-line aids for this process will require file structures suitable for making on-line changes.

d. Support the construction of new report and output formats as organizational requirements change. One example of an on-line aid to this process would be an output report format to be filled in partially by a person supplemented by machine stored information. In similar fashion, stored formatting elements could be rearranged or added to on-line by human intervention to create new output or report formats.

e. Provide storage space and access means for individual or private files, structured in accordance with individual user requirements. This capability, promised quite early in a variety of technical proposals dating back to the early 1960s, is long overdue. Standardized files of equally standardized information have their uses. Their limitations are equally obvious to actual and potential users of complex information systems. To accommodate individual files, once again the computer file structures must accommodate changes.

f. Provide file protection. These requirements involving on-line access to files create an even more imperative need for file protection than exists for the more conventional, change-resistant systems. File protection is feasible. However, whatever means human ingenuity creates to protect files, human ingenuity can undo. The task has always been, both for manual as well as computerized systems, to make the costs and risks of illegitimate file penetration or destruction higher than the urge to penetrate or destroy. The requirements above do not make this task significantly harder to accomplish for any given case and situation.

In the past, at least during the predominance of the third-generation computer systems begun with the IBM 360 series systems, a great deal of inertia had to be overcome in order to develop software satisfying the requirements listed in (a) through (e). The software packages developed to operate with the third-generation computer systems had cost much in programming effort and funding. That such software packages neither met the above requirements nor fulfilled the potential of automated retrieval seems now quite clear to most objective observers. But few wanted to undertake the complete revision of such software packages necessary to permit change oriented file structures, on-line aids to indexing, to search question formulation, and to term list or thesauri construction or revision, and the like. Further, it has been shown that the older software packages became incredibly complex and error prone as various add-ons were found necessary (3).

The situation today represents one of those interesting moments in history when new software is required in any event. The new microminiaturized processors, storage elements, terminals, and taken all together computer systems cannot use the older software packages (4). Perhaps this time around, the software to be produced will be able to satisfy the requirements for on-line and continuous file changes and the other requirements based on the nonlinear assumptions. Those to be involved in the implementation of the new systems should know by this point that the requirement is an essential one for their own success. In this light, we turn to the needed transformations in management policy which are equally important as the transformations required in the technology.

9.4 MANAGEMENT GOALS AND POLICIES

The view that no changes are required in the technology or, alternatively, that the necessary changes have all been made, will continue to be expressed. Meanwhile, we shall continue to live with systems incapable of making simple address changes or correcting errors in timely fashion. A similar view will be offered by management about management goals and policies. Both technologists and management who are inclined to these views would concur with the remarks expressed by the Assistant Secretary of Commerce (United States) recently: ''. . . a relatively modest investment would probably enable us to develop a vast computerized information system tying potential foreign buyers all over the world to potential suppliers all around this nation'' (5).

Given the confusing blend of national and international regulations covering trade, the varieties of restrictions, credit arrangements, exchange rates, methods of payment ranging from barter to gold, to mention a small portion of the kinds of items requiring processing in a time as real as that during which these various items change, our discussion to date would lead us to prefer some slight modifications in the remarks just quoted: ". . . a vast investment would probably enable us to develop a relatively modest computerized information system tying selected suitable foreign buyers to the appropriate participant suppliers within this nation."

Management is supposed to be an art in which realistic goals and a relatively orderly process of attaining the goals are established in what would otherwise be a chaotic world. Achieving a degree of orderly function within an organization is to provide direction for purposeful behavior and to ensure that the organizational environment is conducive to the established purposes and goals. When management sets unrealistic goals, the implied management policy is to create unnecessarily chaotic conditions. Policies that tend to create chaotic conditions tend also to create organizational environments inappropriate to the goals or purposes set, however realistic or unrealistic these may be thought to be. The implementation of complex information systems suffers from the kinds of managerial direction incapable of or unwilling to draw these rather obvious conclusions. Management policies based on the linear assumptions are inappropriate to the extent that the nonlinear assumptions apply to the implementation of complex information systems. The case histories and our discussion to this point have shown that better management policies are required. Even should the nonlinear assumptions be only accepted in part, a look at the managerial approach based on them should be of interest. For those content with existing implementation policies and their results, a different approach is often necessitated by still unresolved problems and the requirements stemming from the next round of applications. For those sufficiently dissatisfied with the current status of complex information systems and the methods for their implementation, a managerial approach compatible with the nonlinear assumptions is imperative. Let us consider what such an approach might more specifically be.

9.4.1 The Decision To Replace or Abet Manual Processes

The heresy that the decision to automate is essentially subjective becomes less questionable when one considers only those decisions that are not forced. Furthermore, if the automation appears forced by economic or other considerations, the choice of the path toward automation is based more on wishful thinking and its exploitation than on solid information and a realistic assessment of the feasible or desirable. Despite all the paraphernalia of modern management decision processes, one relevant factor produces the essential subjectivity of the decision to automate. Knowledge of what is feasible and desirable is obtained only through the process of implementation. To opt for vast or grandiose systems is to opt also for the very long time interval, measured in years, of development and implementation. One seldom chooses such systems without establishing at the same time an equally vast or grandiose set of fixed requirements to be satisfied. The time from decision to operational system implementation is more than long enough to ensure that what is thought to be feasible and desirable no longer is the same or even resembles the original description. As the first nonlinear assumption puts it, the decision to automate "settles very little for very long." The usual result of supposedly objective decisions for large-scale and fixed automated systems is simply to involve the organization in a prolonged and uncontrolled experiment with unknown outcomes. The question arises, "Would not the exercise of prudence and rationality admit the subjective basis for such decisions and, therefore, opt instead for a more controlled experiment?"

To the extent that the experimental nature of the implementation process is denied or not recognized, there is little managerial support for an attempt to set up controls appropriate to an experimental implementation program. In contrast, by emphasizing the subjective elements of the decision to automate for complex information system applications, the requirement for establishing a controlled experimental implementation program becomes clear. The relevant management policy is then based on the recognition of the experimental nature of the implementation path chosen and the acceptance of the need to establish appropriate controls. The problem for management is to establish a framework within the organization conducive to carrying out the controlled experiment of an implementation process regarded as a series of planned interim steps toward automation.

Management must establish methods by which each interim step is based on what has been learned from the previous steps. This is not to "think small." Rather, it is to "think slow" about the vastness of the automation initially attempted. It is also to think and concentrate largely on those many intellectual processes needing computer support and which are essential to the successful functioning of any automated complex information system. To date management too often has been backed into this sort of experimental program, forced finally by the results of attempted implementation based on the linear assumptions. The nonlinear assumptions suggest that a better management policy would be to start out with the acceptance of the experimental nature of implementation and to simultaneously accept the responsibilities for the establishment of the proper organizational framework for undertaking a controlled experiment. In establishing the appropriate organizational framework and policies management should consider:

a. Establishing the requirement for more flexible technology and accepting the burden of participating in its development and implementation.
b. Creating an implementation staff, giving this staff a rather long temporal

charter (up to ten years) and establishing the managerial policy of strongly supporting this staff.

c. Establishing a clear set of initial short-term goals which are organizationally accepted and can be accomplished without unforeseen disruption of existing processes.

d. Establishing a set of interim longer-term goals that focus on providing computer support to the more intellectual, difficult, and costly tasks and ensure that those now performing these tasks directly participate in the development and implementation of the computer support.

e. Establishing a management policy to ensure that participation in item (d) work is required for promotion or career advancement.

f. Ensuring that such longer-term goals are truly interim by making additional funding easily available only on the revision of the initial goals. At a minimum, establishing that such funds for revision of longer-term goals are made available at the request of implementation staff or the participant users.

g. Establishing a management policy that sets up a very difficult process for obtaining additional funding for the accomplishment of the original set of interim longer-term goals. At a minimum, establishing the policy of unanimity among management, users, and implementation staff before such additional implementation funds can be requested or made available.

h. Establishing an ongoing requirements and evaluation study group at a high managerial level with four specific tasks:

1. Reporting the fulfillment or lack of fulfillment of the short-term program. This includes stipulating the organizational changes deemed necessary as a result of fulfillment or nonfulfillment and arranging for their acceptance by management, implementation staff, and users.

2. Establishing which of the interim longer-term goals can be accepted as short-term goals and arranging for their acceptance as such by management, implementation staff, and users.

3. Reporting on the developing technological state of the art, with emphasis on the changes in the implementation program to be expected or encouraged as a consequence.

4. Reporting on the developing organizational requirements and overall organizational changes, with emphasis on their impact upon the implementation program.

9.4.2 The Justification of the Decision To Automate

Whatever other means may be used or regarded as necessary for the justification of a decision to automate, there is only one relevant method we seriously consider. If a set of short-term implementable goals can be defined and combined with a reasonable cost estimate for their achievement and an equally reasonable estimate of the benefits to be obtained for the organization, a decision to automate can be justified. Further, if the interim longer-term goals can be shown to be compatible with the developing technology and with a development program acceptable to the organization and if they are compatible with the staff now performing the intellectual work associated with information systems, the decision to automate is probably a sound one, independent of any cost-benefit analyses made at the time of decision. However, both short-term and longer-term interim goals must be understood in terms of the discussion in Section 9.4.1. In this sense, no justification of the decision to automate is sound without the specification of short-term goals achievable without unforeseen disruption to the organization and within the existing and proven technological state of the art. At the same time, no justification can be regarded as final. The initial justification can be expected to be proven wrong in several important aspects. This is why some of the short-term goals will be given up and some of the longer-term interim goals will be established as new short-term goals. In general, cost-benefit analyses are likely to be the least reliable predictors of the actual outcomes during implementation. A more relevant indicator of the virtues of the decision to automate is whether managment has been able to set up the organizational framework for implementation suggested in Section 9.4.1.

9.4.3 The Statement of Requirements

One should spend little money and managerial time on the development of an overall statement of requirements so that one can spend more money and managerial time on the development of an implementation program capable of ascertaining the actual requirements over a period of time and adjusting to meet these. Once the short-term goals are established and the interim longer-term goals defined as *interim*, little more specification of requirements tends to be reliable. All further effort and funding for statements of requirements should be applied to the requirements and evaluation group described in Section 9.4.1. As Robert Townsend might put it, "You've set up an implementation program to determine and satisfy the requirements as discovered in actuality. Instead of being frivolous, support it" (6). No one-time study of requirements produced by any number of inside and outside experts can do as much for you as your own implementation program.

9.4.4 The State of the Art

The fact that descriptions of the state of the art relating to complex information systems are usually outmoded by the time a given system becomes operational does not in itself rule out the utility of obtaining a realistic description of the technically feasible. The question for management is bound up in the meaning of the term "realistic". Is it necessary for management to experience for themselves the difficulties of implementation before they obtain some insight about the realities of the technological capabilities? In general, and unfortunately, this seems to be the case. There are, however, a few available hints for management before implementation. The relevance and validity of any description of the technically feasible at any given time can be tested by posing the following questions:

a. What support is to be made available for file construction, input, correction, and update, and the admission of information collections considered necessary to the files?
b. What support is to be made available for describing the information in files in a manner suitable for the formulation of search requests within this organization?
c. What search formulation aids are to be made available?
d. What indexing, classification, or other content descriptive aids are to be made available?
e. What will it take to make use of any of the aids or support to be made available?

If the answers to these questions amount roughly to none or if the technological solutions offered make such questions irrelevant, obtain another description of the technically feasible.

Other relevant questions capable of providing management with insight about the relevancy of the technology described can be summed up in the following two queries:

a. What amount of filtering of irrelevant, erroneous, or useless information will be required on the average giving upper and lower bounds?
b. What aids to the filtering process are to be made available and what will it take for the organization to use them?

Again, if the answers to those questions amount to none, the need for another description of the state of the art is indicated.

These are precisely the questions that management will have answered during implementation. The answers obtained at that point are often not very pleasant ones. If the experts in technology cannot answer these questions more accurately in advance, their expertise is likely to be irrelevant to managerial and organizational needs. At the minimum, managerial acceptance of the none answers should carry along with it the requirement for an initial experimental phase, strictly designed to check these answers. If the experts and management cannot design such an experiment capable of providing clear and realistic answers to these questions in a relatively short time, one must obtain another group of managers and technological experts. For management tending blindly to sign up for "vast systems developed at relatively low cost", these questions should serve as eye-openers. Beware of one-eyed experts leading the managerial blind.

9.4.5 Systems Performance and Costs

For each case of potential interest, it is practically impossible to determine the worth of a piece of reliable information, however defined. In general a complete informational whole is worth more than the sum of its parts. Usually, information systems deliver only some of the relevant parts and not all of the informational parts delivered are relevant or accurate. Some relevant parts are worth more than others, and some of the excess baggage delivered is more disrupting or dangerously inaccurate than others. Yet even here the worth or disworth of the informational parts delivered is as much a function of the order in which they are delivered and their context, as it is a matter of their intrinsic utility or lack thereof.

It is well to state these facts bluntly. Mathematical smoothing functions producing curves averaged over values about which we are essentially ignorant or confused seldom provide us with valid measures of system performance.

Indirect means of determining systems performance in terms of user satisfaction are also overdependent on context and case as well as questionnaire format. In addition, the comparative approach which analyzes the relative performance of the old system versus the new is usually oversimplified. Very often the old system cannot be compared to the new in all relevant aspects. As we have noted, some of the services performed by the old system cannot be duplicated by the new and vice versa. In both cases the problem of how worth is to be determined arises. How much is user satisfaction worth or better, how much is this degree of user satisfaction (or the lack of it) worth? How much were the old nonduplicable services worth? How much worth are the new services not previously available?

The question about system costs is a little clearer. Presumably, management has established controls sufficient to determine the operating costs of the older system. Presumably, the same sort of management controls will permit the determination of the operating costs of the new system. However, the costs involved in both closing down the older system and bringing the new system into operation are not small and cannot safely be ignored. Managerial controls can be set up to determine these costs as well, but as with the determination of the costs of operations for the new system, such costs can be determined accurately only after the fact. Such estimates are prone to optimism or pessimism but seldom to accuracy.

Assuming that management has achieved a reasonably good handle on both performance and costs of the existing system, there is an equally reasonable way to obtain a ballpark judgment about both performance and costs of the new system and its implementation process. It involves two steps. The first is to add the question, "How much will it cost?", to each and all of the questions stipulated in Section 9.4.4. If no answer is obtainable, the cost estimate is worthless. Assuming that answers are obtained, they should be treated as estimates to be taken with a large degree of plus or minus. The second step is to proceed as described in Section 9.4.1 and to establish an experimental program attempting to achieve selected short-term goals in accordance with both the requirements and the assessment of feasibility as temporarily and tentatively understood. By drastically limiting funding and time allocated for this first phase to what can be accomplished within six months to one year, much insight can be obtained within this time period about the degree of accuracy, or lack of it, in the estimates of costs and technical feasibility.

A similar procedure should help to clarify a great deal concerning systems performance. Will obtaining the aids or computer support established as goals for the interim system:

a. Increase the amount or quality of the searchable information?
b. Provide better means of file description for users interested in knowing what information may be available?
c. Decrease the number of search formulations and searches necessary to obtain a satisfactory result?
d. Reduce the time required for users to translate their search requests into system-acceptable search questions or to evaluate search questions formulated for them?
e. Increase the accuracy and utility of the information obtained (decrease the irrelevancy and excess information obtained as a ratio of all information obtained)?
f. Reduce filtering time and the need to retrieve and check through externally stored information carriers?

Again one begins with estimates with unknown probabilities as to their accuracy. One therefore sees to it that the probability of such performance estimates is significantly better known, as determined within the experimental implementation program, before proceeding much further. This process calls for direct managerial participation, something so often noted before. It is perhaps the best way, however, for management to determine just how much all those information pieces delivered by their information systems are worth, and how much it really costs to deliver and make use of them!

9.4.6 The Last Three Nonlinear Assumptions

For convenience and to place them in the context of the above discussion, the remaining nonlinear assumptions are repeated below. Their relevance for management should now be clear enough:

- Management can rely on and make use of experts only by becoming sufficiently expert in the fields involved themselves.
- Fixes are possible only for fixed organizations satisfied and able to live tomorrow with what they thought they wanted yesterday.
- Given the surprises discovered during implementation, anything can happen, including the achievement of success. But there usually is a sense in which it can be said that all concerned get what they deserve.

We have tried to show that there are better management goals and policies available for the implementation of complex information systems. We turn now to the problems of the users and their roles in the implementation processes.

9.5 USERS

Discussions of different forms of actual or attempted information system automation, as well as common sense, indicate that it is difficult, if not impossible, to pin down exactly the varieties of potential users. One repeated theme throughout the preceding discussions, however, is that a distinction should be made between two general types of system users: the new breed of information specialists in close contact and interaction with both system and client-users and the client or customer users with their wide variety of backgrounds, needs, and interests. This distinction should not be taken to mean that the same individuals never exchange roles or that customers of information system services may never serve themselves. In fact, the question remains open about whether the ideal information system of the future should be a functioning automated cafeteria offering its informational wares on a self-service basis.

At present and for quite some time in the foreseeable future, the need for highly skilled information specialists, be they librarians or information engineers, functioning as middlemen has been well established. Not all requestors of information prefer to search for themselves, and most automated systems have made the proper formulation of search requests a highly skilled specialty. In any event, file development and maintenance remain tasks filled more with drudgery than intellectually appealing labor, as we have been repeatedly reminded by all the applications discussed. Low-quality files make acceptable-quality search results very difficult to obtain even by "search experts," let alone lay users. Because of this, the discussion of users will refer to these two user types, the servers and the served. Both have a role in proper system development and implementation. To date such users have played essentially passive roles, being more the objects of requirements studies than active participants in either development or implementation. Under such circumstances it is not strange that user attitudes, whether information specialists or clients of system services, have been negative. Chapter Eight showed that these negative attitudes in industry are about the same as user attitudes in research institutions (Chapter Five) and the Patent Office (Chapter Four). These, in turn, simply reflect the almost universal experience during implementation of complex information systems. To the extent that such negative attitudes are not merely tied to the normal tendencies expressed in resistance to change, any change, perhaps the transitions called for by the nonlinear assumptions as these pertain to user roles could help to create more positive user attitudes.

9.5.1 Those To Be Served

It might be possible for certain individuals to define accurately their informational requirements, even without a realistic appreciation of what kinds of requirements could in fact be satisfied. The danger here is not so much establishing requirements that cannot be satisfied. It is difficult to order a satisfying dinner in a strange restaurant without an understandable and accurate menu showing what may be available and at what cost. In such cases one tends to order what one knows from past experience. It is just as difficult for potential users of information services to specify their appropriate requirements without some kind of realistic "menu" showing what is actually feasible and at what cost. Without this, one tends to rely on experience with past services, specifying one's requirements in terms of the old and soon to be outmoded services. Systems built to satisfy such requirements look not surprisingly very much like the old systems they were to replace. On the other hand, when users are encouraged to request their "wish-book," the same lack of a reliable appreciation of the possible can produce requirements incapable of being satisfied by any system at any reasonable cost.

Of course, one can be lucky. There are cases where user requirements have indeed been met. The problem here is that the time of satisfaction too often occurs long after the requirements were valid. One needs simply to ask whether such users can specify what their requirements for informational services will be with any degree of accuracy three or more years from whenever now happens to be. That, as has been clearly shown, is the time period required for implementation. Try specifying what information you will need as a function of your workload and position three years or more from now! This is a far more difficult task to accomplish with any degree of success than it is to order that dinner in the strange restaurant without a menu. And it is far more important to specify such informational requirements accurately and well. One can pass up the dinner or eat it with little probable pain. It is a one-time affair. One has to live and work with the ordered information on a daily basis for an extended time period.

Of course, system designers claim to understand this situation. This is why most user requirement studies are farcical and not taken too seriously during system design. The experts know better what users will want by the time the system is brought into operation (7).

When experts know more about the specification of user requirements than the users, it can mean one of two things. It can mean that experts are able to define the user requirements sufficiently in advance to permit system design, development, and implementation to proceed, based on the statement of requirements so derived. This perspective is expressed by the linear assumptions. The cases discussed clearly show that experts can do no such thing except in the most general and vague ways, and even then they are usually wrong. Our statement about expert knowledge can mean something else, however. It would amount to the explicit admission by the experts that no specific statement of requirements is likely to be valid three years from its date of creation. Such an admission would lead us to the nonlinear assumptions. It would lead us as such into an experimental program during which the users as participants would learn better how to determine what their informational requirements might be. It would create the menu of potential options in a form understandable to the participant users, just because such users participated in its creation.

Obviously, not every user could so participate. It is up to management to see to it that a reasonably representative number of client-users are made and wish to be made available as participants. It is up to technology to provide the appropriate systemsware for such an experimental phase. This means to provide systemsware and system functions that are accessible to users so that the experimental phase is relatively comfortable. Preceding sections have covered these matters. But it is up to such users to be willing to participate in such an experimental program. Why should they?

It is neither sufficient nor correct to claim that only through this process can users determine validly what their informational requirements may be and what can, in reality, be satisfied for all time and for all users. Actively participating in development and implementation can help users better appreciate the problems and possibilities intrinsic to automated information systems. It can expand the users' knowledge of the range of potential informational resources and services. Further, such participation can make users more aware of the manner in which informational sources are handled and processed, offering them in this way some notion as to the range of reliabilities and accuracies of the results obtained. However, in so far as the accurate determination of user requirements is concerned, active user participation is a help but by no means a cure-all.

There are two other grounds for requiring active participation of the client-users during development and implementation of more importance to the achievement of a more satisfactory information system. Such participation puts users in the position of exercising sufficient clout concerning both the technical characteristics of the system and the operational environment created by management. This improves chances for the system of obtaining the necessary system and operational flexibility sufficient to better meet user requirements as these develop over time. The costs to client-users of being forced to live with inflexible systems are high. Once systems are developed and implemented, the feasibility of the system's adapting to later changes depends on both the technical characteristics and the managerial environment. Until now, it has been the client-users who have had to do most of the adapting. This would appear to be the major ground for the evident negative attitudes found almost universally among such users. Preceding sections have offered our views concerning the preferred technical characteristics and managerial policies for automated information systems.

A second factor which should encourage client-users to participate during development and implementation has to do with the development of better relationships and mutual understanding with that other group of users, the information specialists. This aspect is explored below.

9.5.2 Those Who Serve

"The Sons of Martha" have never had an easy time of it. Information specialists, be they librarians, documentalists, or credit bureau operators, have had their daily lives and working environments changed at least as much as any other group affected by automation. But unlike some groups, their responsibilities and workloads have increased either because of or in spite of automation. Furthermore, although new titles have been invented, pay scales remain relatively low compared with other trained specialists in industry or public service. At the same time, user expectations have been raised, and the demands for services as well as the varieties of services demanded have increased. The importance of the tasks such information service center staff must perform has been repeatedly emphasized. In order for the automated system to operate at all, the list of tasks includes:

a. Document or other information carrier classifications.
b. Preparation of appropriate bibliographic materials.
c. Content analysis and indexing.
d. Document entry.
e. Construction and maintenance of term lists and thesauri.
f. Preparation of catalogues and other products descriptive of the files.
g. Interpreting user search requests.
h. Formulating search formulas for users and aiding users to formulate search requests and system-acceptable search questions.
i. Preparing abstracts.
j. Preparing citation forms.
k. Obtaining documents or other cited information carriers such as tapes and books.
l. Suggesting supplementary material for users.
m. Preparing summaries of cited material and undertaking other varieties of informational research tasks for users.
n. Accomplishing various forms of clerical or bookkeeping work or aiding the computer in its bookkeeping functions.

One reason for requiring the participation of those who serve as information specialists during development and implementation is to ensure that meaningful forms of computer support for the listed (and other related) service tasks is in fact made an important focal point for the functions of the automated system being implemented. Having the information specialists present is also a good way for management to learn rather quickly whether the technologists responsible for the system understand what automation is supposed to accomplish. If automation increases the workload of the information specialists and if any such increase is deemed unacceptable or unworkable by the information specialists, management can conclude that the technologists have not understood the problem well. It is better for management to discover this all-too-typical effect of automation during the experimental stage rather than after three or more years of implementation of a system that produces precisely this effect. As such, management should be more than willing to encourage the very active participation of their information specialists. A good way to encourage those who will serve the client-users (including management) is to do something quite positive about pay scales for those information specialists willing to cooperate with the new system by participating in the development and implementation stages. This is also an excellent way to transform negative attitudes.

There are two further reasons for requiring such participation. One is obvious. The information specialists learn how to be information specialists within the framework of the new system as the new system comes to life. Waiting until afterwards often effectively kills the new system or ensures that it never will be brought to full fruition. Such learning means that those who serve learn better how to satisfy those to be served. However, this is not accomplished solely by information specialists becoming system experts. More importantly, it requires learning how to understand client-user needs and requirements. Here we have the crux of the matter. This is perhaps the most important reason for the active participation during development and implementation of both forms of the user populations, user-clients and client servers. Both groups in performing their active roles during the experimental stages of the introduction of automation are thrust into an environment where learning how to work with each other becomes an essential part of learning how to work with the experimental system. When both management and technologists as well as users understand this simple fact and create the appropriate technology and organizational environment called for by the acceptance of the nonlinear assumptions, we shall come much closer to achieving the kinds of automated information systems we need.

NOTES

1. For further insight into the reasons for this situation, see Wessel, CAIR, particularly Chapter 5.2, "Reasons and Unreasons."
2. See Wessel, CAIR and Social Use of Information.

3. Wessel, CAIR.

4. Paul L. Hazan, "March of the Microprocessors," *Johns Hopkins Magazine,* November 1976, pp. 10 ff.

5. Frank Weil, Assistant Secretary of Commerce, in a speech to the Chicago World Trade Conference, April, 1978.

6. Robert Townsend, *Up the Organization,* Knopf, New York, 1970.

7. If any critic wishing to damn this book without understanding it wants to choose one sentence for his purpose, this one will do.

Chapter Ten

An Example of an Experimental First Phase Implementation Project

This is a multipurpose chapter. Several of the major themes running through the book will reappear as working principles shown in their practical application. The illustrative data and material were obtained from a project recently conducted within an industrial technical library (1). The primary focus of the project was to develop and prove within the realistic environment of an already functioing major information service the means to improve the existing methods of book classification and content description. The existing methods covering classification, indexing, and search were in use by both the technical library staff and the in-house industrial clients served. The clients consisted of engineers, scientists, and other professionals from management, R&D laboratories, production divisions, marketing, and so forth.

The project attempted a direct attack on some of the "intellectual processes needing computer support and which are essential to the successful functioning of any automated complex information system" as stated in Section 9.4.1. It covered a significant portion of the key interface area described in Section 9.2.2 as the "Intellectual Description of Documents" for both indexing and search.

Furthermore, this project represents the kind of first phase experimental implementation stage we have claimed is essential in order to establish the required groundwork and environment for successful automation. Computer support was provided rather early but within an intellectually developing context

177

given as much or more weight as the computer. Data processing aids and applications were developed, but only simultaneously with the managerial and supporting staff capable of making the most efficient and rational use of the technical capabilitites.

The experimental project was short, covering four months. Its short-term output was promptly tested in an operational framework. A practical and operationally sensible follow-on phase was, as such, readily determinable from the initial results. Lastly, the project began and ended with a harmonious but by no means uniform team consisting of high-level management, operational management, library staff, and technical and informational field specific experts, some of whom were also client-users. Many of the project's characteristics and much of its approach should be of general interest, particularly for those considering upgrading existing information and documentation or library services. For other applications, it may be considered as a negative yardstick for testing the decision to automate or upgrade most forms of complex information systems. It was based on the nonlinear assumptions for the implementation of complex information systems. If this sort of effort (or a similar one) cannot be accomplished, the decision to automate should be reconsidered. For multiuser, multiinterest search services and systems, this form of first phase implementation experiment reveals a great deal about the capabilities of the existing management, technology, and service staffs and realistically indicates the chances for success or failure of more extensive attempts to automate.

10.1 THE DEVELOPMENT AND TEST OF A NEW STRUCTURAL FRAMEWORK FOR A TECHNICAL LIBRARY BOOK THESAURUS

Using methods and techniques (2) adapted to the then manual operations of a major industrial technical library, new thesaurus structural frameworks (3) were produced and tested for two distinct informational fields. These fields were (a) industrial management and administration and (b) data processing. At the time of the project these two fields each had approximately 5000 books assigned to library shelves. For alphabetical shelf location, all books classified as belonging to data processing were coded DV and all books belonging to industrial management and adminstration were coded WW. We shall use these same library shelf codes DV and WW to refer to their respective fields. The choice of the two fields, DV and WW, from among the 20 or so basic book field categories in use at the library was an attempt to determine the general utility of the methods to be tested. Book content, vocabulary, topics and subject matter covered, and so forth, although containing some small amount of overlap, were sufficiently different in these two fields. If the new thesaurus sections produced for the two fields proved useful for classification, indexing, and search under normal library operations, it could be assumed with some degree of reliability that the same methods could be applied to most if not all the remaining fields then recognized for book classification.

It was agreed that library personnel responsible for the classification and indexing of books and for helping client-users searching for information in these fields would participate as active project members. Library and information and documentation (I&D) management would also participate. Further, it was agreed that those responsible for the technical development and application of the methodology would phase themselves out after the project. The project was to provide training and documentation sufficient to permit the library staff participants to continue the effort if experimentally justified for the remaining informational fields. The "phase-out technologists phase-in library staff" agreement, once management made clear to all concerned that it was to be taken seriously, more than any other factor created a favorable attitude and enthusiastic response on the part of the user particpants (4).

Beyond these basic implementation project agreements, there were several other features of the project of particular interest to those interested in the nonlinear approach for the introduction of new techniques and methods associated with automation. These nonlinear features of the project will be emphasized as our discussion proceeds.

10.2 THE PROJECT FRAMEWORK

Most thesauri consist of variously structured term lists organized to reflect the subject matter pertinent to the given field or fields covered by the thesauri. From the perspective of indexers or searchers, such thesauri offer little more than lists of system-acceptable terms or phrases in a relatively impenetrable fashion. That is to say, the thesauri structures themselves do not provide effective guidance through the term lists to terms desired for indexing or search question formulation.

Previous books described certain practical methods by which it was felt that thesauri could be restructured to provide more accessible guidance to the terms therein for indexing and search (5). These essentially involved the development of a semilogical ordering directly connected with associated multiple choice formats containing selected terms pertinent to either basic indexing choices or search term descriptors. Once the basic choices were made by indexer or searcher, the formats were intended to offer selected lists of variously associated terms as additional choices for refinement or expansion of indexing or search question formulation. Further choices by the indexer or searcher would lead to additional preselected formats, and so on, until the indexing or search question formulation process was halted. The indexer or searcher could in fact halt the process at any time felt desirable. However, for this project and its application to a technical book thesaurus, indexers were to be encouraged to continue this process until at least three but not more than eight terms were selected. (These boundaries are more or less artificial and can be changed to suit organizational requirements, i.e., for fewer or more indexing terms per indexed book.)

It was agreed that two fields, DV and WW, were to be selected for the development of new structural frameworks and that these would then be subjected to indexing tests to determine whether the guidance offered by the associated formats would lead to better accuracy, consistency, and completeness (within the limits of current organizational requirements). Should such tests lead to positive results at little or no cost in indexing time, extension of these methods would be considered for the remaining fields of the book thesaurus. At some time in the near future, should these methods be applied, search tests could be conducted to determine the full range of utility of the format structural frameworks. Such search tests, however, were not included as tasks under the initial project effort.

We shall now describe the development of the new structural frameworks for both DV and WW and the indexing test methodology and test analyses. Both the DV and WW tests had surprisingly positive results. However, one important note of caution is indicated. Positive test results do not in themselves offer conclusive evidence that these methods are universally applicable. Such a conclusion can only be drawn after at least six months of operational usage of the new structural frameworks. In fact, it should be expected that long-term operational usage will further refine both the given format structures and, in part, the basic methodology itself.

10.3 THE INITIAL WORKING METHODS

The initial steps involved an intellectual analysis of the existing book thesaurus (existing DV and WW structural frameworks and term lists) and current indexing practices and results. The existing state of affairs is described below.

10.3.1 Analysis of the Existing Thesaurus (DV and WW)

Intellectual inspection of the existing thesaurus term lists for both DV and WW indicated that various inconsistencies and nonlogical term assignments existed. For example:

a. Free terms can be found within the thesaurus term lists.
b. Various thesaurus terms should be treated as free terms. These are essentially names such as PL (programming language).

c. Inconsistent and sometimes incorrect thesaurus numeration of terms are used.
d. Thesaurus words in the hierarchical section are not always found in the alphabetical section, and vice versa.
e. There are illogical hierarchical levels.
f. There are illogical word selections.

10.3.2 Analysis of Existing Indexing Practices and Indexing Results

Discussions with indexers and actually attempting to use the existing DV and WW thesaurus parts for indexing produced the following observations:

a. There is great individual variation in indexing practices and methods not only at the central technical library but also throughout the other in-house technical libraries.
b. There are very few terms (an average of one and a half terms per book) assigned to books, and even this small number is assigned without guidance or rules for selection.
c. There are no thesaurus aids for indexing or search.
d. Indexing and classification are nonetheless time consuming—apparently an average of about 10 minutes per book with, however, a large variation from this average.
e. Quality control is almost nonexistent and essentially dependent on overburdened indexers at the central library (or wherever checks are made of externally indexed books from other centers).

For introducing automation to replace or to support existing processes, the first implementation working principle is:

FIND OUT WHAT IS GOING ON IN PRACTICE NOT IN THEORY.

For example, it had been taken as gospel that books were entered into the technical library with an average of three index terms per book. Where this number had come from, no one knew. Nor had anyone before the experimental project deemed it necessary to check the number. The fact that library staff indexers and classifiers were project participants forced management and the technical developer to pay some attention to what the library staff were doing. It was quickly determined, as mentioned above, that the average number of terms per book was more like one and a half than three. It had been further assumed that relatively strict controls existed covering book classification and indexing. By forcing all concerned with the project to observe the actual working processes, it was soon discovered that such controls existed only on paper. It is precisely this sort of fact that is not obtained from study of organizational charts and paper organizational studies. Being aware of such facts makes quite a difference for the success or failure of any implementation process. It is certainly no new notion that systems and organizations work often in spite of rather than because of the regulations. Introducing automation under such conditions had better preserve or help what makes things work rather than merely attempt to copy what is supposed to make things work and doesn't! One advantage of the attempt to automate is that one usually brings to light what makes things work and what does not. One advantage of the nonlinear assumptions is that this advantage is introduced very consciously and quite early. Too often one learns what makes things work too late.

10.3.3 Analyses of Computer Printout Usage Statistics

Computer printouts showing the actual usage of index terms, both thesauri and free terms, were produced. Because the WW part of the thesaurus had been recently redone, a special printout showing the new WW categories was produced. Used in conjunction with the technical book thesaurus and external thesauri covering some of the same fields as well as various reference works pertinent to DV and WW, the computer printouts provided some very useful input. Some general areas of interest for which data was obtained were:

a. Very low usage terms (such terms were checked to determine whether low usage was produced by poor fit under existing categories, whether upper headings correspondingly were getting overused instead of the lower-level terms covered, and whether such low-usage terms should be removed from the thesaurus or perhaps better listed as free terms, etc.).
b. Usage patterns as a function of the spread of such terms under their own and other category headings (often terms from one category were found listed under other thesaurus categories applied to given books—a valuable indicator that the existing thesaurus structures might be inadequate and a specific pointer toward those particular terms and categories requiring investigation).
c. High-usage terms (lists were set up for high-usage terms, and their usage patterns—spread among existing thesaurus categories—were checked. This helped to determine both valid term groupings and potential linking among thesaurus categories. By this means checks could be made to determine whether terms from other fields as well as other in-field categories were getting picked when necessary for valid book descriptions.)
d. Most-used categories (to determine whether some categories are overused, underused, or misused, and whether thesaurus terms are well spread among important categories, i.e., high-usage categories).

The second implementation working principle is:

USE THE COMPUTER FIRST TO FIND OUT WHAT IS GOING ON BE-
FORE YOU USE THE COMPUTER TO REPLACE OR SUPPORT WHAT IS
GOING ON.

This principle is relevant also in negative terms. If the team of management, technical, and user experts cannot get the computer to help them find out what is going on in the processes to be improved or automated, it is more than likely that this same team will be unable to get the computer to improve or automate the very same processes. One advantage of proceeding in accordance with this working principle is that one starts by using computers to do what computers have been taught to do, analyze data. Working principle No. 1, if followed, ensures that the data to be analyzed by the computer are in fact the data that need to be analyzed. This in itself does not ensure that the computer analyses will be the right ones. For that the second working principle is established.

10.4 TOWARD A NEW STRUCTURAL FRAMEWORK FOR DV AND WW

In developing a new structural framework for thesauri, a balance must be struck between the attempt to achieve a more perfect logical ordering and the need to develop a workable, though still imperfect, framework that can be used for test purposes. It should be emphasized that purely intellectual attempts to produce perfect thesauri structures by consensus of experts or arbitrary decree become quickly counterproductive. Every structural framework must undergo a testing period. It is through the testing period and the resultant feedback of test data and indexer experiences that the framework can be further refined. The key to temporarily halting the intellectual processes of thesauri structural development is the successful development of what we have called structural formats that are sufficiently adequate for use during tests (indexing and search). Should both formats and structural frameworks hold up reasonably well during the test phases, it can be assumed that the overall structure is sound and that most later changes will occur within the new framework structures and formats. However, only after a significant period of operational usage, about six months, can this assumption be confirmed.

Given the nonlinear implementation philosophy, the following specific steps were accomplished to develop an experimental test structure for DV and WW.

10.4.1 Most-Used Terms

The lists (Section 10.3.) of the terms most often used were checked as to their existing thesaurus placement and the relevance and logic of their categorical assignment and place. For all terms that appeared misplaced, new tentative category groupings were established. Furthermore, both frequency of usage and spread among other existing categories were checked for those terms felt misplaced within a given category or within the existing hierarchy.

10.4.2 Inappropriate Categories

The categories themselves (higher-level grouping terms) felt inappropriate as a function of the analysis of the spread patterns of most-used terms (see Section 10.3) were inspected for all terms therein, independent of the frequency of usage of those remaining terms. This was done as a means of discovering new tentative grouping categories for such terms, to check for additional discrepancies within existing categories, and to attempt better subdivisions within categories.

10.4.3 Suspicious or Questionable Terms

Questionable terms, terms with double or multiple meanings, or unclear terms are indicated by their relatively widespread usage under differing categories. Other indications of questionable terms are illogical placement in the hierarchy or any strange thesaurus location and/or spread and usage as determined from the thesaurus lists compared to expert knowledge of the field. For example, when the term "small-sized computer" is confused with what is today called "minicomputer" or when the word part "-lehre" ("-theory", "doctrine") as used within WW appears to cover both subjects of university study and objects of business enterprise.* Often separate categories must be set up for such questionable terms and/or new term groupings in order to clarify their meanings as thesaurus descriptors.

10.4.4 Remaining Category Groupings

Many existing category groupings or upper-level hierarchical terms will remain as is. However, these must be set up with a better logical ordering and connected to the new categories and term groupings developed by the preceding steps.

10.4.5 Tentative New Structural Framework Overview

By accomplishing steps 10.4.1 through 10.4.4, including the more logical ordering of new and old term grouping categories or higher-level hierarchical terms, an overview of the new structural framework for a given field is produced (see Sections 10.8.1 and 10.8.4 for the DV and WW overviews). These overviews were presented to appropriate specialists in the fields concerned for their critique and input. However, care must be taken to avoid perfectionism at this point. Not all potential controversies among experts can be resolved intellectually. What is

---

*The technical book thesaurus was, of course, in German. The example given here indicates one of the major ambiguities within the WW part. As such, the example is relevant even for English readers; "-lehre" appeared quite often in the older WW thesaurus in this form and with the ambiguity mentioned above unresolved.

required is more-or-less agreement among such experts that ''the tentative structural framework is good enough for test purposes and subject to further revision and critique once test data are available.''

The third implementation working principle is:

THE OPERATIVE WORD IS ''TENTATIVE.''

Generally, systems and solution methods tend to get cast in concrete before testing. This has meant that if the test feedback is to be taken seriously, a crowbar must be first applied. Methods and systems set up for test need to be hard enough for test purposes but should equally be soft enough for the necessary revisions expected after testing. This means that we have to learn how to build tentative or nonlinear, if you like, systemsware.

10.4.6 Completion of the New Test Structural Framework

The overviews of the new DV and WW structural frameworks consist of a logical ordering of the basic thesaurus categories. This is now to be extended by filling in the basic categories by listing the terms for which the basic categories serve as grouping headings. One begins by using the remaining high-usage terms (see Section 10.3) and then completes the process by adding the remaining terms. During this process a gradual expansion of the structural framework will take place, including the introduction of subcategories. Slight modifications of the overview categories can occur; however, most of the changes should involve the creation of new subcategories. Terms felt unimportant and seldom used can be eliminated at this point. This would include redundant terms and terms resisting clarification.

Should extensive modifications of the basic categories be required during the fitting in of the remaining terms deemed desirable, we would have the first indication that the new tentative structural frameworks may be unworkable. We should be careful in rejecting low-usage terms, because the low use of a term may have resulted from its poor location within the older thesaurus. However, low-usage terms deemed unimportant or essentially functioning as proper names should be rejected as thesaurus descriptors but remain options within a free term list.

10.4.7 Format Development

The resultant new structural framework constitutes a new hierarchy and/or a many-leveled field thesaurus composed with better logic and level balance and providing for more rational term location. The many-leveled structural framework in effect constitutes a group of relatively simple formats that reflect the new structure and term locations. Whether a given format will contain several structural levels unified under a given grouping or constitute exactly one level in itself will depend upon the number of terms involved and common sense. As such, a certain degree of imperfection may be produced by the particular determination of the specific formats that complete or fill out the new structural framework (see Sections 10.8.2 and 10.8.5 for the DV and WW formats). It is important to check the resultant structure and its formats for proper location and the consistency and correctness of their interpretations with field experts. Much more important, however, will be the feedback from indexing and/or search tests.

Format structuring reflects the structural framework. But it is much more important to note that the formats are an attempt to reflect or abet an "ideal" indexing process using the new framework. Please note we have used the word "an," not "the." The formats constitute a form of the logical flow of the indexing processes using the structural framework. However, it must be a logical flow that allows for indexer (or searcher) freedom of choice throughout the process. In fact, the use of one or another of the formats will depend upon the initial choices of terms by an indexer or searcher. However, at any time an indexer or searcher must be free to reject the suggested format and the terms it offers, freely choosing some other format for consideration. Entry into the process through formats can proceed by the initial selection of general terms, by using the alphabetical listing of all terms showing their structural framework place and format location, or by following the indexer's intuitions based on experience with the formats and the field. The same remark applies to searchers. However, whatever the entry point may have been, format guidance to other potentially relevant term groupings is then available.

10.4.8 Specific Format Development Procedures

At the risk of some redundancy, we shall list as far as possible the various working steps employed in developing the formats associated with a given structural framework.

List of Work Points:

a. Develop the structural framework overview, providing a very loosely organized format structure. The overview in itself is a logically ordered collection of basic categories or term groupings. It may not appear significantly different from the older categories, insofar as the older thesaurus in fact reflected correctly the basic categorization pertinent to a given field.

b. Attempt, in extending the overview structure by means of constructive formats, to group all terms under existing term headings, creating new term headings and subcategories when necessary and establishing related terms and groups.

c. Develop further breakdowns within groups, particularly where many terms exist, and establish headings for such lower-level groupings. During this process new terms not in the older term list may be added and older terms deemed useless or too infrequently used may be rejected.

d. Carefully establish logical connections between the different groups and levels, remembering that certain subgroups or terms may be linked to more than one group and/or linked to groups in other structural frameworks. Here is where ''see also'' and ''use instead of'' references are established.

e. Check all groups for term balance and further breakdown if too many terms remain under one heading; remove redundant, unnecessary terms.

f. Go through the full alphabetical list of terms for the given field (using the computer printouts) as a final check of any terms not yet covered. Terms deemed inappropriate may be rejected or reserved as candidates for free term lists.

g. Establish the relationships among the formats so that specific formats serve as introductions to the other formats. The number of formats for any given field-specific structural framework should be held down to a practical number, say ten to fifteen, with one to three of these functioning as the introductory points to the remainder.

h. Develop an alphabetical listing of all terms now covered by the structural framework and its formats, showing their structural place and format location. For those terms that appear in more than one place or format, clarification or short definitions should be made, indicating the special meanings of these terms as a function of which structural place or format location is referenced. For example, the term ''simulation'' may be regarded as an area for computer application, or it may be regarded as a technique used in developing software or hardware under the DV structural framework, or it may appear in the WW structural framework as a tool for management planning.

i. Code the structural framework overview to refer to the developed formats. At this point, the overview, the formats, and the alphabetical list with the appropriate clarifying definitions constitute the new thesaurus structure. The new structural framework (see Section 10.8) is ready for test use, however, only after the addition of the indexing rules and procedures (Section 10.8.7) described in Section 10.5 following.

10.4.9 Special Note on Formal Document Descriptors

It was deemed advisable to establish a separate format called format F for both DV and WW to cover formal document descriptors rather than having such terms appear scattered throughout the lists of content descriptors. It should be noted that the construction of a list of formal document descriptors is more properly a function of the librarians, as they know best what formal characteristics of books may be of interest in a given library and are probably best suited to develop the structural format. As such, the two formats F (for DV and WW) for formal document descriptors should be regarded as no more than models for the construction of these formats in a proper manner by the library staff themselves. However, the preceding working principles and discussion of format development will be found generally appropriate to the development of a format for formal document descriptors.

A last point is that it should be possible to construct one format F covering the required formal document descriptors applicable to all given technical book thesaurus fields. The important formal characteristics of books are far more dependent on the special library requirements than on the disciplinary field or the content pertinent to the books.

10.5 THE INDEXING EXPERIMENTS

A standard indexing test was developed for potential application to any of the technical book thesaurus fields for which the new structural framework and formats are constructed. The indexing tests have been concluded. This section will describe the experimental design, test procedures, and test analysis methods applicable to both DV and WW and probably to any future fields for which a structural framework may be constructed. Section 10.6 will present the test results obtained.

10.5.1 Experimental Design

Any comparison of indexing or later search between the older processes and the newer (using the formats and new developed structural framework) inevitably involves us with the problems of the learning curve. We are forced to compare results obtained using an older process with which the indexers are familiar to results obtained using a relatively unfamiliar structural framework and its associated indexing processes. Because of this, a certain bias could exist in favor of the older system. In this case, because of the relatively uncontrolled indexing procedures under the older system and an inconsistently applied rule to restrict the number of descriptors per book, a counterbias in favor of the new structural framework may well exist. The experiment was designed to overcome as much as possible both biases and, more importantly, to provide us with meaningful data. The experimental design features are as follows:

a. It may be repeated or extended to other fields without complication.
b. Comparisons between and among the individual indexers can be accomplished.
c. Comparisons of the individual indexer at points along the learning curve can be made.

d. All such comparisons of individual indexer and all indexers combined can be made at selected points along the learning curve and can be compared on an overall basis to "ideal indexing" that has been established by expert group consensus.

e. Overall and individual comparisons between indexing resulting from the use of the new structural framework and formats and indexing accomplished by the older processes (past indexing patterns) can be made.

f. The simplest valid design and test methods were chosen. Complications that might have been introduced to avoid one or another of the biases explicitly identified above would only produce differing biases. Rather than attempt an overly complicated experiment, it was deemed better, should serious questions remain after the tests, to establish an operational period of time for use of the new structural framework in a normal operating environment. A quality control check at some later point might then be used to confirm test results and/or to make further comparisons to the average indexing quality obtained in the past using the older methods. Furthermore, it would always be possible, if necessary, to set up for a short period of time parallel indexing processes using both old and new methods, permitting the most objective quality control comparison possible.

The fourth implementation working principle is:

THE BEST TEST IS OPERATIONAL EXPERIENCE.

However, neither test results nor operational experience will help matters much unless the technology, the operations, the management, and the users are set up to encourage participation in the evaluation and acceptance of the indicated changes.

10.5.2 Test Book Selection

Fifty books from each field involved (DV and WW) were selected at random by the library staff. In order to permit more useful comparisons between older methods and the new, books published in 1972 or later were used. This stipulation is a function of the timing of the introduction and use of the original book thesaurus and/or term lists. Indexing according to such term lists can be identified by noting whether the existing indexing assignments use terms from the thesaurus lists. Most books with a 1972 or later publication date were indexed using the technical book thesaurus.

10.5.3 Test Indexers

For DV, three indexers were used during the test. Of those one was highly experienced and familiar with the DV field, one was fairly experienced with the existing indexing processes and familiar as well with the DV field, and the third was unfamiliar with the older indexing procedures but familiar with the DV field and the new structural framework formats.

For WW, the indexing pattern was similar but not identical; one very experienced indexer very familiar with the WW field, one less experienced as an indexer but very familiar with the WW field, and the third familiar with the formats, less familiar with the older indexing practices, and unfamiliar with the field. For WW, however, a fourth indexer was added, an experienced indexer unfamiliar with the WW field but familiar with the formats through experience as an indexer for the DV test. Note that one of the test indexers accomplished test indexing for both the DV and WW tests, a possible means of comparison between the use of formats by specific field.

10.5.4 Indexing Instruction

The instruction period was minimal. Five books were jointly indexed under the guidance of the structural framework builder. Consensus rapidly obtained to proceed with the actual test rather than continue preindexing together. However, the indexing of the first test book was carefully observed to determine if significant misunderstanding of the format usage was present.

Experienced indexers tend to revert quickly to their older and familiar indexing practices, and because of this may also tend to ignore the formats. Indexers were requested to avoid this tendency, even if, initially, indexing times might be longer. The point of the test was to test, and to test the formats. Generally this was accepted and understood by all indexers, but it did require emphasis during the initial indexing period.

Indexers were given a test instruction sheet (see Section 10.8.7) which established "the rule of three and eight," the number of descriptors less than which formats should continue to be considered and more than which indexing by format could halt. Beyond this indexers were provided with the structural framework overview, formats, and alphabetical lists showing format location and structural framework place along with the instruction sheet. Indexers then proceeded as they deemed fit.

German-English lexicons and basic field reference materials were available to the indexers during the test periods, just as such reference material is available to indexers normally. Generally something like 30−40% of the books were in English.

10.5.5 Test Indexing

Each indexer indexed the same 30 books in the same order, one after the other. Form sheets (see Section 10.8.8) for indexing were provided. These indexing form sheets were identified as to book, indexer, and free term or thesaurus descriptors, and a space was made available to indicate formats used. Further space was available for indexer comments.

Initially a time limit of a maximum of 15 minutes per book was established. However, this was found unnecessary since books were indexed in about the same time (10 minutes) as normal. Fifteen books were indexed each day for two days. The actual indexing sessions including training, waiting periods, and so forth, were approximately 3½ hours each. This indexing break was established to avoid boredom and to permit comparison between two learning points: initial use of formats and later use of formats after an overnight pause.

10.5.6 Existing Indexing Patterns

The indexing (previous indexing assignments according to the older library methods and term lists) of the 50 books selected for the indexing tests were obtained from the library staff. These were made available in convenient form listed on a copy of the front page (title page) of each of the books. This sheet had also the classification category and shelf location number. This material was made available for only analysis and was not given to the test indexers.

10.5.7 The Construction of "Ideal" Indexing Lists

A group of three individuals knowledgeable in the field and containing one of the original test indexers composed an "ideal" or group consensus indexing for each of the 30 books indexed. This was accomplished by taking the indexing lists per book of each indexer and requiring unanimity among the consensus indexing group for accepting terms from the individual indexers' lists. Additional terms could be suggested by any consensus group member and were accepted as part of an "ideal" list on unanimous agreement by the group. An "ideal" of group indexing could exceed eight index terms but was restricted to less than ten for future tests. (For DV this restriction was not made explicit, and occasionally more than ten terms appear in an "ideal" list per book.)

10.5.8 Test Scoring

There were two methods considered for scoring the indexing test results. An "ideal" list was formed by group consensus concerning the basic subject matter or topics covered by a given book. To keep within the technical library's standards, the identification of a maximum of eight such basic subjects or topics was allowed per book. The actual selection of descriptors for each book involved the selection of the "best" descriptors (or free text terms) reflecting the basic sub-

Given: Indexer's set of descriptors $\quad A = \{a_1, a_2, \ldots, a_n\}$ test set
and
Ideal set of descriptors $\quad\quad B = \{b_1, b_2, \ldots, b_m\}$

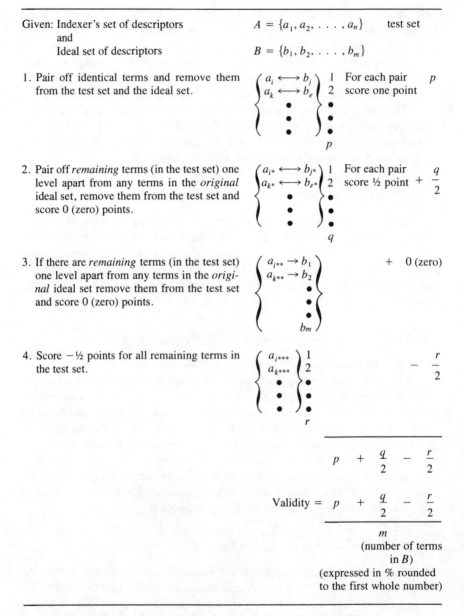

1. Pair off identical terms and remove them from the test set and the ideal set.

$\left.\begin{array}{l} a_i \longleftrightarrow b_j \\ a_k \longleftrightarrow b_e \\ \quad \bullet \\ \quad \bullet \\ \quad \bullet \end{array}\right\}$ $\begin{array}{l}1\\2\\ \bullet \\ \bullet \\ \bullet \\ p\end{array}$ For each pair p
score one point

2. Pair off *remaining* terms (in the test set) one level apart from any terms in the *original* ideal set, remove them from the test set and score 0 (zero) points.

$\left.\begin{array}{l} a_{i*} \longleftrightarrow b_{j*} \\ a_{k*} \longleftrightarrow b_{e*} \\ \quad \bullet \\ \quad \bullet \\ \quad \bullet \end{array}\right\}$ $\begin{array}{l}1\\2\\ \bullet \\ \bullet \\ \bullet \\ q\end{array}$ For each pair $+ \dfrac{q}{2}$
score ½ point

3. If there are *remaining* terms (in the test set) one level apart from any terms in the *original* ideal set remove them from the test set and score 0 (zero) points.

$\left.\begin{array}{l} a_{i**} \rightarrow b_1 \\ a_{k**} \rightarrow b_2 \\ \quad \bullet \\ \quad \bullet \\ \quad \bullet \\ \quad b_m \end{array}\right\}$ $+ \quad 0 \text{ (zero)}$

4. Score $-½$ points for all remaining terms in the test set.

$\left.\begin{array}{l} a_{i***} \\ a_{k***} \\ \quad \bullet \\ \quad \bullet \end{array}\right\}$ $\begin{array}{l}1\\2\\ \bullet \\ \bullet \\ r\end{array}$ $- \dfrac{r}{2}$

$$p \quad + \quad \frac{q}{2} \quad - \quad \frac{r}{2}$$

$$\text{Validity} = \frac{p \quad + \quad \dfrac{q}{2} \quad - \quad \dfrac{r}{2}}{m}$$

(number of terms in B)
(expressed in % rounded to the first whole number)

Figure 1   Test scoring calculation methods and formulas (validity).

jects or topics. Indexers could choose other descriptors covering these same subjects or topics which were more specific, more general, or simply parallel to the "best" descriptors for covering these same book subjects or topics. If such indexer selections were regarded as "correct" by the group responsible for constructing an "ideal" list, the indexer could be said to have covered the appropriate book subject or topic. Scoring here involved merely the determination of the percentages of the number of basic book subjects or topics correctly covered.

Scoring on this basis involved an unavoidable degree of subjectivity. However, it was used as one of the scoring methods because of its intrinsic interest and for its value in providing data that could be compared to data achieved by a more precise and objective scoring method. The more objective method was to require identity of descriptor selections for comparisons among indexers and to an "ideal" list, as well as the comparisons to the older indexing. For this purpose, each indexer's list of terms per book was compared both to an "ideal" list and to each other's indexing choices for that book. The older indexing for each book was also compared to an "ideal" thus permitting a comparison on that basis between the older indexing per book and each indexer's lists, and the combined averages of all indexers. This method also permitted a comparison of the overlap among indexers on the basis of the part identity of their indexing lists per book. Figures 1 and 2 show the actual scoring formulas.

Given: Indexer 1's set $A = \{a_1, a_2, \ldots, a_n\}$

Indexer 2's set $B = \{b_1, b_2, \ldots, b_m\}$

1. Pick all a_i such that a_i is identical with a term in B

$$\left\{ \begin{array}{c} a_1 \longleftrightarrow b_j \\ \bullet \\ \bullet \\ \bullet \\ a_i \longleftrightarrow b_e \end{array} \right\} \begin{array}{c} 1 \\ \bullet \\ \bullet \\ \bullet \\ i \end{array} \right\} \ i \text{ terms}$$

$$\begin{array}{cc} \text{def.} & \text{def.} \\ p = \dfrac{i}{n} & q = \dfrac{i}{m} \end{array}$$

(n — number of terms in A)
(m — number of terms in B)

The agreement is taken to be the lesser of p, q

Figure 2 Test scoring and calculation methods and formulas (consistency–overlap among indexers).

10.6 TEST RESULTS

The more subjective measure of indexing performance with the new structural framework indicated that descriptors were correctly selected covering roughly six out of eight basic book subjects or topics. When the actual indexing selections were routinely extended in accordance with the structural framework (an automatic process of selecting the next higher term), something like seven out of the eight basic book subjects were correctly covered. The actual percantages averaged are given in Table 1.

These percentages are rather interesting when compared to the average percantage of correct coverage derived from the old indexing lists for these same books. This was a low 37.5% or two out of every eight basic subjects or topics identified by "ideal"'lists.

This rather broad and admittedly subjective measure of indexing coverage and the roughly 100% improvement achieved using the new structural framework compared to the older thesaurus were confirmed by the more objective and precise scores shown in Figures 3 and 4. These figures show the detailed results for the DV test.

The original indexing was automatically extended by using the structural framework to add one term higher in the hierarchy to those the indexer had chosen if this did not produce duplication. The learning curve effects were checked by computing averages for the first ten, second ten, and third ten of the 30 books indexed. Since the books were indexed over two days, 15 books per day, overnight learning was checked by also computing averages for the first 15 and second 15 books indexed. Clean learning curve effects were obscured by difficulties with two books within the books numbered 16 to 20 which indexer No. 1 failed to note had been previously incorrectly assigned to DV. These two books produced indexer No. 1's lowest scores of 47.7% and 50.9% in the 16−30 rows of the original and extended indexing. Nonetheless, it appeared that after the first 10 books were indexed all indexers had achieved a relatively stable usage of the new structural frameworks and formats. All averages in Figures 3 and 4 were computed from real data and rounded to one decimal point. Overall aver-

Table 1   Correctness of Book Subject Matter Identification

Indexer	Original indexing (%)	Extended indexing (%)
I_1	75	87.5
I_2	62.5	87.5
I_3	87.5	87.5
AI	75	87.5
	(6 out of 8 subjects)	(7 out of 8 subjects)

Original	I_1 (%)	I_2 (%)	I_3 (%)	AI (%)	Old Indexing (%)
1–10	49.6	49.6	54.5	—	—
11–20	56.8	52.0	75.6	—	—
21–30	55.6	50.3	68.1	—	—
1–15	60.3	50.7	62.5	—	—
16–30	47.7	50.5	69.7	—	—
T=30	54.0	50.8	66.1	56.9	30.1

Extended	I_1 (%)	I_2 (%)	I_3 (%)	AI (%)	Old Indexing (%)
1–10	52.4	55.0	61.0	—	—
11–20	60.5	61.2	80.8	—	—
21–30	58.4	55.8	70.9	—	—
1–15	63.7	57.5	67.9	—	—
16–30	50.9	57.1	73.9	—	—
T=30	57.3	57.3	70.9	61.8	29.8

Figure 3   Comparison of DV indexing validity to an "ideal."

ages (AI) were also computed from real data and not from the rounded percentages given for the individual indexers. The older indexing was similarly scored. However, the extension of the older indexing naturally used the older thesaurus structure. Every means to interpret the older indexing favorably was used in arriving at these averages, thus any bias here is in favor of the older thesaurus.

The check for specific term indexing consistency was more a test of the extension principle than anything else because there was no means of obtaining a measure of the indexing consistency among the indexers who had produced the older indexing. Indirectly, however, Figure 4 does indicate that most indexers were often merely one term apart in hierarchical level when using the new structural framework. This indication is given by the roughly 10% improvement

Overlap	T = 30 Original (%)	Extended (%)
$I_1 - I_2$	46.5	52.6
$I_1 - I_3$	32.3	42.3
$I_2 - I_3$	38.6	49.4
AI	39.1	48.1

Figure 4   Specific term indexing consistency for DV.

in indexing consistency for extended indexing. As far as the broader subject topic coverage was concerned, a much higher consistency among indexers, roughly 75%, increasing to 87.5% when extended, was obtained. Probably for book indexing more consistent indexing may prove unobtainable, and certainly the use of the new structural framework did not degrade matters.

The group responsible for creating "ideal" lists, for scoring the indexing, and, with the exception of the one common indexer noted before, the indexers themselves for WW were different than those used for DV. Despite this and the equally different term lists and book subject matter, the WW test results were essentially the same as those for DV shown above. A variation within two or three percentage points, in most cases better than DV results, was found for WW. Possibly this was because all 30 WW books used for test indexing had been previously correctly classified, whereas two of the 30 for DV had been incorrectly assigned to DV.

For original indexing, the overall average for all indexers for the 30 books was 59.9%. Even the one indexer with no previous WW experience scored 50%. The extended indexing produced an average score almost 10% higher for all indexers. As with DV, the improvement over the older indexing was at least 100% for indexers taken individually or for the four indexers taken together. Obtaining this result again for WW is of particular interest, since all WW books had been reindexed by specialists during the last two years. Thus the older indexing for WW presumably had been better accomplished or better controlled than the older indexing for DV.

The scoring methods shown in Figures 1 and 2 gave an indirect measure of error rates, that is, the number of wrong descriptors assigned as a ratio of all descriptors assigned. The error rate appears to be rather low. To ascertain this more clearly, a direct check of the error rate was made using the indexing for 15 of the WW books. The sum of the incorrect descriptors assigned by each indexer for these 15 books was obtained. This was then compared to the sum of all descriptors assigned by each indexer. The indication that a low error rate was produced using the new structural framework was confirmed. An error rate of only 10% or one out of every ten descriptor assignments was found. The four indexers assigned a total of 275 descriptors to the 15 books. Of these only 27 were wrong. Given the variation among indexer experience and knowledge in the WW field, the use of the new structural framework produced an accuracy of indexing that went beyond the initial expectations (6).

10.6.1 Feedback for Further Refinements of the New Structural Framework

An important purpose of the test was to obtain feedback useful for refining the structural frameworks and formats. Positive test results for methods applied to the neglected areas of indexing and content description may stem in part from the same factors as those producing improvement by offering placebos to neglected patients. The greater improvement of indexing for both the DV and WW fields with different indexers and scoring groups using the new structural frameworks should therefore be regarded simply as a strong indication to proceed to a period of operational usage and evaluation. The fact that the improved indexing obtained by using the formats and structural frameworks did not increase indexing time is just as important as the improvement itself. More important is that the feedback from the tests was used to further refine the formats and structural frameworks to make them still more effective and easier to use. In summary form it was shown that:

a. The overviews (see Sections 10.8.1 and 10.8.4) for the structural frameworks could and should be simplified. The basic category terms used there needed better explanations for indexers unfamiliar with the respective fields or the contents and characteristics of books assigned to those fields.

b. A complete revision of format F, used for formal descriptors indicating standard book characteristics, should be produced by the library staff. Format F was necessary to keep such descriptors from cluttering up the descriptors for the contents of books.

c. The formats should be further compressed to single sheet forms if possible. Only slight modifications of the formats are necessary if these are combined with printing techniques and the use of occasional double columns.

d. Short clarifying definitions or explanations for the higher-level structural framework categories would prove useful for unskilled indexers. This should include all terms with multiple meanings.

e. At least one further check through the computer printout listings should be made to correct spelling or other minor errors and to add those few terms felt desirable by most of the indexers. These terms were usually added as free terms during indexing.

f. Attempts to reduce the number of formats, particularly for WW, should continue. However, it was discovered that the maximum number of formats could run to 15 rather than the 10 initially thought feasible.

g. These suggested refinements should be accomplished before using the frameworks and their formats for operational indexing and classification of books.

Such feedback and its importance can be underlined by the fifth implementation working principle:

IF THE INITIAL TEST DURING AN IMPLEMENTATION PROJECT SHOWS THAT EVERYTHING IS ALL RIGHT, THE TEST IS PROBABLY ALL WRONG.

10.7 CHANGING ATTITUDES TOWARD AUTOMATION

The implementation project described above through its introduction of the use of computer printout listings gave some of the participants their first direct contact with potentially more sophisticated computer support. At the end of the project user attitudes toward computers had begun to change to the favorable. Furthermore, the participatory development of the structural frameworks and their formats created a certain vested interest in seeing to it that these would become part of the operational processes. Thus the notion that such formats and structural frameworks could be stored in computers and displayed on demand or on term selection by indexers frightened no one. Because of this, some rather specific, highly interactive, and relatively sophisticated computer-supporting functions could be envisaged, accepted by the library staff, and readily accomplished. This would constitute a new short-term goal for the ongoing implementation program, perhaps the most profound result of the experimental implementation project.

The sixth implementation working principle is:

LONG-TERM GOALS MUST BECOME SHORT-TERM GOALS WITHIN A
REASONABLE TIME.

If long-term goals persist in remaining long-term, get some new ones.

10.8 THE NEW STRUCTURAL FRAMEWORKS

For readers interested in more detail, this section presents portions of the new structural frameworks, their overviews and formats, examples of the alphabetical listings with the format and structural term locations, and the indexing test instructions and test forms. A complete version exists in the German language. The portions of the structural framework and formats appear here (in translation) just as they were at the time of the indexing tests. They contain errors that were later corrected and require refinement along the lines described in Section 10.6.1. Section 10.9 returns to the theme of participatory implementation.

10.8.1 DV (Data Processing) Overview

0.0 − 0.4   *Formal descriptors*

0.1   Introductions
0.2   General reference materials
0.3   Field specific reference materials
0.4   History/future of DV

1 – 1.3   *General aspects*

    1   Data processing

          1.1   Systems (e.g., Siemens 4004, documentation system)
          1.2   Methods/techniques
          1.3   Applications

(Indexing formats F and G belong to this part of the structural framework. The lower-level terms for this part of the structural framework are found in formats F and G. A look through indexing formats F and G will show that these formats lead to other parts of the structural framework).

10 – 15   *Hardware*

    11   Computer

          11.1   Design and construction
          11.2   Periphery
          11.3   Switching computer
          11.4   Firmware
          11.5   Types
          11.6   Computer applications USE 30 Applications

    12   R&D (research and development) areas
    13   Problem areas
    14   Components
    15   Remote data processing SA NT 240

(See also Indexing formats H and H1. The remarks for formats F and G apply here as well.)

20 – 25   *Software*

    21   R&D areas

          Formal systems
          Automata theory
          Artificial intelligence
          Other R&D areas

    22   Programming

          Formal logic theories
          Data organization
          Operating systems
          Compilers
          Modular systems

> Microprogramming
> Sorting Programs
> Machine instructions (assembly language)
> System programming

23   Preparation of automation (see also WW . . .)

24   Programming languages

25   System performance (see also WW . . .)

(See also formats S, S1, S2. The remarks for formats F and G apply here as well.)

30 – 33   *Applications*

33   Application problems

32   Special application techniques

31   Application (general)

(See also format A. The remarks for formats F and G apply here as well.)

10.8.2 DV Formats – Examples

Format H   *Hardware*

10   Hardware

   11   Computer

      11.1   Design and construction
      11.2   Periphery
      11.3   Switching computer
      11.4   Firmware (trade/firm names)   } *see* Format H1
      11.5   Types
      11.6   Computer application USE 30
              applications

   12   R&D areas

   • Computer design
   • Data output
   • Data input
   • Magnetic thin film

- Magnetic signal display
- Optical storage
- Storage

13   Problem areas   USE 32 application problems

14   Components

Adder, analog-to-digital converter, analog circuit, code converter, magnetic thin film—*SA storage,* magnetic card, magnetic signal display, magnetic disk, magnetic film storage, microprocessor, optical storage, gate circuit, source computer

15   Remote data processing   SA NU 240 data transmission

Format H1   *Design and Construction, Periphery, Switching Computer, Firmware, Types*

11.1   Design and Construction

Adder, analog circuit (SA 14 components), index register, core storage, arithmetic unit, simulator, storage, central unit

11.2   Periphery

- Adapter
- Data acquisition
- Data carrier
  Punch card, punch tape
- Printout
  Page printer, graphic printer, plotter, high-speed printer
- Input/Output
  Display unit, COM (computer output to microfilm), data output, data input, card puncher, light pen, visual indicator, optical reader
- Storage
  Mass storage, semiconductor storage, integrated data storage, magnetic tape, magnetic film storage, disk, shift register, drum
- Terminal
  Communication terminal, data display terminal

11.3   Switching computer

Data exchange, remote data processing (SA NU 240 data transmission)

11.4   Firmware   (trade/firm names)

(Open name list: brand names, firm names)
ERA 1101, Honeywell 200, IBM, Robotron 300, Siemens 2002, Siemens 4004, Univac

11.5   Types

Analog computer, digital computer, hybrid computer, small-sized computer, microcomputer, minicomputer, modular system, desk computer

Format S   *Software*

20   Software

21   R&D areas   SA programming

- Automata theory
- Formal systems
- Artificial intelligence
- Other R&D areas

see format S1

22   Programming   SA R&D areas

- Operating system   *see* format S3
- Compiler
- Data organization
- Formal logic technique   *see* format S2
- Machine instruction (assembly language)
- Microprogramming
- Modular system
- Sorting program
  - Sorting procedure
- System programming

23   Preparation of automation   (SA WW)

Data organization, problem analysis, search procedure, systems analysis

24   Programming languages   (Open name list)

Algol, Algol 60, Algol 80, APL, Assembler, Balgol, Basic, Cobol, Compiler, Fortran, Fortran 4, Hicop, Iitran, IPL, Joss, Jovial, Lisp, Macro language, Ordvac, PLI, Prosa 300, RPG, Simscript, Simula, Soap, Stress, Vega, Zeus
• Program library   SA 1 Formal descriptors

25   System performance

• System optimization
Automatic error recognition, data protection, fault diagnosis, error recognition, error correction, correcting code, redundancy, availability
• Cost-benefit analysis   SA WW

Format S1   Software R&D areas: *"Automata Theory," "Formal Systems," "Artificial Intelligence," "Other R&D areas"*

Automata theory   SA artificial intelligence

• Algorithm SA logic (22 formal logic techniques)
• Automata table
• Finite automata
• Learning machines
• Linear automata
• Learning models
• Turing machine

Formal systems   SA automata theory SA logic (22 formal logic techniques)

• Code SA other formal logic programming techniques
• Formal grammars
• Formal languages
• Formal syntax
• Symbolic languages

Artificial intelligence   SA automata theory

Automatic language translation, automatic character recognition, image recognition, data acquisition, Delphi method SA other R&D areas, decision SA other R&D areas, decision tables SA other R&D areas, learning models, model theory, natural language, optical reader, language processing, speech recognition, language translation, search procedures, synthetic languages, translation machine, character recognition, random processes

Other R&D areas

- Computer graphics
- Data protection
- Index value determination
- Language processing SA artificial intelligence
- Search procedure
- Random process

Format S2   22 Programming   *"Formal logic techniques"*

Formal logic techniques

- Digital technique

    - Analog-to-digital converter
    - Coding
    - Digital information
    - Digital signals
    - Digital systems

- Logic   SA formal systems (R&D areas)

    - Algorithm SA automata theory
    - Logical instruction
    - Logical circuit
    - Logical network

- Numeric algebra

    - Binary logic
    - Binary numbers
    - Coding
    - Numeric system
    - Switching algebra
    - Number systems

- Special programming techniques

    - Real time programming
    - Iteration

- for office computers (as opposed to general-purpose computers)
- Recursive programming

Other formal logic programming techniques

Process control, addressing system, code, code converter, data flowchart, decision, decision tables, list processing, Monte Carlo method, problem analysis, simulation, language processing SA artificial intelligence, data acquisition

Format A   *"Applications"*

30   Applications

   33   Application problems

- Computer criminality
- Data acquisition
- Remote data processing
- Data protection
- Privacy
- Legal issues

   32   Special application techniques SA 21 R&D areas

- Automatic language translation
- CAD
- Computer graphics
- Learning machines
- Man-machine dialog
- Simulation
- Character recognition

   31   Application (general)

- Automation
- Inventory control
- Office machines
- Data bank
- Data bases
- Data processing system
- Data processing center
- Documentation

- Information system
- Payroll accounting
- Management
- Seat reservation
- Problem analyses
- Process control SA MR 300 process computer MR 300 process automation
- Real time processing SA operating system
- Computerized printing machine
- Computer center
- Batch processing system
- Traffic control computer
- Sales, computer application
- Administration, computer application

Format F   *"Formal descriptors"*

0.1   Introductions

- General introduction
- Specific introduction ("how to . . .")

0.2   General reference materials

- Bibliography, encyclopaedia, dictionary
- General "state of the art" reports, e.g.:
  - Yearbook
  - Performance evaluation
  - Conference proceedings
  - Technical evaluation
  - Survey . . .

0.3   Field specific reference materials

- Handbook
- Specific "state of the art" reports, e.g.:
  - Yearbook covering specific subjects
  - Performance evaluation
  - Conference proceedings
  - Technical evaluation
  - Other technical reports . . .

0.4   History/future of DV

- Historical survey and historical report
- Futurology

10.8.3   DV Thesaurus Descriptors – Example of Alphabetical Listings

Descriptor	Location in Structural Framework	Format
Data carrier	11.2 Periphery	H1
Data processing system	31 Application (general)	A
Data processing center	31 Application (general)	A
Delphi method SA other R&D areas	21 Artificial intelligence	S1
Digital information	22 Digital technique	S2
Digital signals	22 Digital technique	S2
Digital systems	22 Digital technique	S2
Digital computer	11.5 Types	H1
Digital technique	22 Formal logic techniques	S2
Documentation	31 Application (general)	A
Printout	11.2 Periphery	H1
Real-time programming	22 Special programming techniques	S2
Input/output	11.2 Periphery	H1
Finite automata	21 Automata theory	S1
Decision SA other R&D areas	21 Artificial intelligence	S1
Decision	22 Other formal logic techniques	S2
Decision tables SA other R&D areas	21 Artificial intelligence	S1
Decision tables	22 Other formal logic techniques	S2
ERA 1101	11.4 Firmware	H1
Fault diagnosis	25 System optimization	S
Error recognition	25 System optimization	S
Error correction	25 System optimization	S
Firmware	11.4	H, H1

10.8.4   WW (Industrial Management and Administration) Overview

000   *Formal descriptors*   USE format F
    010   Introductions
    020   General reference materials
    030   Field specific reference materials
    040   History

100   *General theories and models*   USE format T/M
    110   Theories
    120   Models

200 *General management* USE format U

210 *Working fields* USE format U1
211 R&D
212 Production
213 Financing
214 Marketing
215 Disposition
216 Personnel USE WP
217 Human engineering USE WP

220 *Functions* USE format U2
221 Company policy / goals
222 Planning
223 Organization
224 Control
225 Economics / profitability

230 *Types of Enterprise* USE format U3

300 *Methods/Techniques* USE format M/T

301 Accounting
302 Cost accounting
303 Operations research
304 Networking
305 Management stiles / techniques
306 Work techniques
307 Business statistics
308 Market research
309 EDP applications
310 Program planning
311 Systems engineering
312 Simulation
313 Decision methods
314 Information systems

400 *Special business* USE format SB
administration areas

Industrial management, banking, commerce, insurance, service economy, public enterprises, industrial taxation, etc.

500   *Company-related applications of*   USE format A
        operational models and methods

e.g. at Siemens, BASF, BP, ESSO, Xerox

10.8.5   WW Formats – Examples

Format G

000	Formal descriptors
100	General theories and models
200	General Management
300	Methods / techniques
400	Special business administration branches
500	Company-related applications of operational models and methods

Format T/M

110   *Theories*

Balance theory	SA 301
Decision theory	SA 303, 314
Information theory	SA 309, 314
Organization theory	SA 223
Production theory	SA 212
Investment theory	USE investment accounting
Cost theory	SA 302
Cybernetics	USE DV
Price theory	
Systems theory	SA 303, 314
Theory of science	

120   *Models*

Decision model
Management model
Inventory model
Marketing model
Operations research model
etc.

Format U1   (Samples: 211–214)

211   Research and Development

Product innovation
Product development

212	Production	
	Disposition	SA 215
	Operating fund	
	Company-produced assets – outside purchase	
	Individual construction	USE manufacturing procedures
	Manufacturing	
	Supervision of manufacture	SA 224
	Production planning	
	Production control	SA 309
	Manufacturing procedures	
	Prepatory work	
	In-plant transportation	SA 215
	Assembly planning	
	Optimum lot size	
	Production factors	SA 110
	Quality control	SA 224
	Mass production	USE manufacturing procedures

213	Financing	
	Depreciation	SA 301
	Investment activities	USE investments
	Budgeting	USE financial planning
	Self-financing	
	Factoring	
	Financing methods	
	Financial planning	SA 222
	Outside financing	
	Investments	
	Investment planning	SA 222
	Investment accounting	
	Capital structure	
	Leasing	
	Calculation of profitability	USE investment accounting
	Payment conditions	

214   Marketing

Sales planning	SA 222
Marketing policy	SA 221
Industrial marketing	USE marketing
Consumer	
Brand	
Market segmentation	
Price policy	SA 221
Product design	
Product planning	SA 222
Product policy	
Sale	USE marketing
Packaging	
Sales policy	USE marketing policy
Marketing	
Advertising	

Format M/T   (Samples: 302, 314)

302   Cost accounting

Break-even analysis	
Direct costing	USE marginal costing
Calculation	
Types of costs	
Accounting by types of costs	USE cost accounting
Cost control	SA 224
Cost planning	SA 222
Accounting by unit of cost	
Standard cost accounting	USE cost accounting
Contribution margin accounting	USE cost accounting

314   Information systems

Informal information
In-plant reporting
In-plant information
Integrated information system

Communication

Personnel and sociological aspects	USE WP
Management information systems (MIS)	USE MIS

Format F

010   Introductions

General introductions
Introductions to specific fields

020   General reference materials

Bibliography, encyclopaedia, dictionary
Handbook
Overview
Statistical yearbook
Commemorative edition
Conference procedings

030   Field specific reference materials

Bibliography
Handbook
Expertise
Conference proceedings
Commemorative edition

040   History

10.8.6 WW Thesaurus Descriptors — Example of Alphabetical Listings

Descriptor	Location in structural framework	Format
Business statistics	307	M/T
Interfirm comparative studies	307	M/T
Industrial tax theory	400	SB
Bibliography	020	F
	030	

10.8.6. *(Continued)*

Descriptor		Location in structural framework	Format
Balance		301	M/T
Balance theory	SA 301	110	T/M
Bookkeeping		301	M/T
Bookkeeping system		301	M/T
Budgeting	USE financing		
Office organization		223	U2
Office rationalization		225	U2
Office operation		223	U2
Cash flow	SA 301	307	M/T
CPM		304	M/T
Contribution margin accounting		302	M/T
Delegation, responsibility		305	M/T
Direct costing	USE marginal costing		
Disposition		215	U1
Double-entry bookkeeping		310	M/T
Dynamic programming		310	M/T
EDP applications	see 100–500	309	M/T
Company-produced assets/outside purchase		212	U1

10.8.7 Test Indexing Procedures

Instructions — DV. The decision about which descriptors are to be assigned to a given book is left to the indexer. However, instead of confronting the indexer with a list of all available descriptors, the new structural framework and its formats are intended to serve as aids to permit the indexer to focus on selected groups of descriptors and to suggest other groups, as well, for consideration during the indexing process.

This is accomplished in the following manner:

a. There are three different formats serving as entry points to the DV descriptors (formats H, S, and A).

b. There is one supplementary format (G) serving as one means of deciding with which of the formats H, S, or A to begin.

c. There is an alphabetical list of all DV descriptors, indicating their locations in the structural framework and the formats as a further means of deciding with which of the formats H, S, or A to begin.

d. The indexer also is free to proceed directly from one format to any other format or format part.

Note that the selection of the format with which the indexer begins (format H, S, or A) serves merely as a starting point. It does not necessarily eliminate the remaining formats. In fact, all three basic formats may apply to any given book. We have established a simple rule to show when further formats should be considered.

Finally, there is a format for formal descriptors: format F. This format could normally be used at any point during the indexing process. However, for the purposes of this test it is requested that format F be used only at the conclusion of the indexing process, unless the indexer is convinced that a book, such as a DV dictionary, requires only the use of this format.

Instructions — **WW.** The decision about which descriptors are to be assigned to a given book is left to the indexer. However, instead of confronting the indexer with a list of all available descriptors, the new structural framework and its formats are intended to serve as aids which permit the indexer to focus on selected groups of descriptors and suggest other groups as well for consideration during the indexing process.

This is accomplished in the following manner:

a. Seven different formats serve as entry points to the WW descriptors (formats G, F, T/M, U, M/T, SB, A).

b. Using format G, the indexer can determine with which of the formats (F, T/M, U, M/T, SB, A) he might best begin. For general literature, format G with an additional consideration of format F should be sufficient for indexing.

c. An alphabetical listing covering all WW descriptors shows their locations in the structural framework and the appropriate formats. This serves as a further orientation aid for entering the formats.

d. The indexer also is free to proceed directly from one format to any other format and/or format part.

Note that the selection of the format with which the indexer begins serves merely as a starting point. It does not necessarily eliminate the remaining formats. In fact, more than one format can be used for and be applicable to any given book.

The format for formal descriptors, format F, could normally be used at any point during the indexing process. However, for the purposes of this test it is requested that format F be used only at the conclusion of the indexing process, unless the indexer is convinced that a book, such as a dictionary of business administration and industrial management, requires only the direct use of this format.

Rules for the Conclusion of the Indexing Process (**DV** *and* **WW**). For the purposes of this test, we have established two magic numbers, three and eight, to conclude or keep open the indexing process for each book, based on the number of the assigned descriptors.

1. No more than three descriptors were assigned:
   a. After the initially selected format is apparently of no more use, try one of the remaining formats. The selection is left to the indexer.
   b. Try the last remaining formats.
   c. Try to assign free terms.

(The indexer may decide at any point during this process that the book has been incorrectly classified or that the book is so general that further indexing is not required.)

   d. Try to assign at least two descriptors using format F.

2. Eight or more descriptors were assigned:
   a. The indexing process is halted as soon as the indexer feels that the format being used is of no more help.
   b. Try to assign at least two descriptors using format F.

3. Between four and seven descriptors were assigned:
   a. The decision whether the indexing process should be continued is entirely left to the indexer.
   b. Try to assign at least two descriptors using format F.

Lastly, the use of hierarchical descriptors: The new structural framework with its associated formats partially relieves the indexer of the problematic decision about the use of higher-level or lower-level descriptors when both may be appropriate for assignment to a given book. Given the new structural framework and its associated formats, the neighboring higher-level hierarchical descriptor can always be assigned by (manual or automatic) routines after the indexing process for a given book has been concluded.

Higher-level descriptors should only be assigned if the indexer feels that the higher-level descriptor is more appropriate than any one or several of the lower-level descriptors in question. The indexer should remember that after the conclusion of his indexing the next higher descriptors will be added through a routine extension process.

10.8.8 Test Indexing Sheet – WW

Book No.

☐ Mrs. Egger

☐ Mr. Hänsch

☐ Dr. Röcke

☐ Mrs. Thilo

☐ Mr. Zombeck

☐ Team

Format F
   1.
   2.

Format G

Running number	Either thesaurus descriptor	Or free term
1		
2		
3		
4		
5		
6		
7		
8		

10.9 THE USE AND AUTOMATION OF THE STRUCTURAL FRAMEWORKS

Attempts to reduce either the formulation of search requests or the indexing of document contents to a fully logical process will fail to cover all the practical, not to mention the theoretical, possibilities. Nonetheless, the structural frameworks with their formats for descriptor locations are based on a kind of logic pertaining to the selection of descriptors. However, instead of attempting to reduce descriptor selection for either search or indexing to one stipulated process, the formats combined with the alphabetical listings and thesaurus structure offer guidance to indexers or searchers using a variety of approaches.

Searchers and indexers may approach the system-acceptable terms by using more or less normal methods. For example, starting with the concept(s) in mind, the alphabetical lists can be scanned. Should a term or terms be found there presumably corresponding to the concept in mind, reference is made to the thesaurus location and structure and/or the stipulated format(s). This provides the searcher or indexer with a reasonably good indication about whether the close similarity between the given term(s) and the concept(s) in mind suggested on first glance by the spelled-out term(s) is essentially correct or misleading. If a given term is picked up from the alphabetical lists in the belief that it appears to correspond to the concept in mind, a quick check through the format within which that term is embedded should indicate whether the correspondence is valid. The surrounding terms in the format and/or the thesaurus grouping will tend to clarify the meaning of the term. Thus one can determine whether, say, the term ''program'' in fact corresponds to the concept in mind, which could have been something to do with computer programs or, alternatively, with management (or even a theater program, to make the example quite clear). Depending on what one finds embedded within the appropriate format(s) or thesaurus structure(s), possible ambiguities and misunderstandings should vanish.

Naturally, one need not begin as a searcher or indexer with the alphabetical lists. One can proceed directly to the thesaurus with its higher-level categories to determine whether one is in the right ball park for finding terms corresponding to the concepts in mind. If successful, one is then led to more detailed terms and to the formats where the specific terms are embedded in association with other plausible terms. This process would certainly be followed, should scan of the alphabetical lists fail to turn up any potentially corresponding terms.

However, whichever approach to the initial term selection may be used, all such approaches lead to the formats with their surrounding terms offered for consideration. And each such further term choice continues the process leading to the individual formats. Thus the formulation of search requests, as well as the indexing of document contents can proceed with guidance but without the processes being reduced or restricted to any one standard method.

With or without the additional sophistication of the PRIMAS SUGGEST mode or the use of extensional relationships, the structural frameworks can be computer-stored. Presentation of the formats, the relevant portions of the thesaurus, or the alphabetical lists can be offered on-line in response to indexer or searcher request. The search through the alphabetical lists could be initiated by entry of any term spelled by the indexer or searcher for that matter. Further, the input of any system-acceptable term selected could further trigger the display of the appropriate format. A great deal of manual look-up and scan through the formats could be eliminated in this manner in combination with this form of computer-aided guidance. Since the test results to date show that the use of the structural frameworks and formats even in a purely manual mode improves indexing quality, this further step toward automation seems sensible. Nonetheless, the success of any step involving automation to produce computer-aids for the indexing or search processes lies with the direct participation of all concerned in developing and testing the methods.

Having what gets automated and how it gets automated flow from a participatory program is the key to successful automation of just about any process or method involving the critical interface areas, as we have strongly emphasized. It is in this sense that the case history discussed here constitutes an example of the type of experimental implementation stage we regard as a prerequisite to the successful implementation of complex information systems.

NOTES

1. The project took place under the auspices of the Central Technical Library, Siemens AG, with participation from the Erlangen, Berlin, and Munich Library Centers and staff. It began in September, 1977, and concluded in January, 1978.
2. Wessel, CAIR, Chapters Seven and Eight.
3. In German the term used is "Systematik" which would directly translate into English as "systematic(s)." It means both the systematic structural skeletons and the arrangement of the terms or thesaurus descriptors which flesh them out.
4. User participants were U. Algermissen, H. Bauer, I. Egger, H. Graml, R. Hänsch, W. Kühnel, Dr. L. Röcke, M. Thilo, K. Zombeck — all of Siemens AG and representing management, library staff, field experts, and, to a lesser degree, library users. Other Siemens field experts were called in for short consultations from time to time, as were other library users. Should user search tests take place in future, the library users could be better represented during that phase of implementation of the new technology.
5. Wessel, CAIR and Social Use.
6. According to K. Zombeck, a Siemens AG WW expert and project participant.

Chapter Eleven

Some Unfinished Business

This chapter closes the last of a series of three volumes, each focusing on different aspects of information systems technology and problems. This book has attempted an exploration of the problems of implementation and, with the contributed case histories, emphasized some of the neglected interface areas and tasks. The neglect of these interface areas and the failure to provide significant computer support to the intellectual activities forming an inherent part of any information system (discussed also in Computer-Aided Information Retrieval) continues to date. As such, the issues concerning the poor distribution of information systems remain with us, in part, because of technology inappropriate to the better spread of computers throughout our societies (as described also in The Social Use of Information).

Solutions, in part detailed and in part protocol, to the problems raised are also found in each of these three books. However, the interrelationships among the different aspects, although observed initially, become as we have proceeded even more significant. That "interlocked triad of user organization, thesauri builder, and computer technologist" mentioned in the first book still has not completed its necessary evolution into a functioning implementation team, as we have seen in the preceding chapters. Information scientists, computer scientists, organizational management, and users continue to travel their separate roads with all too few exceptions. This situation is likely to persist. The required transformations we have discussed in some detail will occur only slowly and intermittently.

In fact, all concerned with these matters may be caught up in a rather vicious circle. Without enough knowledgeable and experienced users and managers, sufficient pressures will not be generated to develop and produce the appropriate technology. Without the appropriate technology to encourage user participation, knowledgeable and experienced users and managers will remain few indeed. And we certainly do not have enough workable solutions to the problems of providing useful interactive aids for the intellectual tasks intrinsic to and surrounding information systems. Under such circumstances, users, managers, and technologists willing to endure each other and the rigors of participatory developmental and implementation programs will be truly exceptional. Unless we discover how to break out of this vicious circle, we shall continue to live with inadequate technology, inadequately distributed, implemented, and used.

If this situation concerns no other groups, it should disturb those of us who call ourselves information scientists. Computer systems, as machinery, will continue to develop and flourish whether we find means to create and implement truly acceptable information systems. The organizational world and the public have learned to put up with inadequate information systems and get on with whatever they in fact are doing. With an occasional grumble or complaint, most of us have learned to make do with misaddressed or incorrect bills or payments, reservations, bank account statements, the large amount of erroneous information in files, and the high costs and problems of obtaining needed and relevant information.

However, there are some indications that a flash point is not that far away. Once general discontent reaches sufficient levels, the reaction can be severe. Physicists and engineers involved in the implementation of atomic energy plants have learned that the underlying mood of public disquiet about their doings can become quite unruly. Information scientists may also find that the managers and users have reached the flash point and that their reaction to the inadequacies of information systems is far from mild.

We have been told often enough that we are dealing with an explosion. But the information explosion is only part of a more extensive reaction indicated by the formula:

Information explosion ⟶ Cost explosion ⟶ User explosion

with information systems functioning as catalysts at each step.

Over the past 10 years, the overall costs of asking questions and getting useful answers from information systems, manual or automated, have actually and radically increased. These increased costs stem only in part from normal inflationary factors. The costs, kinds, and amounts of labor-intensive work required to develop information and data collections and to support search services and facilities for just about all informational fields have not been reduced by automation. Furthermore, it has become less and less feasible to establish acceptable limits for any given information collection and its users. User expectations have been raised to ever higher levels. These impose still broader requirements on information retrieval services and facilities. Computer technology as implemented to date has increased rather than decreased costs and expectations. Both the size and scope of services offered and the services expected have grown. Document and information collections have expanded to match the growth of computer storage capacities. The number and variety of users, clients, and customers has grown to match the always increasing number of terminals that can be connected on-line. The technology sold to reduce costs and replace the labor-intensive work and tasks associated with information systems and services breeds only new requirements for larger and larger information collections and for a greater and greater variety of users with their multidimensional interests and needs and ever increasing expectations—all of which results in the requirement for more and more labor-intensive and costly services. The vicious circle of the implementation problem is turned into an explosive spiral by inappropriate technology.

Information science cannot in itself create the appropriate transformations of user and managerial methods and attitudes that we have described in preceding chapters. But the information scientists certainly can welcome user and managerial participation and provide the appropriate technology required for participatory development and implementation programs and projects. Continuing to focus our efforts as if we believed that the replacement of human functions by black boxes with easy-to-push buttons creates the friendly systems users need to solve the problems of complex information systems makes neither scientific nor practical sense. It does not provide the welcome, encouragement, and the appropriate technology for participatory development and implementation. A way out of the vicious circle of implementation problems and the spiraling costs of providing information system services is more likely to be found by concentrating far more heavily in our work as information scientists upon tasks such as these:

a. Information system and documentation language construction and maintenance (search and indexing term lists and thesauri).
b. Information system and documentation language utilization (search request formulation and reformulation; information or document entry and analysis, including error-correction and guidance techniques).
c. Post search result analyses, filtering, and conversion of search outputs into more useable forms (i.e., aids for the conversion of citations to information content carriers, getting rid of redundant, irrelevant, or useless output).
d. Information collection and file construction, development, maintenance, and revision (including the means to describe adequately such files and information collections by using techniques that clearly expose the existent file structures as they may be according to empirically determined time slices for any given file).
e. Design and implementation of multiple data base and networking techniques (including the means to formulate supplementary search questions through external or "foreign" files).

Effective means and methods must be developed to permit better sharing of the costs and the information collections and facilities. The ability to share information among differing user groups and organizations with special information collections and processes is essential if we are also to have the ability to share and reduce the costs. This means that we must find means to reduce unnecessary reduplication of information collection, maintenance, and the labor-intensive processes involved in providing acceptable dissemination and search services and facilities. In short, we must reduce the high costs of providing broader informational bases and processes with which to better satisfy both special and general information needs.

Specifically, this means that the techniques and methods to bridge and link data banks and information collections with differing technical specifications must be developed. This in turn requires that we develop and test better methods of constructing search languages, term lists, and thesauri for newly established documentation and information systems. We need to achieve more efficient as well as broader use of those systems already in process by providing better means to bridge or integrate information and data collections covering various fields and established according to particular user interests, technical characteristics and designs, and organizational processes. Finally, we must determine the feasibility of translation methods among the differing documentation languages and/or determine the means and methods by which supplementary search languages can be established to permit system-independent search.

These are the labor-intensive and overcostly processes that must be accomplished for special user groups and their "unique" information collections and requirements as well as for multiuser groups with their wider variety of information collections and requirements.

If we intend to develop and use information collection and distribution systems and further to develop such systems within the context of a rational network of systems and facilities, cost-effective, user-acceptable, and technically feasible solutions that reduce the overwhelming labor and costs associated with these basic tasks and processes are a necessity.

Readers who have come this far will have noticed that the tasks described as essential for the information sciences are also the tasks with which this and the previous books have been concerned. Is it merely then that we are suggesting that all information scientists concentrate on the same tasks we favor or find important?

Certainly, the notion that one should have investigated the tasks one proposes as necessary cannot be faulted. Further, to have shown that potential solution paths are feasible for the problems one has defined and clarified usually is considered a prerequisite to proposing "researchable" or "do-able" tasks. This work and its companion volumes have attempted to describe the prerequisite investigations and endeavored to provide the necessary clarifications and demonstrations of feasible solutions. Further, we simply point to the explosive spiral of costs associated with existing information systems and the description of the sources from which these costs stem. For readers exercising that modicum of care mentioned in the Preface this should be justification enough.

The steps and methods described in these chapters for the implementation processes should help users and managers reduce costs and eliminate some of the more severe problems and disappointments associated with the application of computer technology to complex information systems. However, it remains necessary to develop the more appropriate kinds of technology that we have described for such applications. It would appear also that the best of the many ways to proceed for information scientists as well as for managers and users is to begin with implementation. The actual experiences gained by at least one real-world attempt to apply modern computer technology toward satisfying the requirements and resolving the problems of complex information systems would underline again the urgency for the accomplishment of these suggested tasks.

This book has been based on such experiences and has offered what we have learned from them. The test of the methods we have described is found in the same arena of experiences—the implementation of complex information systems.

Index